DISCOVERY WALKS IN THE YORKSHIRE DALES

The Northern Dales

David Johnson

Published by Sigma Leisure – an imprint of
Sigma Press, 1 South Oak Lane, Wilmslow, Cheshire SK9 6AR, England.

British Library Cataloguing in Publication Data
A CIP record for this book is available from the British Library.

ISBN: 1-85058-465-6

Typesetting and Design by: Sigma Press, Wilmslow, Cheshire.

Cover design: The Agency, Wilmslow, Cheshire

Maps: Perrott Cartographics

Photographs and illustrations: The author, except where indicated

Printed by: MFP Design & Print

Preface

In the Preface to The Southern Dales companion to this book, I expressed the hope that the two would fuse together straightforward route description and deeper interpretative background material. I explained that the rationale of the books lies within the use of the word "discovery". My aim has been to provide the walker and the reader with a detailed analysis of the Dales landscape in its broadest sense, in the temporal as well as spatial dimension.

It will be clear to those who have read The Southern Dales that there is an indispensable wealth of history in the area. Visible and identifiable history, be it monuments, great buildings or simply lumps and bumps in a field, is all around us in the Dales. There is also the spatial element: subtle changes and nuances in the "natural" vegetation, roads and farming patterns. Village form, the local economy, and a host of other variables reflect spatial differences in geology, relief, soils, micro-climate and, of course, the human response.

Each dale has its own individuality and charm. This applies to the Northern Dales just as much as to the Southern. I have been, perhaps, rather subjective in where I drew the line. I am confident no one would question the inclusion of Swaledale, Wensleydale and their tributary dales in this collection. The subjectivity comes with the selection of Dentdale and Coverdale. I do not find a conflict, though, as these seem to me to be more akin to Wensleydale than to Ribblesdale or Wharfedale. And they are, of course, based on the younger rocks of the Carboniferous, the Wensleydale Group, rather than on the Great Scar Limestone of the more southerly Dales. The real conflict has been in deciding which twelve walks to include. I could just as well have included a dozen more, such is the variety within the northern part of the Dales.

Another big thankyou to ...
I owe the same debt as with the first book to those who have inspired me either on foot or in print. I owe the same debt of gratitude to Judith Allinson for her sterling support and invaluable comments on the text. Many have been the occasions when she has put me right botanically, though any errors of fact or interpretation remain mine. I should also like to thank Karen Holmes for again translating my scrawl into typescript; Robin Zahler for his sketches on pages 114 and 135; and dp Design and Print for converting my rough illustrations into final copy. I should also like to acknowledge the assistance of various National Park officers who supplied information, and particularly the staff of the Access section for checking the legality of chosen routes.

For permission to reproduce the tune Dentdale I acknowledge and thank Oxford University Press. Scientific plant nomenclature follows Stace's *New Flora of the British Isles* (1991) and Kent's *List of Vascular Plants of the British Isles* (1992).

David Johnson

Contents

Introduction

In this and the previous book, *The Southern Dales*, there are 24 Discovery Walks. My primary aim has been to present a selection of walks that will encourage you to explore further within the Dales. It has been my hope that the walks I have selected will stimulate you to devise your own elsewhere. After all, I could have selected 12 contrasting routes just in Swaledale, never mind the rest of the northern dales. As with the companion volume, I have tried to avoid the honeypots – in this case Hawes, Aysgarth Falls and Richmond – though inevitably some of the walks do touch upon or start from popular villages. I can almost guarantee you peace and seclusion on some of the walks all the time, and on all of the walks some of the time.

There has been a common theme running through the two books. Most of the walks follow ancient paths and tracks, not using them as an end in themselves, but as a vehicle for understanding and appreciating the many facets of the area. The emphasis in both books has been very much on interpretation and discussion of the landscape in detail.

The other common theme is flexibility and adaptability. Most chapters contain a basic walk as well as the option of extending or shortening the distance to suit your needs of the day.

Distances and other details

Walk	Location	Distance
1.	Dentdale and Deepdale	7.5 to 10.5km (4.7 to 6.5 miles)
2.	Grisedale	8.0km (5 miles)
3.	Cotterdale and the High Way	9.0km (5.6 miles)
4.	Raydale	7.8 to 8.3km (4.8 to 5.2 miles)
5.	Askrigg and Bainbridge	8.4 to 8.7km (5.2 to 5.4 miles)
6.	Castle Bolton and Carperby	8.8 to 11.1km (5.5 to 6.9 miles)
7.	Bishopdale	6 to 14km (3.7 to 8.7 miles)
8.	Coverdale	9 to 12.5km (5.6 to 7.8 miles)
9.	Kisdon	9.5 to 10.5km (5.9 to 6.5 miles)
10.	Gunnerside Gill	8 to 12.5km (5 to 7.8 miles)
11.	Healaugh and Low Row	12km (7.5 miles)
12.	Arkengarthdale and Calver	7 to 10.8km (4.3 to 6.7 miles)

Each chapter starts with basic planning information such as public transport, local facilities, parking details, map number, and an outline of the route.

On each and every walk you will be on rights of way throughout or on

Access land or permissive routes. As I stated in the first book, I do not subscribe to the "wander where you will" way of thinking.

I have tried to present the facts – and sometimes ideas and theories – in a digestible way. The format of each chapter is essentially the same. There are comprehensive route details for each walk though, again, I would stress the need to carry an Ordnance Survey map. The sketch maps included here are not meant to be maps to follow in the field. Each walk has a number of selected points of interest, inevitably some more than others, and I have described and explained these as the walks unfold. I have tried to make sense for you of the scenery from the perspective of geological and landscape processes. I have discussed in some depth the historical processes and influences from the Bronze Age to the early modern period because they figure so largely in the Dalescape. I have also included a goodly amount of detail on the lead industry because of its enormous impact on the landscape we have inherited and on the lives and livelihoods of many generations of Dales folk. I have included notes on flowers and birdlife where worthy of mention. In *The Southern Dales* I included cameos of common birds found on the walk. In *The Northern Dales* I offer you tree cameos of the more frequently encountered species, such as the one on the facing page.

The walks are presented in no particular order of merit or priority. There is no rising level of complexity or detail and, to avoid possible repetition of recurring themes or ideas, I have put in notes for you to refer to an earlier or later walk.

In the first book I discussed in some detail the geological and historical frameworks, and I would commend those pages to you before you delve into these 12 walks.

If I were asked which of the 24 walks is my greatest favourite, my response would be that of the politician or maybe diplomat. My favourite walk is the one I happen to be following on that particular day, and I hope you enjoy these walks as much as I do. I hope they will enable you to wander in the Dales with a greater depth of knowledge and understanding . . . and to return again and again.

The National Park

The Yorkshire Dales, one of Britain's ten fully designated National Parks, celebrated its fortieth anniversary in 1994 . . . and how vastly different the park is now compared with 1954. I suppose that when you live in an area you tend not to notice the gradual, evolutionary changes but, when you stand back and consider what it was like ten, twenty or forty years ago (not that I can do that – quite), the changes seem immense.

There is a certain degree of misconception in Britain concerning our

Scots Pine
Pinus sylvestris

Status: native to the whole country

Height: average 25 to 35 metres.

Trunk: up to 1m diameter; tall and straight with few low branches.

Bark: heavily ridged; often with a clear reddish tinge. Cones: dull and dark brown; woody; average 5cm long; quite pointed and ovoid (egg shaped).

Crown: conical in young trees; more flattened in mature specimens.

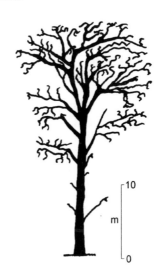

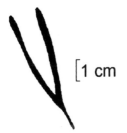

[1 cm

Leaves: needles have a blue green tinge; wide and strong looking; in pairs.

Uses: In the past for pit props and railway sleepers. Now for building and joinery work.

National Parks because they are neither really parks nor national. The National Parks of Africa or North America, for example, have been set aside specifically for conservation and public enjoyment but the Dales, in contrast, have less than three per cent of the total area in public ownership: the vast majority is privately owned by landowners and farmers. The National Park most definitely was not set aside back in 1954 as a museum or massive theme park where the public has open access to whatever form of recreation they might favour: the area within the Park boundaries is a living and working entity where some 20,000 people have their homes and carry out their daily routines.

So why is it a National Park? In its early days the Countryside Commission decided that this was a landscape with special qualities that needed to be granted a high measure of legal protection from possible future unsympathetic development or change, protection not only for the landscape itself but also for life and tradition. But that was forty years ago and our country has undergone changes that were inconceivable then, and our National Parks have not been immune to the immense pressures generated by increased levels of personal prosperity, personal mobility and leisure time.

A journey to the Dales in the 1950s had to be planned well in advance by Mr. and Mrs. Public but now anyone from virtually anywhere can jump into their car for a day out on the fells, even from distant parts of the country. It has been suggested that the Dales, being central, are ideally placed for travelling to all parts of the country. That logic must also work in reverse, and the result is that the very landscapes we all treasure are in danger of being loved to death. Nine million visitor days are made to the Dales each year and, just from 1975 to 1991, there was a 44 per cent increase in road traffic within the Park.

Thus the task of the Park Authority is immeasurably harder now and its role has necessarily changed. In the words of the National Park Committee its

"primary statutory duty is to conserve the landscape character, scenic beauty, wildlife, cultural heritage and the peace and quiet of the area. It also has a duty to promote quiet informal outdoor recreation."

It also recognises better that the needs and interests of residents must be safeguarded and promoted. Alongside conservation we hear more and more of *stewardship* these days, and of the need to promote *sustainable* tourism by encouraging the *thinking* tourist and the *Green* tourist to help the Park and those of us fortunate enough to reside within its bounds to co-exist peacefully and amicably.

I am sure I will not be around in another forty years' time but I sometimes wonder whether our National Parks will indeed be able to sustain their current state of evolutionary change, or whether some of the more extreme solutions to snowballing visitor pressure will be enacted. I know *you* are a

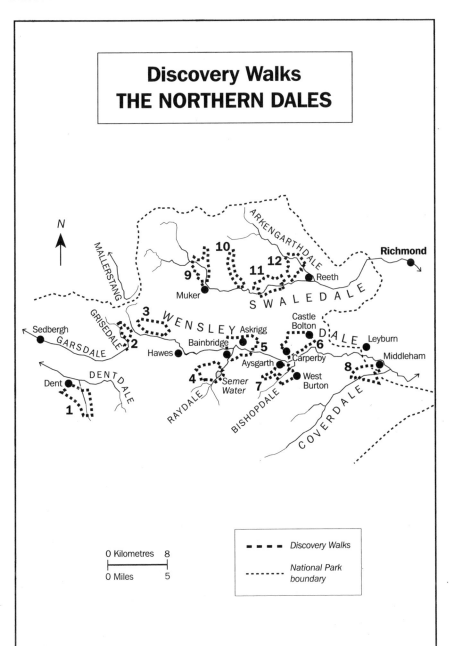

Discovery Walks
THE NORTHERN DALES

N

Richmond

10

12

11

9

Reeth

Muker

S W A L E D A L E

A R K E N G A R T H D A L E

M A L L E R S T A N G

3

W E N S L E Y

Askrigg

Castle Bolton

D A L E

Leyburn

Sedbergh

G R I S E D A L E

2

G A R S D A L E

Bainbridge

Hawes

5

6

Carperby

Middleham

Aysgarth

8

Dent

D E N T D A L E

4

Semer Water

7

West Burton

1

R A Y D A L E

B I S H O P D A L E

C O V E R D A L E

0 Kilometres   8

0 Miles   5

▬ ▬ ▬ *Discovery Walks*

- - - - - - - *National Park boundary*

thinking and Green tourist: just encourage your friends likewise and always remember to respect the Park's "lifestyle, work and customs" and to "support local skills, services and produce" and follow the Yorkshire Dales Visitor Code.

The Yorkshire Dales Visitor Code

¤ Keep to public rights of way or access areas.

¤ Use gates and stiles to cross dry stone walls, hedges and fences.

¤ Leave all gates as you find them.

¤ Stay in single file through uncut hay or silage meadows.

¤ Leave wildlife and flowers alone for others to enjoy.

¤ Keep your dog under close control.

¤ Do not interfere with farm animals, machinery or work.

¤ Take your litter home.

¤ Do not start fires.

¤ Do not pollute rivers or lakes.

¤ Use public transport, whenever you can, or park thoughtfully.

¤ Respect the lifestyles, work and customs of the Dales and show consideration for other legitimate countryside users.

Keep these points in mind and you will receive a warm welcome in our "Treasured Landscape".

Old Roads

We tend to take roads, of whatever variety, very much for granted and rarely give them a thought. We expect them to be there and to be able to cope better with the volume of traffic that is holding us back and preventing us from going the speed we feel we have a right to go. How many of us ever give thought to why this road is here, why that lane twists and turns so much, why the road from A to B takes such a tortuous route, or how old this road is and why did it first develop?

You can be absolutely certain of one fact. Apart from motorways and modern relief roads, very few roads were created as such; very few were planned out in an office before being carved across the landscape. Most roads evolved over a very long period of time, modified their precise course in response to change of local circumstances, or gradually went out of use to become mere footpaths, or even to disappear without trace. The lost road from Semer Water to Deepdale in Langstrothdale is a case in point where no vestige survives on the ground.

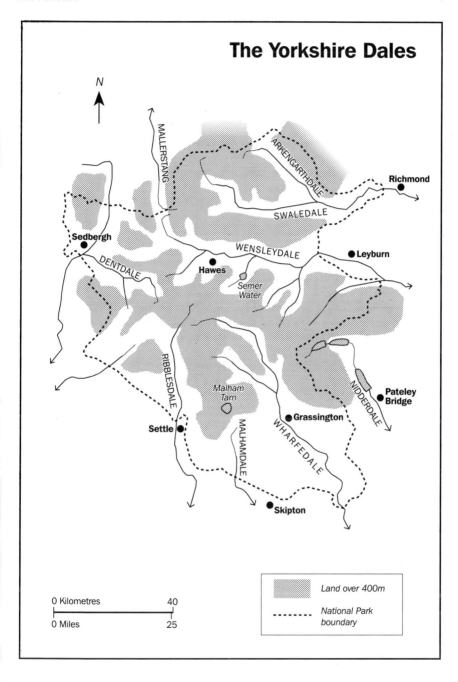

The Yorkshire Dales

N

MALLERSTANG

ARKENGARTHDALE

● Richmond

SWALEDALE

WENSLEYDALE

● Sedbergh

● Leyburn

DENTDALE

● Hawes

Semer Water

RIBBLESDALE

Malham Tarn

NIDDERDALE

● Pateley Bridge

● Grassington

Settle ●

MALHAMDALE

WHARFEDALE

● Skipton

▒▒▒	*Land over 400m*	
- - - - -	*National Park boundary*	

0 Kilometres	40
0 Miles	25

The word "road" only came into common usage in 1596, in the reign of Elizabeth I. Prior to that there were *highways* (major routes) and *ways* (local routes).

Early Development

Before the coming of the Romans no one had ever talked of a road, or way, as a deliberately planned concept. Obviously people moved from one place to another from the time of the earliest settlements. Nomadic hunters and later farmers moved in search of game or virgin land: trade goes back at least into the Neolithic period and certainly mushroomed in scale and extent during the ensuing Bronze Age. All of these needed "roads" in the sense of the means to move around. People then as now, given half the chance, took the line of least resistance, avoiding dense forests, swamps and steep slopes, preferring ridges where possible for safety as well as ease of movement.

Ever so slowly "roads" evolved and became etched onto the surface. Tradition, custom and the herd instinct focussed travel along emerging routeways . . . until the Romans arrived. They had rather different ideas.

The Romans laid out an extensive network of well engineered roads – or *streets* – connecting all population centres and frontier zones with often ruler-straight courses. Many of their roads have become modern tarred roads, others can still be discerned on the ground as present-day footpaths or hedgerows, or from aerial photographs as vegetation or crop marks. The approximate route of others is known but the exact line can only remain conjecture. It is known, for example, that a Roman road led down Wensleydale from Bainbridge to Catterick – but which line did it follow on the ground? However, the exact line of one Roman road in the northern Dales is known and can be walked today (see *Discovery Walk 4*).

After the Roman abandonment of these islands, the country sank back into relative chaos and its different parts became inward looking. The economy collapsed, trade became a mere fragment of what it had been, and roads were no longer maintained. No one needed them to be maintained: there was no social or political structure to have them maintained.

It was in the Anglo-Saxon period that we see the mention of transport routes again as their various kingdoms became established and organised. Into the local vocabulary came the word way to replace the Roman streets. The Anglo-Saxons, of course, were Germanic peoples and our word *way* is derived from their German word *weg*.

In succeeding centuries, as the Norsemen arrived with their families to settle the Dales, roads began to be called *gates*.

The Medieval Period

The road system began to take on a more organised complexion in the monastic period. For the first time since the Roman demise, we can identify road networks, linking monastic houses with their scattered granges and with ports for exporting wool and other products to the continent. On the more local scale roads connected granges with outlying farms and mines on monastic properties. Many of them were to remain as important routeways into the early modern period. Many of these early roads no longer carry traffic but they do form the basis of much of the rights of way system in the Dales.

Market charters were granted to a number of towns in the Dales during the Middle Ages, all connected by roads. It was generally accepted in the country as a whole that market towns should be no more than about 11 kilometres apart, thus enabling villagers to make the return journey and to complete their business within the day. As with many rules and regulations today this probably had more of a theoretical than a practical application, given the appalling state of most roads in all but dry periods.

It is interesting to note that the verb "to travel" comes from the French "travail" which means work or labour. This speaks volumes for the condition of the roads.

Such a state of affairs could not be allowed to continue forever so an attempt at improvement was made in 1285. The Statute of Winchester decreed that individual landowners were henceforth duty bound to maintain roads within their domain. Furthermore highways had to be wide enough, and kept clear of undergrowth at the edges, so that no one with evil intent could lie in wait to ambush travellers and traders.

Further progress was made by the Highway Act of 1555. This maintained the status quo for byways: the lords of the manors had to keep these in good order. Upkeep of highways now became a parish responsibility. Each parish had to appoint – or more than likely pressgang – unpaid surveyors or *waywardens*, to oversee road maintenance. Villagers had to give four – and later six – days of service every year, again unpaid, so you can well imagine how reluctant the waywardens were to enforce this *statute labour* (. . . and no analogies with traffic wardens here please!). In theory roads would now be kept free of hindrance and open to all, on pain of a fine, but the Act was about as successful as the previous statute. In 1771, for example, Arthur Young wrote that the road to Askrigg was "fit only for a goat to travel". This confirms the picture painted at the opening of the previous century by one John Taylor who described one road within the Dales "so fowle and moorish as the inhabitants cannot pass but with great danger" and others as "so rocky, stony, boggy and mountainous".

Of course, you might say, many green lanes are in that state today.

The Act of 1555 was not repealed until the nineteenth century, despite its failings. Matters must have become immeasurably worse from the 1560s as the heavy and lumbering stage-waggons first came to prominence then. This must have been the century of the road because it was in 1596 that we observe in the written record the first usage of the word *road*.

Packhorse Roads

Before the advent of the waggon there was only one way to carry goods and that was on horseback. Waggons only appeared well after the Dissolution of the monastic houses so packhorse traffic had had at least 300 years of history behind it by then. Imagine, though, taking a waggon into the Dales. Unthinkable, so packhorse traffic remained important until the late nineteenth century in upland areas as there was no alternative.

The first packhorse trains were developed by the monastic houses to transport wool from farm to grange to abbey and on to the ports. Very quickly other forms of trade utilised the same method: it was versatile, relatively maintenance-free, and entirely flexible. A hierarchy of packhorse routes evolved, the major arteries, called *prime ways*, focussing on major trading centres like Kendal, Barnard Castle and Kirkby Stephen. These routes were the motorways of the time, but there was a whole web of routes spreading into all corners of the Dales linking village to village, mine to smelter, corn mill to farm, and road to road.

Within the northern dales there were several major pack routes. One came from Tan Hill along what is now the Pennine Way to Keld, and south to Hawes. Another crossed The Stang from Barnard Castle to Arkengarthdale, meeting the dale at C.B., the focus of a number of routes. From there, from Lilly Jocks inn as it was, one important road led down dale to Reeth on the line of the modern road, and another led over by Surrender Bridge to Feetham, and thence to Askrigg.

Packhorse trains did not use horses but ponies of a breed descended from the German *jaeger* ponies, tough and able to carry 100 kilograms up hill and down on a wooden back frame or in side panniers. The word was corrupted into jagger and the pack men were known as jaggers or jaggermen – hence the surname.

Some of the biggest companies of today began life in this way. The removals giant Pickfords was established in the seventeenth century as a packhorse concern transporting from Manchester to London, and the brewers Bass started around 1720 primarily as packhorse transporters offering ale as an incentive to prospective customers.

Many settlements within the Dales owed their existence and prosperity to packhorse trains. The end of the system often sounded the death knell for remote villages. Thorns (see *The Southern Dales*) died out totally. Skell Gill, just west of Askrigg, has shrunk to a fragment of its former self. In the height of packhorse days there were three inns serving what was then a stop on the road from Askrigg to Kirkby Stephen and Sedbergh.

Some packhorse roads were renowned for the transporting of salt, evaporated out from sea water until the development of mining around 1670. Such roads were often named as salt roads or *salterways*. One can be traced by place-name evidence, running from Slaidburn near Clitheroe to Tebay.

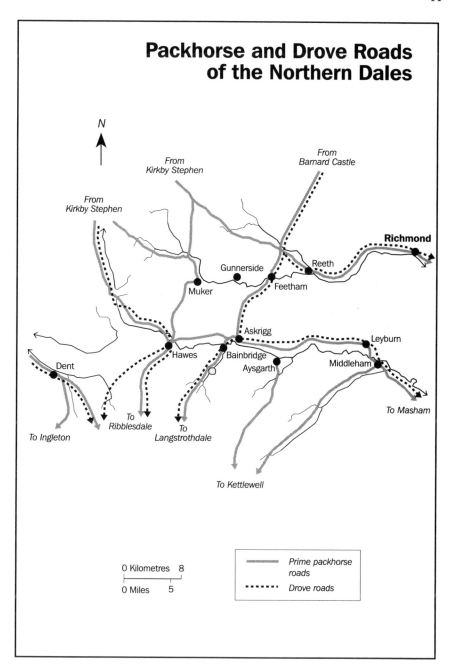

Packhorse and Drove Roads of the Northern Dales

N

From
Kirkby Stephen

From
Barnard Castle

From
Kirkby Stephen

Richmond

Gunnerside

Reeth

Muker

Feetham

Askrigg

Leyburn

Hawes

Bainbridge

Dent

Aysgarth

Middleham

To Masham

To
Ribblesdale

To
Langstrothdale

To Ingleton

To Kettlewell

0 Kilometres 8

0 Miles 5

Prime packhorse roads

Drove roads

The earliest bridges owe their construction to the packhorse trade. Merchants and transporters could not risk losing animals and goods to a risky fording of the rivers, nor could they afford to wait, idle, for floods to subside. Thus bridges appeared on the prime ways early on in the monastic period: the archetypal hump-backed packhorse bridge is a familiar sight in the Dales. Early narrow bridges had no parapets: they would have been in the way of panniers or back-frames. Early bridges across rivers, too broad for the simple stone arch, were of timber. Leland, who journeyed through the Dales in 1546, mentions bridges at Middleham, Wensley, Grinton and Richmond.

Drove Roads

Drove roads pre-date the monastic period but reached peak usage from the mid eighteenth century to the coming of the railways in the mid to late nineteenth century. Long distance cattle droving is in the written record from the twelfth century, and from Scotland from two centuries later. The Act of Union of 1603, uniting Scotland and England as one, acted as the catalyst for expansion of droving from Scotland. Peace had come to the borders, and the troublesome border reivers – basically cattle thieves and plunderers – had been pacified. Indeed some drovers had been reivers: they had been given a sound apprenticeship!

This union of the crowns also stimulated "technological" developments in the sense that the Galloway breed of cattle was introduced by selective breeding to replace the smaller stock of hitherto.

The cattle trade represented large-scale business and involved huge investments of cash. The trade had to be regulated and it was Elizabeth I who entered the first qualifications in the statute books. Drove leaders had to be at least 30 years old, married and a householder to be granted a licence, which was to be renewed annually. Vast amounts of money were tied up in cattle or sheep. One famous drover, John Birtwhistle of Skipton, had up to 15,000 head on the hoof at any time in the late eighteenth century. No wonder, then, that the larger drovers acted as mobile bankers, carrying promissory notes rather than huge amounts of money.

The drove trade also brought welcome cash to farmers en route from the hire of pasturage. Some farmers planted clumps of Scots pines as a signal that drovers were welcome.

It must have been a sight to behold when the drove came through, 200 cattle or up to 2000 sheep making their usual noises and leaving their usual trade mark on the ground. The arrival of the drove team in the township must have been a real social occasion with news and gossip being exchanged, quantities of ale consumed, with no doubt the odd argument or two.

For an evocative picture of droving, I can do no better than refer you to the writing of Sir Walter Scott, whose ancestors had been reivers, whose grandfather was a drover, and whose character Rob Roy was also a drover. He is a fictional character but based on a real-life Rob Roy. This factual Rob

Roy had been a drover who turned to outlawry after being accused of Jacobite sympathies.

The chief drove roads in the northern Dales are shown on the accompanying map.

Post-Roads and Coach Roads

Coaches are normally associated in the mind with the Wild West but they were an integral part of our transport system from the 1640s. For those who had cause to travel long distances the coach was the only alternative to horseback. The coaches, usually seating six, could hardly be described as offering any comfort, however. They were unsprung, unglazed and unheated and must have been purgatory on stony roads.

In the late seventeenth century only two post-roads touched the Dales: the Lancaster-York-Newcastle road; and the London-Skipton-Richmond road which came into Kettlewell, Agglethorpe in Coverdale and Middleham. As the term suggests post-roads were routes along which horse riders transferred documents, changing mounts at staging posts.

Stage-coaches (people carriers), as opposed to coaches, began in 1784 and were noted for their speed: 16 kilometres per hour, which was no mean feat for a coach given the state of many roads. Passengers were carried to cover the costs of operating the mail service and, in response to this new development, coaching inns were either established or grew out of existing inns. They can be seen in all our Dales towns, often typified by the archway to a cobbled courtyard.

Turnpike Roads

Mail coaches relied on roads being kept in good order to maintain their average speed, and to adhere to their timetables. The improved state of the roads was, in turn, due to the creation of Turnpike Trusts following the passing of an Act of Parliament in 1663, the first useful traffic legislation since the Act of 1555.

The first Trust to be established was on what is now the southern third of the A1 and the Acts were enacted "for the repairing of highways". It was only at the end of that century that barriers began to be erected at toll booths to force travellers to stop. The travellers, drovers, packhorse men and whoever saw the tolls as another form of taxation. The system was as popular as the ill-fated "Poll Tax" levied on us a few years ago, and travellers went to extremes to avoid passing through the tolls.

The creation of the turnpike road network was spread over a long period of time but most of the important routes were eventually drawn into the net. The first one in the northern Dales connected Lancaster with Richmond by way of Wensleydale. You will be walking part of this road as it climbs from Bainbridge over to Cam and Chapel-le-Dale (see *Discovery Walk 4*). This was set in motion in 1751, though the upland section was re-routed via Widdale (by the present motor road) in 1795.

The last one established in the Dales, in 1824, ran through Garsdale (see *Discovery Walk 2*).

Commentators noted that the turnpike roads in Yorkshire were maintained in a far better state than those in Lancashire (well . . . obviously!) because there was such opposition to turnpikes and tolls in the latter, leading to resistance and sabotaging of installations.

Just as railway growth killed off the drove and packhorse trades, so too were turnpikes doomed. The Acts were allowed to expire in the 1870s, with roads being "de-turnpiked", and the very last Trust was wound up in 1895. They had served a purpose, and have bequeathed to us hundreds of tiny turnpike cottages and probably thousands of mileposts, most of which were erected in the 1820s, so it is said.

To bring the roads story up to date, county councils were given responsibility for road maintenance in 1888, while six years later all except main roads were transferred to the care of Rural District Councils . . . and that is more or less how matters have remained.

Local Roads

In addition to the types of roads I have discussed – all of which were designed to move people, livestock or goods – there are two other roads worthy of mention. Corpse roads were for transporting the deceased on their last journey (see *Discovery Walk 2* and *9*). Enclosure Roads allowed access from the village through intake fields to the common pastures up on the fells (see *Discovery Walk 11*).

Place-names

I gain my pleasure from walking in a number of ways, all of them fairly simple. I enjoy the physical act of walking, sometimes fast, sometimes at a dawdle. I enjoy the scenery and the views, even if I have seen them countless times already. I enjoy trying to make sense of the landscape and of all the diverse elements that add together to make the patchwork quilt that is the Dales. And, not least, I enjoy the hunt to untangle the meaning and origin of place names.

Some names are easy to disentangle. It is fairly obvious that Middleham means the middle settlement, or that Bainbridge was the bridge over the River Bain. Others are easy to crack if you know what individual elements of the place name mean: *rigg*, for example, was a ridge in the days of yore so Askrigg was the ash ridge. If you know that a *thwaite* was a forest clearing, then it is easy to come up with Langthwaite having started as a long clearing whereas Thwaite was simply a clearing (rather unimaginative, methinks).

Other names are exceedingly perplexing as some place names have changed through the centuries. For example Oxnop was Oxhoppe in 1538 and Muker was Mewacre. Down the centuries the original names have become transmuted. It requires very little mental effort to see how such changes can come about. Names can change, early map surveyors probably misheard a name given in local dialect, or maybe they just guessed at the spelling of a word that until then had not been written down.

Place names must reflect the language spoken, and the ethnic origins, of each particular area. If an area has been linguistically homogenous for millennia, you would expect the majority of place names to reflect that so it would come as no surprise to find so many Welsh place names in Wales. That might equally apply to England – or perhaps not. In the Dales English *is* a veritable hotchpotch. Many of the words in use today are not really English but are more akin to the languages of Scandinavia, as the various waves of settlement have all left their mark in topographical terminology, in place names and in the local dictionary of life.

Very few local words have survived from the early Celtic period. Some of the rivers still bear British (i.e. Celtic) names: Dee, Ure, Cover are all pre-English, as is Penhill which stands proud to proclaim its Celtic ancestry. The Angles took up residence in the lowlands within the Dales and you can trace the extent of their settlement in the early period by place names. Anglian (ie. early English) settlements of the early period typically have names ending in *ham* or *burn*: Middleham and Coverham and Leyburn. A later wave of Anglian settlers spread their new roots around farmsteads or *tuns* (first settled between 750 and 950) like Grinton, Carlton, Ellerton and West Burton. Later still Anglian farmsteads often have *ley* in the name like Cringley and Wensley. This is not to say, though, that all Anglian place names end in ham, burn, ley or ton. Far from it.

The next lot of off-comers were the Danes, who spread in from the Vale of York and intermingled with the Anglians, fairly peacefully it would seem. Places containing the element *booth* or *thorpe* are usually Danish (like Agglethorpe), and *by* is a typically Danish suffix also, though we must beware here, as some later Anglian, and even Norse, names include *by*, especially in the northern Dales.

Last, but by no means least, were the Norse who settled the higher and remoter parts of the Dales. In certain areas there is a pronounced proliferation of Norse place and topographic names. Many of the names for landscape features that you see peppered across Ordnance Survey maps are Norse, signifying the enormous importance of their linguistic influence and penetration. In modern Dales-speak many words in common usage are distinctly Norse, and readily understandable by modern Norwegians; beck, gill, dale, scar, pike, force (or foss), to mention but a few. Did these Norse words replace earlier English or Celtic names, or did the Anglians not bother with the upland areas, fearing them in much the same way as eighteenth century travellers and diarists scorned the fells? Just something else we shall probably never know.

At the end of each chapter I have listed the meanings and origins of the place names en route, as they add to an understanding of the total landscape. The lists in these chapters are paltry compared with those in *The Southern Dales*. Far more research has been carried out in the former West Riding than in the North Riding. The English Place Name Society published seven volumes for the former . . . and one for the latter! I assure you I have done my best.

In the lists the following abbreviations are used:

Brit	British, i.e. Celtic
O. Dan	Old Danish
O.E.	Old English, i.e. Anglian
O.I.N.	Old Irish-Norse, i.e. Norse with an Irish flavour
O.N.	Old Norse
O.Fr.	Old French
M.E.	Middle English i.e. early Medieval
O. Welsh	Old Welsh
O. WSc.	Old West Scandinavian

Access in The Dales

There are those – and emphatically I am not one of them – who would argue their "rights" to wander at will within the Dales, or any other upland area for that matter. Personally I believe there are enough points of access for walkers to leave the straight and narrow and head for the tops and nether regions, and I could never advocate deliberately going where I know I should not be. Whether the situation will change, if legislation being proposed and debated at the time of my writing these books ever reaches the statutes books, remains to be seen. Certainly there is one school of thought that advocated transferring trespass from the civil to the criminal law list. There again another school proposes increased access to open spaces: if this school wins the legal arguments, fine – the more the merrier, but legally so.

Here are a few figures. Within the National Park there were, when I started writing the books . . ..

¤ 1450km of public footpath (about 900 miles)

¤ 600km of public bridleway (over 360 miles)

¤ 18km of RUPPs and BOATs (around 5 miles)

We all know what a footpath is, and what our rights are on them – to pass unhindered from A to B on foot. Most of us know that a bridleway gives us the right to ride a horse or pedal cycle, though both should still give way to walkers. RUPPs are a legalistic anachronism. Once upon a time they were roads, but you would find it hard to get your car along them now. In fact we have only one section of RUPP in the northern Dales, above Mallerstang.

What do the letters stand for? Road Used as a Public Path. A BOAT is a Byway Open to All Traffic, from foot sloggers to motorised "adventurers".

What about Green Lanes? They have no legal status: they may be a RUPP or a BOAT or simply an unsurfaced and unclassified County Road. If it is the latter you can, in theory, drive along it. The National Park Authority is, as I write, looking into the whole thorny issue of Green Lanes as confusion has merrily reigned, tempers have become frayed over what is or is not permissible, and many of them can only be described as a mess, a linear quagmire in winter when the ground never gets chance to dry out. So, ultimately, when the processes of consultation and enquiry have been finalised, and objections overcome, there will be re-classification "up" to County Road status or "across" to BOAT status.

However, one point transcends all arguments and legal disputes: the vast majority of Rights Of Way (ROWs) in the Dales have ancient origins, sometimes back in prehistoric times. Most of the routes in this book are based on Old Roads, and there are very few corners of the Dales that I have not managed to explore and discover by path or track.

Apart from legal definitions, another change is afoot. The National Park is beginning to phase out the ubiquitous hardwood ladder stiles, on cost and ecological grounds. Some have already been replaced with stone stiles. If you come upon a stile that I have said is a ladder stile, and it is not, you now know why.

Be Prepared!

These days most people who go out walking seem to be adequately equipped and prepared for the worst. In fact I am sure I have seen more ill-shod and ill-clad groups in the high Lakeland fells than in the Dales. Perhaps the Lake District attracts more of the train spotter types of walker, keen to tick off "Wainwrights" or "authorised tops", whereas the Dales attracts the connoisseurs: probably not, but I should like to maintain this illusion in my mind.

None of the walks in this book takes you on to the mountain tops: indeed some of them are largely low-level routes. This does not mean you can venture forth improperly equipped, though, and basic mountain gear should always be carried as our weather can be notoriously fickle. In one dale it can be dry and bright while just over the watershed it is dull and miserable. We sometimes seem to experience three seasons in one day. A decent set of waterproofs, warm clothing, a sound pair of walking shoes or boots are essential. There is rough terrain on parts of all these walks and trainers are not to be recommended, particularly in wet conditions. It might also be useful to carry a compass, and to know how to use it, as a morale booster when the mist suddenly envelops you on some remote section of moor.

A map, too, is an indispensable item. The Dales are covered by three of the Outdoor Leisure series at a scale of 1:25,000 (2½ inches to the mile or 40mm to the km). To complete all the walks in this book you will need two of them, but unfortunately they do not extend to the extremities of the Park. Grisedale and Cotterdale, for example, are omitted (Walks 2 and 3) so you will need the 1:25,000 Pathfinder map numbers 608 and 617. Better news is that almost all of the Dales is shown on the 1:50,000 Landranger map number 98 (Wensleydale and Wharfedale), though again not the north-east which appears on numbers 91 (Appleby) and 99 (Northallerton and Ripon). Even better news is that the entire Park is depicted admirably on the Ordnance Survey's Touring Map and Guide number 6 (Yorkshire Dales) published in 1992 at a scale of 1:63,360 (1 inch to the mile or 16mm to the km). For gaining a general overview and for planning a walking holiday, this map is excellent.

I cannot stress too strongly that the sketch maps in this book are not meant to be maps to walk by. Take the appropriate O.S. map with you.

Take with you, too, a pair of binoculars and your trusted flower and bird guide and, if the weather is at all doubtful, a weather forecast. This can be obtained for the Dales from any National Park Centre or by telephone. As I write, the talking forecast can be gleaned on 0891 500417.

Meanings of common topographical terms

bark	ON	hill
beck	ON	stream
ber	ON	hill
dale	ON	valley
fell	ON	hill
force/foss	ON/OWSc	waterfall
gayle	OWSc	ravine
gill	ON/OWSc	ravine
knott	OE	rocky hill top
keld	ON	spring
pike	ON	peak
rigg	ON	ridge
scar	ON	cliff
sike	OE/ON	small stream or ditch
tarn	ON	lake or pond

Discovery Walk 1

Twixt Great Coum and Aye Gill Pike: a walk in Dentdale and Deepdale

Start and Finish: Dent village, south-east of Sedbergh. Grid reference SD704 870.

Parking: pay and display car park near the western edge of the village.

Public Transport: a limited bus service links Sedbergh to Lea Yeat (below Dent Station) via Dent, operated by Woof (015396 20414).

Facilities en Route: Dent has a village store and a post office, 2 public houses, tea shops, craft shops and galleries; a National Park Information Point; public toilets. There are no facilities on the walk itself.

Outline of the Walk: Dent – Flintergill – Green Lane – Nun House Outrake – Mire Garth – Bridge End – Dent.

Length: 10.5km (6.5 miles) for the full route, or 7.5km (4.7 miles) for the shorter option.

Ordnance Survey Map: 1:25 000 Outdoor Leisure 2 1:50 000 Landranger 98

Introduction

When central government felt itself compelled to alter the centuries old boundaries of our counties, more than 20 years ago, Dentdale was hived off from the West Riding and grafted onto Cumbria. In a way that made more sense because the dale is geographically detached from the major dales, and faces west to the South Lakes rather than east to Richmondshire or south to Craven. There is, too, a hint of Westmorland (now part of Cumbria) in the vernacular architecture. The huge, corbelled chimney stacks on many of the farm houses are not at all Yorkshire.

It is a narrow dale, hemmed in by high fell ridges, the "great dangerous mountains" of an early sixteenth century document. Unless you go via Sedbergh, the only way out by car is over high passes: by Denthead to Ribblesdale, by Deepdale Head to Ingleton, or through Barbondale to Kirkby Lonsdale.

Dentdale – the lowest section anyway – can make a claim unique in the National Park. If you hope to see Squirrel Nutkin in the Dales you must explore the woods on the way to Sedbergh. Elsewhere in the Dales the handsome red squirrel has been evicted by its more robust and fecund cousin the grey squirrel. The red is also more prone to population crashes and succumbs more easily to disease. He quite simply cannot compete with the grey.

This first walk guides you through the central part of Dentdale and into its subsidiary and aptly named Deepdale. You have the option to follow the full course, or to shorten the walk by omitting the upper parts of Deepdale. It is clear in the text where the ways part company. You are, however, committed to about 5 miles at the minimum.

We shall be exploring Dentdale's fascinating past. If I can remind you of what the great eighteenth century political thinker Edmund Burke said, "people will not look forward to posterity who never look backward to their ancestors." Hear, hear, say I.

St Andrew's Church, Dent

Dent Town

Until the construction of the turnpike road from Sedbergh to Kirkby Stephen, Kendal and Kirkby Lonsdale, after 1761, Dent was the main centre for the dale rather than Sedbergh. It was Dent Town – and still is to some local residents. The road up the dale over Denthead was only turnpiked in 1802, by which time Dent had slipped into relative economic oblivion.

The village can proclaim a colourful and chequered history, dating from the Anglo-Saxon invasions. It is said the name Dent may be derived from the name of a late Celtic chieftain, defeated in the final Anglian push west. In the medieval period the dale belonged to the noble Earl of Carlisle who met a gruesome end being one of those unfortunates for whom being hung, drawn and quartered was the way out of earthly life. Apparently he had failed to stop Scots raiders from plunder and pillage. His lands in the dale were granted to Le Scrope of Bolton Castle, one of the Earl's accusers. Le Scrope must have suffered from recurring nightmares, as he soon granted his illgotten gains to Coverham Abbey which held the church and lands of Dentdale until the Dissolution almost exactly 200 years later.

Dent folk were heavily implicated in the rebellion against Henry VIII in 1539, the Pilgrimage of Grace. It was said at the time that 10,000 men stood armed in the dale! In the following century the village found itself embroiled in the Civil War with local families divided in allegiance and squabbling.

I would certainly recommend an inspection of St. Andrew's church, a Norman foundation considerably altered through the ensuing centuries, and of the outside of the Grammar School at the corner of the churchyard. Now houses, this building operated as a grammar school in the true sense of the word, offering a liberal education, from 1604 until almost the end of the nineteenth century.

I mentioned the Corpse Roads in the Introduction. One came from Garsdale to Dent church until the mid sixteenth century as the former had no consecrated ground and no right of burial. If you look at the Ordnance Survey map, you will see a walled lane from Cowgill running along High Ellershaw Edge but stopping at the parish boundary at Peggy's Hill. The present lane is an Enclosure road following the line of the early track. The original route actually continues north to Dandra Garth in Garsdale. It is not marked on the map, is often impossible to find on the ground . . . but is still a County Road. I feel sure this route was the Corpse Road.

Adam Sedgwick, Pioneer Geologist

On the cobbled main street stands a large granite monument to Adam Sedgwick. He was born in Dent, in 1785, of a family that can trace its roots with certainty back to 1379. Adam's family had been curates at St Andrew's since 1768 and he took holy orders himself. He entered into academic life, eventually being appointed Professor of Zoology first at Imperial College and later at Cambridge. His real vocation was rocks

Sedgwick Monument, Dent

and fossils and he was rewarded with the professorship of geology at Cambridge, a post he held for many years. He is recognised as one of the pioneering geologists and founders of the subject as an academic discipline. He died in 1873 and lies in the chapel in Trinity College.

At the bicentenary of his birth a 1.5 kilometre Geological Trail was developed and laid out along the Clough Valley north of Sedbergh. An explanatory leaflet is available from National Park centres.

"The Terrible Knitters e'Dent"

A literary contemporary of Wordsworth, Robert Southey (1774 – 1843) immortalised the knitting industry of Dentdale in his book of miscellany called *The Doctor, etc.* Southey is not one of our best remembered poets, despite his voluminous writings, perhaps because he wrote in a rather ponderous style. His account of the knitters appears in Chapter XXIV of the 7th volume of this 694 page book. The chapter in question is entitled

"A true story of the terrible knitters e'Dent which
will be read with interest by humane manufacturers,
and by masters of Spinning Jennies with a smile."

As I said, he was inclined to be ponderous. Oh, and the story is written in dialect!

The tale relates the experiences of a young girl, probably in the 1760s. She had been sent, along with her brother, from her home in Langdale (in the Lake District) to learn the trade in Dent. Children had this to look forward to from the age of six or seven. The girl in question had to fulfil her daily quota after school and was forbidden evening food until the work was complete. As she says

"Neet a' Day ther was
nought but this knitting" of . . .

"quorse wosset stockings –
some gloves – an' peticwoats."

A session with the knitting stick or needles could last up to six hours. Perhaps it would not surprise you to be told that this eight year old girl and her even younger brother of six ran away and walked back home, such were the conditions they had to endure.

Dent town is described as "t'poorest plaace in t'world" and the paltry income earned from spare time knitting helped keep families throughout Dentdale and Deepdale out of the workhouse.

Agents travelled through the twin dales distributing wool and worsted on a fortnightly basis, collecting knitted hose – mainly stockings and gloves – at the same time. The agents' packhorse trains would have been a welcome sight in the farms and houses of the area. The industry began to flourish in the late sixteenth century, and Dent was renowned for the number of people involved in the production process. Southey uses the word *terrible* not in the sense of awful but in the sense of being so productive.

Much of the raw wool was spun in a mill that stood near the chapel at Cowgill near the junction with the road to Garsdale. The mill has gone but the row of mill cottages is instantly identifiable. There was also a weaving shed up Flintergill on the first few hundred metres of this walk, and many of the farms in Deepdale also carded, or combed, raw wool.

The finished products were transported to Kendal which was *the* hosiery trading centre of the north.

The cobbled streets and ginnels of Dent Town were renowned for the wooden galleries that ran along house frontages at first floor level, nearly touching those of the houses across the street. Women spent many hours here spinning, knitting . . . and socialising.

The industry shares one common feature with the modern arms industry. Though there was always a demand for stockings and gloves, there was a boom in times of war. The Napoleonic Wars and the Seven Years War from 1756 to 1763, for example, brought increased prosperity to Dentdale as army contracts demanded mountains of hose as well as caps and jerseys.

Eventually changing clothing styles in the form of long trousers killed the industry off.

The Walk

Cross the road opposite the car park entrance and walk up the lane alongside the old National School, past the village green and straight ahead uphill beyond the Zion chapel. When the tarred road ends continue climbing on the steep and stony lane. This lane is called Flintergill Outrake. **Climb over the step-over stile by the gate** and take your mind off the steepness by concentrating on the gill below – quite a spectacle when in full spate – and the beauty of the sessile oak and sycamore woodland with its ground flora carpet. In spring your olfactory senses will be put to the test by the mass of ramsons *(Allium ursinum)* or wild garlic.

Beyond the second gate the nature of the wood changes as wych elm becomes a dominant tree. The wych elm, incidentally, is not so prone to disease as its English cousin. It is interesting to note that the pollen record highlights a dramatic elm decline about 3000 BC, so the present crash is by no means unique. It is also worth mentioning that elm leaves were collected as fodder for livestock.

The gill is now more of a gorge than a ravine. Eventually this delightful linear wood peters out and the gradient eases considerably. The ground flora also changes as the soil is better drained and less acidic. Tormentil *(Potentilla erecta)* grows everywhere – it has gleaming, four-petalled, bright yellow flowers, low to the ground – and bedstraw *(Galium sp.)* with its tiny white flowers and narrow leaves in whorls of six is also common. This latter prefers

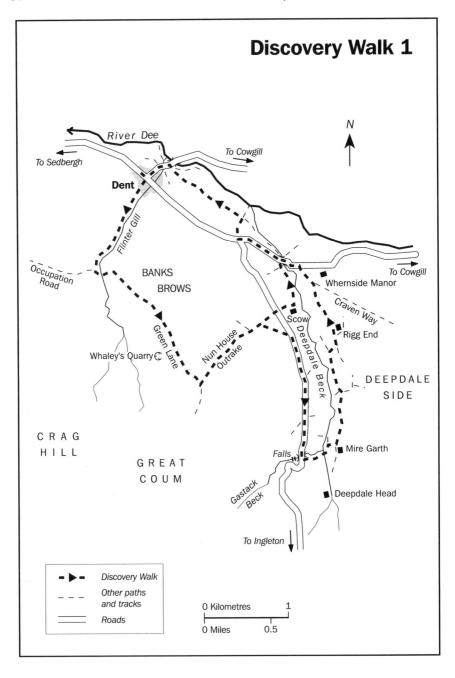

Discovery Walk 1

River Dee

To Sedbergh

To Cowgill

Dent

N

Flinter Gill

Occupation Road

BANKS BROWS

Whernside Manor

Craven Way

Green Lane

Scow

Rigg End

Nun House Outrake

Deepdale Beck

DEEPDALE SIDE

Whaley's Quarry

CRAG HILL

GREAT COUM

Falls

Mire Garth

Gastack Beck

Deepdale Head

To Cowgill

To Ingleton

- ▶ - Discovery Walk

- - - Other paths and tracks

—— Roads

0 Kilometres   1

0 Miles   0.5

acidic conditions so, despite the bedrock being limestone, the glacial cover and the high rainfall total increase the acidity of the soil.

The bird community also changes here. You may well have heard various woodland species twittering away in the wooded gill. Up here the skylark and meadow pipit hold sway.

You will soon reach a constriction in the track walls, just beyond a solitary holly tree. Here the stream disappears into the limestone, except in wet periods, from a higher sandstone layer. This is typical of the Wensleydale Group of rocks which I have discussed in later walks.

At the top of the outrake you reach a track junction. To the right is a track that is called Wideron Gait on the branch climbing up Wold End Moss and the Occupation Road on South Lord's Land: to the left is Green Lane. Both of these, like the one you have climbed up, date from the period when the open fells were being enclosed (see *Walk 11*). The Occupation Road began life as a packhorse road from Dent to Kirkby Lonsdale. The wide, walled lanes you are walking along here date from 1859 when this wide fell was enclosed and the roads re-aligned or created afresh.

Green Lane

Turn left at the track junction for a 2 kilometre walk along Green Lane. Before you head off, though, there is an obligatory view stop here. Due west, beyond Barbondale, lies the bulk of Middleton Fell, the highest point of which is Calf Top (609 metres) facing you. In the distance, to the right of Middleton Fell, you can see the little known area of fells south of Shap. To their right, and slightly nearer, are the Howgill Fells. Across Dentdale to the north-east the skyline is dominated by Aye Gill Pike (556 metres) and Rise Hill (517 metres), a fell with no right of access at all. East-north-east, beyond the head of Dentdale, is Great Knoutberry Hill (672 metres) which was opened up to the walking fraternity for the first time in 1995 by way of a permissive path over the summit. Behind that lies access-less Widdale Fell.

In summer there is a vivid indication on this bit of lane of the impact of sheep grazing on the plant community. You may have noticed how tall the heath bedstraw grows on the lane compared with the usual ground-hugging plants that one sees on the fells. Only the most persistent sheep get onto the lane so the bedstraw can afford to hang its head high. Notice also the heather and bilberry on the lane, but not in the fields.

Anyway, off you go over Flintergill and along the lane as it contours round the slopes of Great Coum. Up above you is a collection of stone "men", the Megger Stones. Such curiosities are found on a number of hills – Nine Standards Rigg near Kirkby Stephen comes to mind. When they were built, and why, is difficult to fathom.

As you progress you swing round into Deepdale and directly across the valley is an eroded track rising over the north side of Whernside. This track is the Craven Way, once an important link in the Pennine packhorse network.

Wych or Scotch or Mountain Elm
Ulmus glabra

Status: native to Britain; more common from Yorkshire northwards. More native than the disease prone English elm.

Height: average 40 metres.

Trunk: relatively short, soon splitting into several boles; very heavy; buttressed at the base on largest specimens.

Bark: smooth and grey in young trees; deeply ridged and cracked, dark grey to brown in mature trees.

Crown: domed and broad spreading; "majestic"; often split into several domes; large, drooping branches; dense canopy.

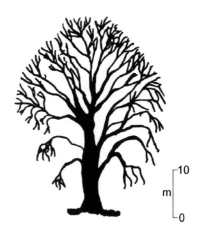

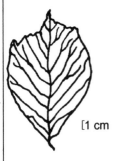

[1 cm

Fruit: quite large (1.5cm), pale green and preceding leaf growth; brown when shed in July.

Leaves: large, up to 18cm long; often shouldered; unequal at the base either side of the stalk (a distinctive feature of elms); rough and dark above, hairy and paler below; acuminate (pointed) and obovate (broadest in middle).

Uses: ideal for chair legs, wheel hubs, wheelbarrows, mallet heads, coffins in the past. Also for riding switches as elm wards off evil spirits! Now widely planted for aesthetic reasons.

The Sunny Side and the Money Side

You also have a clear view up Dentdale. The north side is the Sunny Side, and the improved pastures on that side rise higher up the fell side than on the south side, the Money Side. The first cognomer has an obvious deriva- tion. The slopes are south facing and so potentially receive long hours of sunshine. The second is sarcasm. The land on the Sunny Side is more productive than that on the north-facing Money Side, so in fact the money was made on the Sunny Side. To call the other side the Money Side has more than a touch of humour and pathos.

When you are out walking do you ever feel compelled to burst into song? If so, you may care to sing the English Hymnal's hymn number 23 which is set to the tune Dent Dale. Mind you, the hymn is called *Christmas* so you might feel self-conscious if caught singing it in high summer. The first two verses may be familiar:

1	Hark, how all the welkin rings!
	'Glory to the King of kings,
	Peace on earth and mercy mild,
	God and sinners reconciled.'
2	Joyful, all ye nations, rise,
	Join the triumph of the skies;
	Universal nature say
	'Christ the Lord is born to-day.'

Verse eight has an ecological message, most appropriate as you amble on:

8	Now display thy saving power,
	Ruined nature now restore,
	Now in mystic union join
	Thine to ours, and ours to thine.

It is, of course, the tune that is local to Dent. The words were penned by Charles Wesley.

(arr. Ralph Vaughan Williams (1872 – 1958) from the *English Hymnal*: used by permission of Oxford University Press.)

CHRISTMAS

23

DENT DALE. (7 7.7 7.)
Moderately fast ♩=100.   *English Traditional Melody.*

Welkin is a strange word, not often used now. It is old English (ie. Anglo-Saxon) and can mean sky or sky with clouds.

Walking along Green Lane also illustrates two contemporary problems clearly. Part of the track is very badly rutted and can be horrendous in prolonged wet spells. I own a four-wheel drive vehicle and have cause to go off-road legitimately but I would not consider using a track such as this for fun. It is a growing problem. The other problem is the often parlous state of the walls. They have stood the test of time well but, if you build a wall on a slope, it is bound to give way eventually as gravity, soil creep and surface water dynamics conspire to topple it. Who has the time or the money to rebuild them all?

On a more heart-warming note I have seen, on more than one occasion, kestrel and buzzard patrolling the slopes of Little Combe above you.

Eventually you reach another major junction of tracks. Here the walls open out around the stream, thus allowing space for stock to graze, water and rest on their journey this way or that. Between the junction and the face of Great Combe there is an area of coal pits: poor quality coal was mined and quarried here for use in the nearby dales. You will also have noticed Whaley's Quarry a few minutes earlier. Deepdale and Dentdale were important areas for stone working. Some quarries worked fossil-rich limestones that were sent to Stone House higher up Deepdale to be cut and polished to be sold as Dent Marble, which has found itself in demand as far away as Australia. It can also be seen in the church in Dent. Other quarries, as on High Pike at the head of Deepdale, won sandstone flagstones for roofing and building throughout the two dales.

There are thousands of disused quarries in the Dales, large and small. Today just 13 are in operation.

Turn left down the subsidiary track, Nun House Outrake, often a stream itself in wet weather. An outrake was a road used for bringing sheep down off the fells for lambing and clipping. Ignore the ladder stile on the left just before the small plantation, but please do not ignore the splash of summer colour hereabouts: rowan trees, ragged robin *(Lychnis flos-cuculi)*, meadow buttercup *(Ranunculus acris)*, tall yellow hawkbits *(Leontodon spp.)* and dog-rose *(Rosa sp.)* all congregate here as if to cheer you as you descend from the often bleak fellside tracks.

Carry on down the now rocky track past the plantation to the next ladder stile, on the right.

– Here you have to decide whether to plump for the long or the short route –

The Short Route

Carry on down the outrake to Deepdale Lane. Cross straight over and drop down through a farmyard and two gates onto a rough track along the field

edge. **At the bottom of the field look for the step-over stile at the corner of the house.** It is a long time since anyone lived here at Scow. **From the house head down dale, staying on the banking to a stile in the wall ahead,** next to a field kiln in a remarkably sound state of self-preservation. **Carry on along the line of trees and turn slightly uphill at the far end to a squeeze stile in the old wall-cum-hedgerow. Cross the meadow, keeping to the right of the small building, making for Mill Wood to the right. Drop down on the rough path to Deepdale Beck and through the bridle gate onto the road at Mill Bridge, to rejoin the long route.**

Deepdale: the long route

Just after the plantation there is a ladder stile on the right. Cross the meadow diagonally, slightly downhill, towards the telegraph pole and the hedgerow. Climb over the step-over stile there into the next, cowslip *(Primula veris)* and self-heal *(Prunella vulgaris)* covered meadow. **Pass in front of the barn and through the field gate next to it.** *Be careful here:* **bear left down the grassy track, under the huge sycamore, through a rickety gate, behind Butter Pots house, through a second such gate and into a long, narrow field.** As you proceed there is a low, wooded limestone scar to your right. **At the end is another gate past its prime. Maintain the same course, above the next barn and on to the step-over stile. You are now in the front garden of Holly Bush** – or in its curtilage, to use current Access jargon. **Beyond the house you should turn right up Deepdale Lane** for about one kilometre of level walking.

In that short distance, however, you pass five farms on the roadside, and a further four on the opposite side of the dale. All are small, some especially so, and farming in such a restricted valley can never have been easy. The steepness of the hay and silage meadows between road and beck testifies to this assumption. A glance at the Ordnance Survey map indicates that the farmsteads – and thus the road – were sited at a distinct break of slope. Above them is too steep for building, while below was, and is, too valuable for grass crops to waste on building. The number of abandoned farms in the dale bears added testimony to the marginal nature of the land.

The wild flower display along the lane is colourful, if you forget the nettles and thistles. They are all common plants whose Latin names I have given elsewhere, and include meadowsweet, sweet cicely, meadow cranesbill, campion and a blue vetch.

At the end of the run, the road swings to cross Gastack Beck just below an impressive waterfall where the stream is carving its way through a thick bed of limestone. (This gill is also good caving country with seven cave entrances.) **Just beyond the stream,** next to a stone building, **a footpath cuts off left. Climb through the wall and across to the step-over stile below the building. Head downstream alongside the narrow chasm to a stone step stile under the ash trees. Stay with the stream, over another stile, and onto**

the confluence of Combe Gill and Gastack Beck, the main headwaters of Deepdale Beck.

Ford the narrow gill and follow the beck downstream and across a second stream, to meet the farm track to Mire Garth, once a farm but now holiday cottages. Look out for dipper, incidentally, on the beck, skimming low and fast over the surface or bobbing up and down on a midstream rock.

When you reach Mire Garth turn left and follow the wall through a series of stiles and fields. On the way you pass by an abandoned farm, called Woods. The small size and crudeness of construction, as well as lack of road access, suggest a probable subsistence origin. The independent farmers of Dentdale and Deepdale were known as statesmen. They owned their land and house. A house as humble as Woods was probably tenanted. The relative absence of field barns on this side of the valley, and the former meadows being encroached upon by rushes, again illustrate the marginal nature of agriculture on the east side of Deepdale.

As you walk cast your eyes downdale to the Howgill Fells way beyond Dentdale. Do not let this fell-gazing lead you astray though. When your wall becomes a fence just before a large barn, the line of the path on the ground differs slightly from that on the O.S. map. The path also forks here. **As you approach the barn, pass below the fence that runs alongside the wooded gill. The line of the path is clear beyond this, past two more streams to a very elaborate step-over stile below Blake Rigg. At the end of that field there is a gated stile** with a vicious return spring, designed to snare the unwary, **and beyond the next field is Dyke Hall Lane.** Dyke Hall, now gone, was apparently an impressive statesman's house.

Turn right up the lane and through the first gate to a ruined lime kiln. Leave the lane here by turning left into the field. You will see the next objective, a wall stile, up above, with one more field before the complex of Rigg End farm. One path leads through the farmyard but yours passes through a narrow gate and in front of the house, alongside the edge of the wood. Beyond the stone step stile you should drop downhill, on the same line, to a metal gate by some ruined walls at the bottom. You are back on Dyke Hall Lane.

Follow the lane downhill, noting the junction with the Craven Way. The signpost indicates the distance to Twistleton Scar which is above Ingleton, and the whole route is shown clearly on the Ordnance Survey map. What the map does not show is the important link to Thorns near Ribblehead, because that road has been completely lost unless it meandered through Winterscales rather than cutting across the moor.

Carry on down the lane, at the lower end of which is a young wood on the right. This was planted ten years ago by a very small and select band of National Park workers – including yours truly. Whenever I pass by I cannot suppress a glow of pride to see how well the trees have taken.

Across the field to the east of the wood is Whernside Manor.

The Jamaican Connection

Whernside Manor is not, and never was, a manor house: that is just a name. Indeed the house used to be called West House, but perhaps that did not sound grand enough. The house in its present form was rebuilt by the Gill family of Deepdale who made money in milling and in plantations in Jamaica. Some plantation workers were brought over to the house in the late eighteenth century as servants, though this was still in the days of the slave trade. I am sure this created quite a stir in independent and conservative minded Dentdale. It is not known when these particular slaves were granted their freedom but, even before the Act of 1833 that freed all slaves in the British Empire, laws had been passed to grant freedom to any slave who set foot in Britain.

Nor is it known what became of the freed slaves here. It has been suggested that Dent had a black postman in 1890 but this cannot be safely confirmed.

The Last Lap

At the Methodist Chapel turn left alongside Stubsty Nursery wood to Mill Bridge and Bridge End farm.

– At this point the short and long routes converge –

The mill that used to operate here, Over Mill, was in existence from at least the sixteenth century and probably from several centuries before that. It was a corn mill and was still operating in the early nineteenth century, though I cannot say when it ceased working.

From Mill Bridge you could follow the Dales Way to Church Bridge. **A path leaves the road from across the bridge and hugs Deepdale Beck,** though very often much of the channel is actually dry. The water sinks into the limestone and follows a subterranean course. When in full spate, however, the beck can be violent and the National Park has had to reinforce sections of the crumbling south bank with mesh, stone-filled gabions.

– Because of the delicate state of the path, and the already high pressure of Dales Way walkers, I would prefer you to follow another, less sensitive route –

Follow the road west from Mill Bridge for 600 metres to the junction with Deepdale Lane, the road to Ingleton. Turn right here down the lane to Double (or Douby) Croft. The bridleway continues north to ford the Dee, but I would defy anyone to try and hack their way through the jungle that is the lane.

Immediately before the yard, turn left through a bridle gate, along the field and out through a second such gate at the end of the buildings. You are now on a short stretch of green lane. Carry on, hugging the unkempt

hedgerow in the next field to a step-over stile and a footbridge over the sike. Follow the path alongside the sike to a second stile. If the stream, simply called Keld, is low, you can cross the stream by the stepping stones. Another lane, Garlic Lane, comes down from the road to ford the stream.

If you use the stepping stones, turn right through the gated stile and follow the south bank of the stream through a series of fields and stiles. If the stream is too high, do not panic. There is a right of way along the north bank, too.

In either case you meet up with the Dales Way just before the playing fields. From there it is a short hop to Church Bridge and the village.

Place-name meanings

Aye Gill Pike	ON	(possibly) hay gill peak
Butter Pots	OE/ME	the rich milk pastures near the deep hollow
Dee	Brit	(possibly) a corruption of Dent
Deepdale	OE/ON	the deep valley
Dent	Brit	(possibly) the hill river
Great Knoutberry Hill	ME	the hill with cloudberry
Little Coombe Hill	OE ME	the hill near the small valley or the small hill with peat or coal dust
Mire Garth	ON	the enclosure by the swamp
Nun House	–	a corruption of the family name Moon
Rise Hill	OE/ON	the hill with brushwood
Scow	ON	wood
Whernside	OE/ON	the hillside where querns are made

Discovery Walk 2

Grisedale: the deserted dale

Start and Finish: Garsdale Head below the railway station (SD 787 919)

Parking: there is space for roadside parking between the railway bridge and the road junction.

Public Transport: trains on the Settle-Carlisle railway stop at Garsdale. There is a bus service also, a Dial-a-Ride facility, connecting the station with Hawes (01969 650682 the evening before you want to travel).

Facilities en Route: there is a National Park Information Point and a public telephone box at the start. The Moorcock Inn at the junction of the A684 and B6259 offers the usual facilities. There are no facilities on the walk.

Outline of the Walk: Garsdale Head – South Lunds – Grisedale Brow – Scale – Rowantree – Blake Mire – Garsdale Head.

Length: 8km (5 miles)

Ordnance Survey Map: 1:25,000 Pathfinder 617 1:50,000 Landranger 98

Introduction

No other valley in the Dales has witnessed social upheaval and distress to the extent that Grisedale has. True, all the dales experienced economic misfortune as one industry after another collapsed owing to loss of markets or technological change. Population migration resulting from the retraction of hand-knitting, textiles and lead mining affected all the dales. None of them, however, saw a total clearing out of its people; none of them saw every last house and farm being given up for life elsewhere. Above all, only Grisedale can mourn the loss of 75 per cent of its housing stock. Of the 16 farms in the dale one hundred years ago, no less than 12 fell into a ruinous state, though two have since been saved and restored. Only one farm is still working and the dale no longer has any "natives".

We shall explore the reasons for this decline on today's walk.

Grisedale is hidden away from the outside world, in much the same way as Crummackdale (see *The Southern Dales*). The uninformed motorist, passing down the A684 from Hawes to Sedbergh, would be quite unaware of the dale's existence. The lane into Grisedale branches off another minor road, Old Road, once the main road through Grisedale, the turnpike road of 1824.

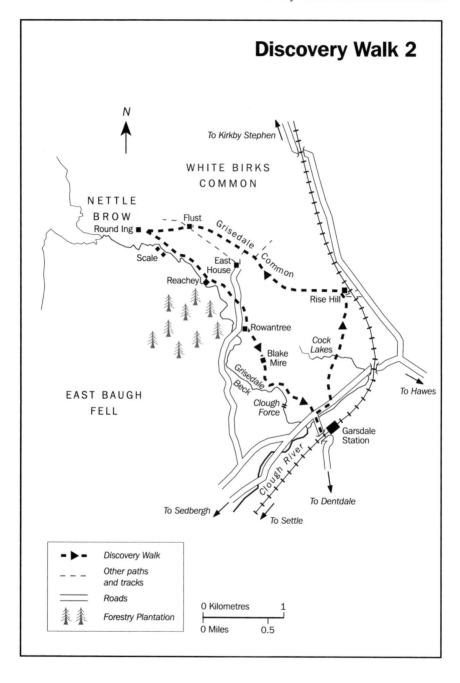

Discovery Walk 2

N

To Kirkby Stephen

WHITE BIRKS
COMMON

NETTLE
BROW
Round Ing ■   Flust
Scale   *Grisedale Common*
East
House
Reachey
Rowantree   Rise Hill
Cock
Lakes
Blake
Mire
EAST BAUGH   *Grisedale Beck*
FELL
Clough
Force   *To Hawes*
Garsdale
Station
Clough River
To Sedbergh   *To Dentdale*
To Settle

■ ▶ ■   Discovery Walk
- - -   Other paths
        and tracks
─────   Roads
🌲 🌲   Forestry Plantation

0 Kilometres   1
0 Miles   0.5

Because of the nature of Grisedale there is only one route to follow today. It seems to me inappropriate to provide a shortened version. Also there is really nowhere to park in the dale, hence the starting point at Knows Foot. Grisedale is very peaceful and unhurried: let's keep it that way and enter on foot.

Garsdale Low Moor

Walk down the road, over the Clough River on Knows Foot Bridge, to the junction and turn right on the main road, but only as far as the houses at Mud Becks. You have 250 metres of road walking to contend with here before you can relax and forget civilisation for the rest of the day. Ahead of you is the viaduct carrying the Settle-Carlisle railway over Dandry Mire. To have built such a structure here demands that we take our hats off to the engineers and navvies. The mire swallowed an almost endless quantity of rock on which to build the piers, and a number of lives were lost in the process. In the initial construction stages the engineers had tried to build an embankment rather than a viaduct, but Nature would not allow them. Incidentally, Garsdale Head station should still be called Hawes Junction.

Opposite Mud Becks a signpost indicates the way to South Lunds. Go over the stile here and pick out the faint path uphill to a gap in the wall. Drop down the dip and head upslope across Garsdale Low Moor to a gap stile in the next wall.

Continue in the same line on a clearer path along a section of moor that is covered in yellow tormentil *(Potentilla erecta)* and the tiny white flower of heath bedstraw *(Galium saxatile)*. **Make for the ladder stile in the third wall.** Just beyond the hummock of Cock Lakes (the boundary between Cumbria, behind you, and North Yorkshire) you can see the cottages of South Lunds with other buildings scattered here and there east of the railway. At one time there was quite a community here, complete with chapel and school. After 1890(ish) the children who lived on Grisedale's scattered farms had to walk to school here at Lunds, summer and winter alike. The path you are to follow soon was their journey to school. There was also a youth hostel up at Shaws – but times have changed, and the community with it.

Look towards the east from Cock Lakes for a long distance view down Wensleydale to Aysgarth Falls. Two hills stand out, on the south side of the dale, both being flat-topped. The smaller one is Addlebrough by Bainbridge while the larger and more distant fell is Penhill beyond Aysgarth.

You also have a view north right up the Mallerstang valley back over the border in Cumbria. There are two prominent hill tops on the east side of the valley, part of a ridge that stretches all the way from Garsdale Head to Nine Standards Rigg near Kirkby Stephen. The prominent top is Hugh Seat.

Rise Hill and Lunds from Cock Lakes

Hugh de Morville

In the twelfth century Sir Hugh de Morville was one of the most powerful men in the north. He held vast lands and numerous manors and castles, including Appleby, Brough and Pendragon. He also held property at Knaresborough. Not only was he in favour with the English Court, he was also on good terms with the Anglophile king David I of Scotland. Sir Hugh was granted large estates in Ayrshire and Lauderdale, and was appointed Constable by David.

Meanwhile, down south, in 1162 Henry II had appointed to the Archbishopric of Canterbury his former Chancellor, Thomas à Becket. This was a purely political appointment and a very unpopular one, not least because Thomas had only been ordained priest the day before his consecration as Archbishop. Thomas was accustomed to living, literally, in regal splendour and he soon lost the confidence of his king, so fled to France for safety two years later. Relations were restored in due course, enabling Thomas to return in 1170. He had obviously learned very little because the king's wrath was aroused again, driving Henry to utter his immortal words "would no one rid me of this troublesome low-born clerk?"

On 29th December, 1170, Sir Hugh de Morville and three knightly comrades accepted the challenge, entered Canterbury Cathedral and slew Thomas who, by all accounts, seemed to welcome the martyrdom he was duly accorded.

Sir Hugh and his partners in crime fled first to Knaresborough and later to France. The king, forced by circumstance to do something punitive, confiscated all of Hugh's (and I suppose, the others') lands. It is amazing, to me at least, that his memory should have been perpetuated in the name of the hill. In the early modern period the hill still bore the name Hughseat Morvill.

South Lunds Pasture

Drop downslope, to the right of the mine spoil heaps, **and head to the corner of the field by Rise Hill cottages: there is a stile set in the corner. Walk round the east side of the houses and over the step-over stile by the field gate.** A bridleway now crosses South Lunds Pasture but you will find little trace of it on the ground. **If you head more or less due west uphill, parallel to but away from the top wall, you will not go astray, and you should pass alongside the collapsed wall of a small enclosure.** Shortly after that the terrain changes dramatically: you are now off the acidic and harsh glacial pasture and onto limestone, shorter and sweeter grass, and a different plant community . . . and altogether easier walking.

Once again, the views from here are stunning. Away to the south-west you can see the unmistakable bulk of Ingleborough with Whernside to its right and Great Coum-Crag Hill beyond that. Due west lies Baugh Fell, with the Howgills stretching away northwards. Turn south and look across Garsdale and pick out the old Coal Road climbing up the flanks of Great Knoutberry Hill. Before the coming of the railways, this was an important link between north and south. It was both a packhorse and a drove road and it is no coincidence the road has also been known as the Driving Road and Galloway Gate.

It is possible that the path you followed from Mud Becks to South Lunds is on the northward line of this road. Further north its route is defined clearly on the ground, rising from what used to be The Bull Inn at Shaw Paddock to Hell Gill Bridge on The High Way.

Listen out, too, for the only sounds you are likely to hear up here – curlew, skylark and meadow pipit. On one of my tramps in this area, I saw absolutely no one and had only the birds, the sheep and the ponies for company. Bliss!

Head on to the ladder stile by the gate, and back into Cumbria. The bridleway suddenly becomes a footpath, so send your horse home. This is also the watershed between streams flowing east into the Ure and the North Sea, and those ultimately heading west to the Irish Sea.

Grisedale Common

You are now well and truly in Grisedale. **The path below Turner Hill is indistinct. Turn half right at the county boundary and walk towards the wall that lies ahead. It soon develops into a tractor track hugging the top**

in-bye wall of the former High Ing and East House farms, and ends at the top of a broken tarred road.

The whole of Upper Grisedale is laid out in front of you now, a natural ampitheatre surrounded by fells: Baugh Fell (639 metres) to the west, Holmes Moss Hill (473 metres) to the west-north-west, then Swarth Fell (681 metres) further round to the north, and Grisedale Brow and White Birks Common up on your right.

Large areas of the Dales were able to supplement paltry farm incomes with a little extra earned in the mines. Alas, Grisedale was not blessed in this respect, though what little mining there existed was up on Grisedale Brow and Common. Copper ores occur in what turned out to be uneconomic quantities, and small amounts of low quality coal were mined in the late nineteenth century. There was no lead.

Grisedale Common was only common to the farmers on this side of Grisedale. They were the *graziers* who held rights to graze stock on the common and to hold an allotted number of *sheep gaits* (one gait gave a farmer the right to put one sheep on the common). The gaits had to be paid for, by a process called *stinting*. If you come across the place-name *heugh* anywhere, it means sheep gait.

The Beginning of the End

From the junction with the broken tarred road you should carry straight on along the rough track as it contours across Grisedale Brow. It is not shown as a right of way on the Ordnance Survey map, but do not fear. It is still officially a County Road. **The track sticks to the head wall, passes by the ruined field kiln of Fea Fow below you.** This is one of the many "lost" farms in the dale and, personally, I find it sad in a way to see meadows that were once tended and valued now reverting to rushes and coarse grasses. At least the house at Fea Fow has been saved from decay.

The road soon reaches a small mixed wood and drops to ford Flust Gill, where there is a barn and some ruinous structures. This was the farmhouse of Flust. Higher up the gill are the unrecognisable remains of High Flust farm.

The original Norse settlers were attracted to Grisedale by its potential for stock rearing and subsistence cultivation. Or was there no better land available elsewhere, leaving the settlers no choice? Whatever the case, the valley was later deemed worthy of the monasteries. Much of the dale was granted to Jervaulx Abbey with the rest going to Easby Abbey near Richmond.

Later residents, however, found the land less rewarding and for many it was a case of hanging on and making the best of very little. Matters came to a head in the second half of the nineteenth century when a series of cold and wet summers caused grief in many upland farming areas. This was compounded by an agricultural slump in the 1870s. In the inter-censal period 1871 – 81 no less than 100,000 men and their families abandoned the land in England and Wales.

Up until this period rural folk had been in a Catch-22 situation. The land could not support them but where could they go? There was no alternative for the majority. Matters changed, however, in the second half of the century. The railways made travel easier, and the phenomenal growth of cotton and woollen textiles in Lancashire and the West Riding, and coal mining in Durham, provided the golden opportunity. These burgeoning industries had, it seemed, an insatiable appetite for women and children to labour "at t'mill" or "down t'pit".

In the 1870s and 1880s half of Grisedale's farms were abandoned. The tenants left one by one and no one came to take up the tenancies. All of them are now either ruins or have gone, no longer recognisable as houses. The names and locations of the deserted farms are shown on the accompanying map.

Also to disappear from the scene was the dale's only school. A dame-school had served the local families' needs but the abandonment of High Ing farm, the location of the school, sounded its death knell. Henceforth the children had to walk over the top to the school at Lunds.

It was some consolation that the surviving eight farms now had much more land to share between them, to increase their viability. Even isolated Round Ing managed to survive, but only as a very poor holding. Further trouble was in store, though. In 1889 came the Great Flood which devastated the lower meadows and pastures, swept away walls and bridges and caused havoc in Garsdale as well as Grisedale. However, the farms all hung on.

Pass through the two gates either side of the barn at Flust. Perhaps you might like to brush up on the Country Code at the second gate! The farmer has a sense of humour – you will come across several of these notices today, not to mention a "beware of the farmer" sign. I suppose you need a sense of humour up here, especially in winter.

Round Ing

At the gate the track forks. The one straight ahead crosses the watershed of Holmes Moss and ends beyond Uldale in the Rawthey valley on the Sedbergh – Kirkby Stephen road. I can almost guarantee you would not see a soul were you to venture that way. I have walked it on several occasions and have encountered nobody. I can commend it to you for another day.

You need to turn left at Flust, down the side track but be careful. Almost immediately you should cut off to the right across the pasture, through a broken wall and then clipping the bottom corner of a second wall, heading just south of west. At this point look for the crown of what looks like a single tree and make a beeline for it. In fact "it" is a sycamore and an ash

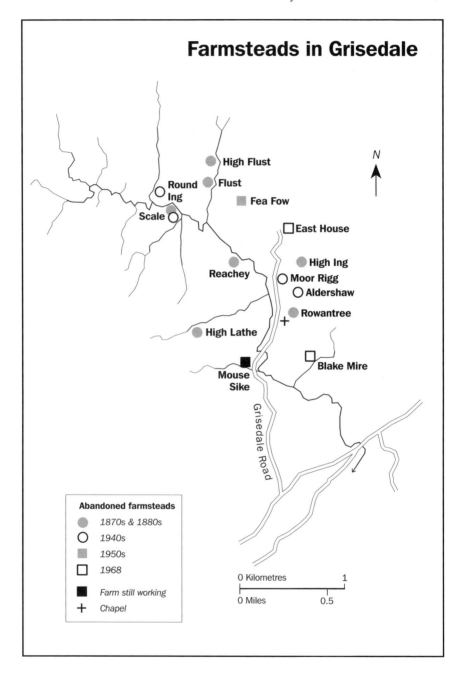

Farmsteads in Grisedale

N

Round Ing

High Flust

Flust

Fea Fow

Scale

East House

Reachey

High Ing

Moor Rigg

Aldershaw

Rowantree

High Lathe

Blake Mire

Mouse Sike

Grisedale Road

Abandoned farmsteads

- 1870s & 1880s
- ○ 1940s
- 1950s
- □ 1968
- ■ Farm still working
- + Chapel

0 Kilometres 1

0 Miles 0.5

sheltering the scant ruins of Round Ing farm. This was the uppermost farm in the dale, though not the highest. Peppered among the rubble are discarded bits and bobs – the stuff to make future archaeologists swoon, perhaps – including a copper posser in which the lady of the house did the laundry, having first carried the water up from the beck. Life was different indeed from what most of us could tolerate nowadays.

It was the terrible winter of 1947 that caused the folk at Round Ing to call it a day. Mind you, I find it surprising that they battled on for so long. No road access, only peat from the moor as fuel, no water other than in the stream . . . the list of reasons not to live and farm here is long.

Scale and the Society of Friends

Double back from Round Ing and follow the beck downstream, staying above the valley bottom. Shortly you pass another derelict farmhouse – West Scale – with its recently collapsed barn. The house roof does not look too happy, either. Notice the rounded addition at the rear of the house. This housed the staircase and would have been added on later, as access upstairs was invariably by ladder in early seventeenth century houses. This house is simple – as were most farm houses of that era – but some fine, original mullions have survived in situ, despite the house having been given up in the 1870s or 80s.

Just beyond West Scale is the twin farm of East Scale, abandoned before 1950, not derelict but not exactly full of home comforts either. This house is larger but does not have the original architectural delights of its neighbour. The two are linked by a paved pathway. Between East Scale and the beck, in the wooded field, is a now disused Quaker cemetery, functional from 1679 to 1863. They are certainly resting in peace here.

The year 1652 was a momentous one for George Fox and for the Quaker movement, the Society of Friends, that he founded.

In 1652 he had his famous *vision* on Pendle Hill in Lancashire, and in June of that year he preached to a gathering in excess of 1000 people on Firbank Fell near Sedbergh. This sermon is seen as instrumental in the founding of the movement. It was in between times in 1652 that Fox passed through the Dales, including Grisedale, preaching and *convincing* many folk. He may well have stayed overnight in Grisedale, perhaps at East Scale itself. One matter is certain, however: this farm was an early meeting place for converts in Grisedale.

There is no right of access to the two houses at Scale but I am sure nobody would object to your looking at, and perhaps reflecting on, the graveyard and on the hardy and independent minded folk who farmed what would have been a close-knit community, in tune with that dale and its vagaries, but probably divorced from the rest of the world.

Bridge at East Scale

Down Grisedale Beck

The path leaves Scale bridge, rebuilt after the Great Flood, and follows Grisedale Beck, keeping to the east bank below Galey Hill. During the summer months you are likely to have your peace shattered by the resident oystercatcher. Not only are they gaudily dressed, they just cannot shut up either. The valley bottom is not exactly botanically rich but there is a smattering of blue and yellow forget-me-nots *(Myosotis sp.)* and the pale mauve lady's smock or cuckoo flower *(Cardamine pratensis)*. Apparently cuckoo flower attracts orange tip butterflies though I doubt they will consider venturing this far.

Head on downstream, through the gate, over a step-over stile and to another gate beyond a large building to the right. From afar it looks like a barn but an inspection of its frontage gives the game away: this, too, was a farmhouse, called Reachey. It is again of seventeenth century date, but you can clearly see where the roofline was altered at some time in the past. With its lost neighbour High Lathe, it would have relied on meadows and improved pastures that have long since been swallowed up by the plantation of Butterbeck.

Pass through the gate beyond the house and soon leave the stream bank to climb up by a ruinous wall to a gap stile. Ahead lies a hay meadow, so single-file please. At the far end of the meadow is a gated squeeze stile. Here

Common or European Ash
Fraxinus excelsior

Status: native to Britain.

Crown: tall, domed with branches spreading out widely; generally open canopy.

Height: up to 40 metres; one of our tallest native species.

Trunk: long and strong; up to 3m in diameter; branches ascend steeply from the main bole; branch and twig ends hang down and then curl up at the ends.

Bark: light grey and smooth in young trees but fluted with distinct vertical ridges in older specimens; distinctly grey in winter.

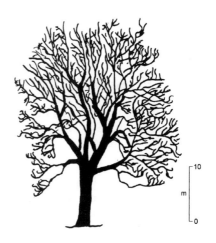

Fruit: ash trees are sexually confused: some are male, some female, some both, so male and female flowers can appear on the same tree. Fruits do not form every year; they occur in dense clusters, bright and pale green, hanging down; wings turn brown in autumn and fall late.

Leaves: pinnate (9 to 11 leaflets set opposite each other on the stem); pale and slightly whitish below; up to 30 cm long; often fall in masses after the first frosts.

Uses: historically a popular hedging tree, with small branches and leaves being spread out in autumn as fodder; used in the past for furniture, farm implements, tool handles and for coach building. Now used for laminates.

I once had one of those experiences with nature that I find uplifting. I was sitting down by the stile, waiting for a rogue cloud to move away so I could take a photograph. After a minute or two a tiny brown head popped out of the wall, and popped back in again. I kept quite still and waited. The head popped out again but this time it stayed awhile to observe me observing it. It was a weasel.

From the stile cross to the road and walk past the gable end of Moor Rigg, another former farm, but this time well and truly lived in. **The path follows the wall, through another wall by the field barn. Drop down the next field, cross the access track to Aldershaw, and go through the stile opposite.**

If you were to turn right at this point, the track would take you down to the road and Grisedale's former chapel. This was built in memory of an evangelical Methodist preacher, Richard Atkinson, who lived in the dale. He died in 1884. The chapel opened for "business" in 1889 and closed down in 1970, having outstayed even the last native family in Grisedale.

Turn left to pass through the farmyard of yet another lost house, Rowantree. Cross the stream and head uphill to another stile just below the field barn in the top corner of the field. Down below, on the other side of the valley, is Mouse Sike, the only working farm left in the dale.

Hill Pastures

Note again, as you walk, how the old meadows are again being surrendered to rushes. **You cross one more field and then pass round the top side of Blake Mire,** yet another . . . yes, you guessed it.

I suppose it has come too late for the ghosts of Grisedale but new initiatives were introduced in late 1995 to help our hill sheep farmers. Something good has come out of Brussels in the shape of Northern Uplands Objective 5(b) money. This is intended, amongst other things, to support farms in disadvantaged areas, including supporting farm diversification schemes and training in new skills, in a four-year plan. Three cheers for this.

You will have noticed that the most accessible houses have been rescued and restored, while the inaccessible and remote ones have been forgotten. Blake Mire is the exception. It is certainly inaccessible but not abandoned. Most people these days seem uninterested if they cannot get the car to the front door. Mind you it is a long tramp with the shopping, and the coal and . . .

Terminal Decline

A series of harsh winters in the 1930s must have made those years of Depression a trial. The exceptionally severe snows of the 1947 winter were the final straw for more of Grisedale's families. Before the end of that decade Round Ing was finally given up, then East Scale, Moor Rigg and Aldershaw.

Fea Fow was abandoned in the late fifties, leaving only three farms still occupied. In 1968 the occupants of Blake Mire and East House decided enough was enough. Only Mouse Syke remained of the original sixteen. The end really seemed nigh in the following year when that was put on the market: its family had decided to leave. This seemed to be the end of the line for Grisedale. For the native population, it was the end of the road: they had all gone, but Mouse Syke was bought by an outsider who intended to run the farm as a going concern. And so it remains.

From Blake Mire the way lies due south across the moor. The path is not at all clear on the ground but you cannot go astray. After five minutes or so you will find yourself standing on the edge of a very deep valley where the stream has cut its way through a natural dam of glacial material into the bedrock below (see *Discovery Walk 3* for a discussion of landform processes).

Do not drop down into the valley. Rather you should follow it round to the left, contouring along the top, passing through a squeeze stile and then dropping down to the road directly opposite the junction ...

... and that was Grisedale. You will have made your own judgement by now but I rank the dale near the top of my personal top ten, for beauty, for tranquility and for being away from the proverbial madding crowd.

Place-name meanings

Aldershaw	OE	the alder copse
Blake Mire	OE	the bleak or dark swamp
Clough River	OE	the river in the ravine
Cock Lakes	OE/ON	the place where (black) cock lek (perform to hens)
Dandry Mire	ON	Andrew's swamp
Galey Hill	OE/ON	gallows hill
Garsdale	ON	Garor's (pers. name) valley
Grisedale	ON	the valley with young pigs
Knows Foot	OE	foot of the hill
Lunds	ON	small wood
Rise Hill	OE/ON	the hill with brushwood
Round Ing	ON	the round meadow or pasture
Scale	ON	a summer shieling
Swarth Fell	OE/ON	the black hill
White Birks Common	ON	the common with white birch trees

Discovery Walk 3

Along the High Way – in and around Cotterdale

Start and Finish: Thwaite Bridge on the A684 (Sedbergh to Hawes road), 6km west of Hawes. Grid reference SD 826 922.

Parking: there is a large lay-by next to the bridge.

Public Transport: Dial-a-Ride buses will stop on their way between Hawes and Garsdale Station (01969 650682 the evening before you want to travel).

Facilities en Route: none.

Outline of the Walk: Thwaite Bridge – Cotter End – High Dike – Tarn Hill – Cotterdale – High Rigg – Thwaite Bridge.

Length: 9km (5.6 miles).

Ordnance Survey Map: 1:25,000 Pathfinder 608 1:50,000 Landranger 98

Introduction

Today's walk, for much of its length, follows two specific old roads. One was the main road from Hawes to Kirkby Stephen until the present tarred road was first constructed as a turnpike road between 1824 and 1826. Even beyond that date, though, it was still in use as a road. In fact its legal designation today is as a RUPP, a Road Used as a Public Path. The second old road was a Corpse Road connecting the hamlet of Cotterdale with the church at Lunds near the headwaters of the Ure. More on both of these follows in due course.

In many of the walks in this collection geology, in the form of the Wensleydale Group of rocks, forms the backdrop. Features that owe their existence to some quirk of geology or geomorphology are seen from below or from afar. Today, however, we can get to grips with landscape forces and processes because we will be experiencing them at close quarters or from above. I believe it is easy to make sense of a landscape when you can look down on it. Thus, the role of geological controls, of glacial action and the weathering processes will become apparent during the day.

We shall also encounter Lady Anne Clifford, one of the most formidable matriarchs of the seventeenth century, the last in a long line of aristocrats who held sway across much of the northern Pennines from Skipton to Appleby and Penrith.

As with *Discovery Walk 2* I offer you only one circuit. There are no shortcuts, and no reason to try and find any. The walk includes a dale similar in some ways to Grisedale, its being hidden from the general view and possessing only one narrow, dead-end road. Cotterdale, too, is a place to approach on foot, not by car.

A preliminary word of caution is in order. As the path approaches the settlement of Cotterdale, it fords West Gill. In times of heavy rain this can be a difficult crossing. In times of spate it is to be avoided, so please think carefully concerning exactly when to undertake this walk. Also, as much of this walk is at high level, reaching 540 metres, you need good visibility. The views are too stunning to venture up in days when the clag has descended.

The entire route is only 9 kilometres: I could do that in two hours if I had a mind to but I prefer to dawdle to the extreme on The High Way. On several occasions, on warm sunny days, I have taken the whole day.

Carr and Cotter Riggs

The road realignment at Thwaite Bridge may have "improved" (ie. speeded up) traffic flow but the results can hardly be described as aesthetically pleasing. More akin to a mess, I would suggest. At least there is a display of summer colour with the rhubarb-like butterbur *(Petasites hybridus)* and the purple of meadow cranesbill *(Geranium pratense)* and melancholy thistle *(Carduus heterophyllum)*. Now quite why it earned the epithet melancholy is beyond me. I would have said it is anything but, especially as it is by no means common.

A friend tells me it is named thus because its very beauty cures the melancholy in us!

If you can tear yourself away from so-called civilisation, **cross over the bridge on the old road loop and go into the wood opposite.** There is a signpost indicating the route. **Walk up the path to the ladder stile at the top of the wood (recently more or less clear felled) onto the steep and rough pasture called Carr. Head straight across the pasture towards the linear wood over to the right.** Looming above you is the ridge of Cotter Clints behind the spoil heaps of a lost mining venture. **At the top corner of the linear wood is a ladder stile. Beyond this continue in more or less the same direction,** passing the mine track almost immediately. **Head north-east through the rushes to meet the long boundary wall rising up Cotter Riggs. Look for the twin stiles in the wall, climb over and turn uphill along the wall side.**

You have here the first of today's many long-range views. Straight ahead, northwards, is Cotterdale, hemmed in by a range of forbidding fells, notably by the massive Great Shunner Fell (716 metres) and its aptly christened subsidiary Black Hill. To your right lies Wensleydale beyond Hawes; behind you across the valley lies the fell separating Widdale from Wensleydale with the prominent gash of Mossdale Gill at the foot.

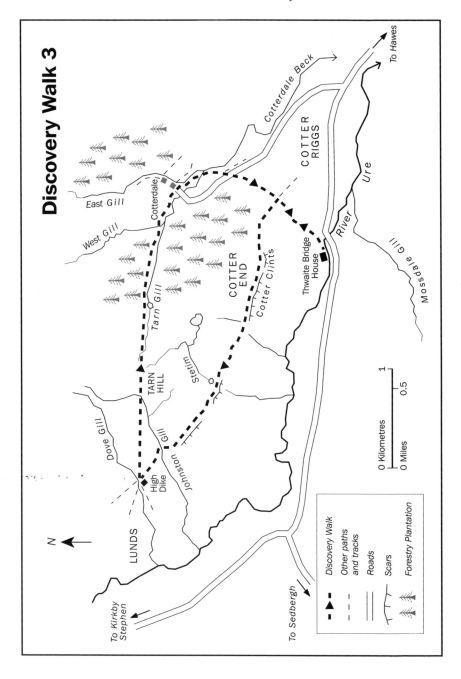

Discovery Walk 3

To Hawes

Cotterdale Beck

COTTER RIGGS

East Gill

Cotterdale

West Gill

River Ure

Mossdale Gill

Tarn Gill

COTTER END

Cotter Clints

Thwaite Bridge House

TARN HILL

Stetim

Dove Gill

Johnston Gill

High Dike

LUNDS

N

To Kirkby Stephen

To Sedbergh

Discovery Walk
Other paths and tracks
Roads
Scars
Forestry Plantation

1
0.5
0 Kilometres
0 Miles

The path up Cotter Riggs is indicated by blue way-marker posts: is the wall not sufficient as a handrail? Blue should signify statutory designation as a bridleway but in fact this path and your next 4 kilometres are designated as a RUPP – a Road Used as a Public Path. It is an anachronism . . . but a timely cue to delve into the past.

The High Way and Lady Anne Clifford

Stand at the stile and look both ways, down the incline to the valley road to your right, and up the incline to the skyline. *That* was a road, the start of The High Way, a high level section of the road from Hawes to Kirkby Stephen. It is, perhaps, hard to accept that this was a road. Take the wall out of the scene, by the way, as it did not exist until near the end of the road's long existence. I dread to think how long it took to jockey a wheeled vehicle to the top, or to prevent disaster happening on the descent. It is little wonder people either rode on horseback or walked. It is little wonder, either, that early commentators condemned the country's roads virtually without exception.

Lady Anne Clifford was the daughter of the 3rd Earl of Cumberland, widow of the 3rd Earl of Dorset and later widow of the 4th Earl of Pembroke and Montgomery. By virtue of being a Clifford she could call the following her homes: Skipton Castle, Pendragon Castle, Brough Castle, Brougham Castle and Appleby Castle, not to mention houses in the capital. When she was a Dorset Sackville, Knole House at Sevenoaks in Kent was her home; and when she was a Pembroke Herbert, Wilton House near Salisbury was home.

She was born in 1590 in the reign of our last Tudor monarch Elizabeth; she lived through the first Stuart period and the Civil War; and died in 1676 well into the final Stuart period. Her story is long and convoluted so suffice it to say here that she inherited her northern estates when she was 60 and twice widowed. She embarked on a massive programme of restoring or even rebuilding her castles and took delight in spending time in all of them. To get from Skipton Castle to her four northern seats meant a journey through Wharfedale, Wensleydale and Mallerstang. The shortest route passed along The High Way, and she is known to have made that journey in October 1663 (aged 74) and again two and a half years later and, for the last time, in July 1667.

Her diaries are available to consult, but they are frustrating in some respects. She goes into detail about who she entertained, what she wore and other such mundane matters. Of the things I want to know – the weather, the state of the road, buildings en route – she is silent.

Lady Anne did not travel lightly. She was a great lady and processed rather than travelled, accompanied by a great retinue of officials and servants, local dignitaries, well-wishers and hangers on. And her luggage . . . and her bed. It has been estimated that up to 300 people were drawn into the cavalcade.

All the luggage went ahead in baggage waggons; the men servants and male retinue rode or walked; her ladies-in-waiting travelled in two coaches. Lady Anne had more sense: she rode in a horse-litter, safe from the bumps and jolts of the unsprung coaches. She was no fool!

She also hired local menfolk to guide her train across particular sections of road, and to carry out emergency repairs to the road surface. By the time the waggons had passed by, I should think the road was in need of repair.

Lady Anne seemed to take delight in going "where never coach went before". This is perhaps indicative of why she still maintains such a presence in the area more than three centuries after her death.

Cotter End

Climb up the old road to the gate in the headwall and follow the track as it zigzags by the remains of the twin lime kilns and attendant quarry. I suppose it was relatively easy to transfer the lime by horse sled to the slopes of the Riggs. The preponderance of rushes now is a sure indication of how vital it was (and still is) to try and neutralise the naturally acidic soil conditions on the glacial drift covered slopes. No such problem existed on Cotter End, however, as the limestone layers here provide a degree of alkalinity.

Kestrels nest in the vicinity. In a recent summer I was fortunate to be able to combine sun bathing here with watching the aerial acrobatics of mother

Limekiln at Cotter End

kestrel teaching her twin offspring how to hover and wheel and dive. My trance and pleasure were soon shattered, though, by a different kind of winged creature. The pilot of a helicopter had decided that time was ripe to start ferrying skips of stone up Black Hill Moss to help in the rehabilitation of a soggy part of the Pennine Way on the shanks of Shunner. Such is progress!

The next section of walking on The High Way, that can take anything upwards from an hour in fine weather, such are its delights, **is easy and relatively flat. You simply follow the wall along the edge of Cotter Clints and beyond.** It is dry underfoot, being limestone, but a short distance to your right presents a different picture. Glimpses of peat haggs confirm the presence of more impermeable sandstones. The old road is actually utilising the top of a band of limestone.

As Cotter End merges imperceptibly into Thwaite Bridge Common – common to the sheep gait holders, not to you and me – another view begins to open up, this time over to the west. You can see beyond Garsdale and Grisedale, beyond Baugh fell to the distant Howgill Fells; to the south-west past Rise Hill (556 metres) to Crag Hill (or Barbon High Fell 682 metres) and the bulkier Middleton Fell (609 metres) the other side of Dent.

The Hawes – Hawes Junction Railway

Down below in the section of upper Wharfedale that is called Mossdale, you can see the old track bed of the railway that connected Hawes on the Wensleydale railway with Hawes Junction, or Garsdale Head, on the Settle-Carlisle railway. The two railways were built and completed within a year of each other (1876 and 1877) but by different companies. The Wensleydale railway, from Northallerton, was built by the North Eastern Railway Company while the Settle-Carlisle was part of the Midland Railway's link from London to Glasgow. The connection through Mossdale came very soon after the other two lines, but was separate from them, though it was built by Midland. The railway link fell foul of the 1964 programme which axed many rural lines.

Thwaite Bridge Common

The old road across the Common passes, for a good 2 kilometres, alongside a line of shakeholes, some small, rounded and grass covered; others vertical and hewn from rock. Erosional processes of dissolution (see *The Southern Dales*) have removed the limestone where surface water percolates down through vertical joints in the rock. The overlying layers of glacial material have collapsed into the voids below to leave shakeholes. One in particular always reminds me of the much-visited Buttertubs on the road from Hawes to Reeth.

At one point a shakehole has developed into a fully fledged swallow hole where the stream called Stetim disappears for a while before resurging on Cotter Side. It is worth having a look at and involves only a short diversion. Where The High Way rises slightly over the limestone outcrop, look for the prominent gully to the right and the sink hole is down there. In times of flood the amount of water exceeds the capacity of the sink hole to absorb it, and the water backfills to form a short-lived pool.

The main line of shakeholes comes to an end at the wall that bounds Thwaite Bridge Common. You will notice that the gateway is too narrow for wheeled traffic, other than bikes, reminding us the road here had been superseded by the valley road before the enclosing of the fells hereabouts.

Pass through the gate and onwards, easily as before. A view up Maller-stang now begins to unfold with Swarth Fell (681 metres) and Wild Boar Fell (708 metres) dominating the skyline across the valley. The latter displays on its steep, east facing edge the clear signs of massive slope failure that most probably occurred in the centuries when the glaciers were melting and retreating. Legend has it that England's last wild boar was killed on the fell in the fifteenth century by Sir Richard Musgrave of the now disappeared Hartley Castle just east of Kirkby Stephen. I am inclined to think the last wild boar in England was like the Holy Grail – everywhere.

Very shortly you come to a limestone scar which needs more than a casual glance to determine whether or not it is natural. Look over the wall and all is revealed. The scar is in fact the face of a quarry that supplied the lime kiln. **Soon after the quarry the road crosses Johnston Gill** which has carved quite a cleft in the hillside.

High Dike

You will no doubt have noticed that sandstone is increasingly replacing limestone in the wall and the former is totally dominant in the vicinity of **the ruin you next reach.** This, complete with its series of paddocks and its own lime kiln, was High Dike. It is also where you must leave The High Way.

If you think about it, is it not strange how perceptions change through the years? Imagine the outcry if a newly privatised railway company were to apply for planning permission now to erect a huge viaduct at Dandry Mire. Imagine, too, the commotion that would follow a decision to build a road across the fells. A High Way today would provoke a tumult of protest as today's vogue is to have roads hidden from sight and to have them avoid scenic areas. Not so in the past. The chief criteria then were to avoid the difficult valley bottoms with their woodland and marsh and their many hidden perils. No, it was far safer to go high where firm ground and an all-round prospect helped to ensure safe travel.

As I have noted earlier, the road up Mallerstang only dates from the mid 1820s so this was *the* road. Travellers needed places to rest and refresh, especially on stretches where the weather can close in and transform a safe journey into peril. High Dike was one such place. It was an inn as late as

High Dike

1877, though I have no clue as to the date of its closure and abandonment. It was a very basic affair: all travellers required was food, ale and somewhere to bed themselves down, and to corral their stock safely.

I do not know how old High Dike is, either, but the present building has a certain air of the seventeenth century about it.

Further north along The High Way are two other ruins: High Hall was a farm and High Way had connections with providing succour to travellers. Opposite High Way, on Grass Gill is an enclosure called Horse Paddock (grid reference SD 796 953) which was used for overnight grazing.

River Capture

An inspection of any map will emphasise how close are the respective sources of the Ure and Eden on the slopes of High Seat. Little more than two kilometres separate Eden Springs from Ure Head. The actual separation in the main valley, between water flowing south and water flowing north, is minute. A similar situation is apparent at Garsdale Head between the tributaries of the River Clough and the feeders of the Ure descending from Wether Fell.

In both cases the fluvial geography experienced a dramatic change in the post-glacial period: at Aisgill and at Garsdale Head the headwaters of the Ure have been captured and spirited away to another ocean. How and why did this happen?

As the glaciers were melting at the end of each successive glacial advance, prodigious quantities of meltwater flowed down the glacially deepened river valleys. Among the areas on which ice accumulated and from which it dispersed were Wild Boar Fell, Baugh Fell and Great Shunner Fell. At first glaciers and then meltwater flowed radially out from these highland masses – north down the Eden Valley, east along Wensleydale and south-west through Garsdale.

These enormous amounts of water had the energy to carve deeper into their valley bottoms. The Clough, flowing westwards, was shorter and had a much steeper gradient than the Ure, and thus possessed more potential energy. This enabled the Clough to cut back at its source, eating into the watershed that had separated it from the Ure-Grisedale Beck system. In time the Clough broke through into Grisedale Beck whose water henceforth took the easier course down the steeply flowing Clough. The Ure had lost this major set of headwaters. Those who have studied the area in detail maintain this happened before the most recent glacial advance.

In the course of future time the Clough could well cut back further across the Dandry Mire watershed to capture the Ure again. If this does happen, all the Ure waters north of the Moorcock will be diverted to Morecambe Bay. Stick around!

Meanwhile, up at Aisgill the Ure fought a losing battle against the Eden, also more steeply flowing and cutting more rapidly into softer New Red Sandstone strata, thus being more energetic than the ambling Ure. Hell Gill is now the infant Eden: it was once the infant Ure.

Life was made even harder for the Ure by direct glacial deposition. Look north from High Dike and you will see that the valley floor is peppered with huge drumlins, elongated hillocks comprising glacial till or boulder clay. These effectively blocked the Ure's pre-glacial course, diverted some of its waters, and made its course more tortuous.

I have discussed drumlins in *The Southern Dales*. Suffice it to note here that the drumlins in Lunds are aligned towards the north-north-west confirming that the dominant ice flow was down from Wild Boar Fell. In Mossdale, however, the orientation is more to the east.

A final thought . . . until pioneering geomorphological fieldwork in the 1840s, it was generally accepted that the covering of what we know as glacial till or drift was laid down during the biblical Noachian flood! How science has progressed in a century and a half.

The Corpse Road

Imagine having to carry the body of a deceased friend or relative, in a wicker basket, from Cotterdale to Lunds church. Having to walk nearly four kilometres, having to climb 230 metres from hamlet to hill top, and having to negotiate the moors of Tarn Hill. Imagine that toil in good weather, never

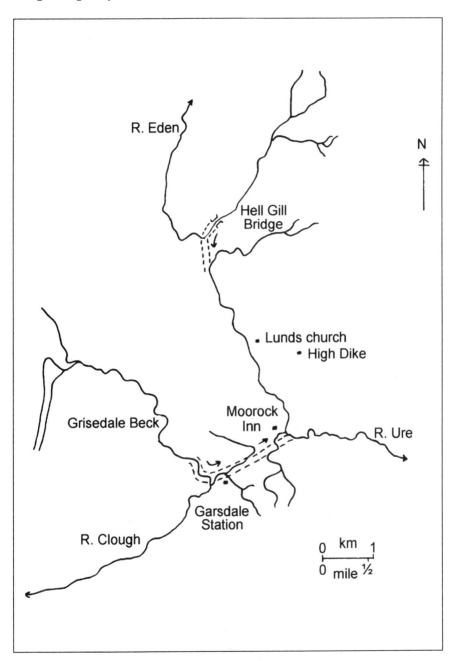

River capture on the Ure

mind against a howling west wind or in the depths of winter. That is what the folk in Cotterdale had to do as Lunds was the only church they could look to.

Without doubt the pall bearers and relatives must have welcomed the first sight of High Dike, as they had welcomed the news of its building, whenever that was.

You are now to follow the Corpse Road in reverse, hopefully only carrying a small rucksack. Think of the members of the cortege as you walk.

High Dike is at the junction of five paths. **If you imagine the ruin as a roundabout, take the last exit to head on a magnetic bearing of 85 degrees, in other words almost due east.** The path is little trodden these days – I have yet to see anybody up here – but it is marked by a line of marker posts.

Before you leave High Dike, however, look back towards the south-west. In the far distance you will see the asymmetrical shape of Whernside, the northern-most of the Three Peaks, and the sweep of fells north from there.

There is another point to note, before you head off on the Corpse Road. Even in dry conditions Dove Gill flows, once you get round the first main bend, and you can see why. The stream runs over a bed of friable but impermeable shale. This was the prime factor in the choice of a site for the inn.

Follow the line of posts up Broats and over the flanks of Dove Gill Hill. Rising away on your left is the hill called Lunds Fell or Sails which has the distinction of possessing the accepted main source of the River Ure. In turn Lunds Fell rises to a hill called Hugh Seat (see *Discovery Walk 2* for an account of Sir Hugh de Morville).

Tarn Hill

As you climb towards the rounded crest a line of grouse butts comes into view. Now, grouse are associated with heather and there is precious little of that left here. But . . . look beyond the fence on Tarn Hill and the picture is markedly different. Controlled grazing on the other side of the fence has preserved heather moorland. In this case the grass is greener on that side at least as far as the grouse are concerned. I have never actually seen or heard grouse up here but I have encountered golden plover with its often mournful call or plaintive one-note whistle.

Cross my dyslexic ancestor's gill again – and the best of luck in soggy weather – and clip the corner of the fence. Maintain the same line past a couple of overgrown puddles and begin the descent off Tarn Hill. **At first the path is quite indistinct, at best, but stick close to the stream all the way down.** Shortly before you reach the western boundary of Blaescar forest, the stream disappears into the depths only to reappear a short way into the plantation as Tarn Gill. **A few metres north of the sink hole a step-over stile allows access to the forest.**

You now have an easy, if steep, descent down the firebreak. The view ahead is obviously restricted but at least there is a "window" ahead to the valley beyond. A climb up this way would give you a mere slit filled with sky, and a seemingly endless trudge. It is better in this case to be going down.

The actual line of the path on the ground does not fully correspond to the map – but do they ever in forestry plantations? **Eventually you drop down onto a forest road and *banjo*,** forestry jargon for a turning area. **Cut across to follow the path through the forest ride that continues downhill, and pick up Tarn Gill again.** This next section is quite pleasant, as plantation walks go!

Then, without warning, you are out of the forest and in Cotterdale. There is a step-over stile in the boundary fence and then West Gill which has to be forded. In very high flow conditions you may have to follow the right bank to the road at Bridge Haw, but it is normally possible to pick your way across.

Spare a last thought for the coffin bearers having to manhandle their macabre load across the beck and up that long drag to Tarn Hill top.

Cotter Dale

There is another step-over stile beyond the beck and the path then turns to follow the riverside past a field barn. Directly across the dale, high up on the slopes of Humesett is a prominent beacon, one of several in that vicinity. The easterly slopes of Cotter Dale and the southern ridge of Shunner were important for coal mining. The track from Hardraw up Shunner, followed by the Pennine Way is still called the Hearne Coal Road. It linked civilisation to a number of scattered workings, mostly small. On much larger scale were the levels of Cotterdale Coal Pit, linked to Hardraw and Cotterdale by track. Believe it or not, coal was still being mined up there in the 1920s. The beacons may have been markers for the mines or the roads.

Cross two more meadows to join the dale road to the immediate left of the farm complex. Exit through the gate ahead, not into the complex, and over the stone stile onto the lane.

– You need to consider the water level now to decide which way to go. If the beck was a problem to ford, I suggest you stick to the road as far south as the cattle grid at Low Rigg, to avoid a difficult stream crossing. Read the next paragraph before proceeding –

If the beck was fairly dry, cross the lane directly opposite that stone stile. There is a path on both sides of the beck. You need the one on the right, or west bank, running alongside the field wall. In less than 200 metres you pass through a bridle gate and cross a meadow, at the far side of which is

West Gill again, just before its confluence with East Gill. The only way to cross this is to jump it.

You then cross another meadow to a handgate next to the barn. Head across the next field following the boundary uphill to another handgate. Turn directly uphill to join the road at the cattle grid. Look back here for the view up the dale (Cotter Dale) beyond the hamlet (Cotterdale) to the enclosing fells.

The last lap begins at the footpath sign (to Thwaite Bridge). Head upslope on the rather indistinct path over Low Rigg, down the dip and up again to the ladder stile in the boundary wall. Cross the next field, to the next wall stile on The High Way, and retrace your steps across Carr to Thwaite Bridge and journey's end. Before you set off, however, look down Cotter Riggs.

Drift Tails

This whole slope, from Cotter End to the road junction at Collier Holme Farm, is made up of glacial deposits. To hit bedrock you would need to drill down a long, long way. It is a feature called a drift tail. To be precise we should call it a drumlinoid drift tail because it is a variation on the drumlin theme.

Bluebell Hill, where the Pennine Way leaves Hardraw, is another drift tail. In both situations the post-glacial streams have been diverted eastwards, in the case of Cotterdale Beck by maybe 1.5 kilometres or so.

Drift tails formed, like drumlins, beneath moving ice tumbling down to the south-east from the fells above. The ice had sufficient energy to dump the material and to shape it in the characteristic tapering form, but not enough to erode and remove its deposits.

It is possible – this is my hypothesis – that the ice coming off Cotter End was squeezed by greater volumes flowing down Cotter Dale and Mossdale, slowing the upland ice down and forcing it to abandon its load.

We shall meet drift tails elsewhere in Wensleydale.

Place-name meanings

Blaescar	OE/ON	the dark scar
Carr	ON	the marsh or brushwood
Cotter Dale	ON	the valley with huts
Mallerstang	Brit/ON	the hill with some kind of landmark
(Great) Shunner Fell	ON	Sjon's (pers. name) hill
Thwaite (Bridge)	ON	the clearing
Ure/Yore	Brit	the strong river
Wensleydale	OE/ON	Waendel's (pers. name) valley
Widdale	ON	the wooded valley

Norway Spruce
Picea abies

Status: not native to Britain but it was known here by Tudor times.

Height: up to 35 metres.

Trunk: up to 2m across; tall and very straight.

Bark: red or copper brown on young trees, becoming darker on older; flaky and papery at first, turning cracked and scaled with age. Cones: 12 to 15cm long; cylindrical; tips of the scales are rounded though blunt ended; turn brown by autumn.

Crown: a true cone shaped tree; lower branches may curve down; dead branches remain on lower trunk.

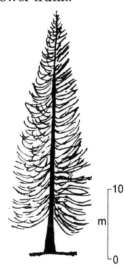

Leaves: the green needles spread 4' each side of a central shoot and beyond the end of the shoot; 1 to 2cm long; dark green, hard and pointed, but softer and less pointed than the sitka spruce.

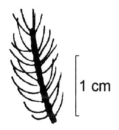

Uses: the Christmas tree. The wood, called deal, is used for housing timbers, packing cases, pulp and paper making; turpentine. It is a very common commercial plantation tree in Britain, along with sitka spruce.

Discovery Walk 4

Semer Water and Raydale

Start and Finish: Semer Water Bridge where the River Bain leaves the lake. Grid reference SD 921 875.

Parking: by the lakeside adjacent to the bridge. A charge (currently £1) is levied and is payable at Low Blean farm nearby.

Public Transport: the nearest bus service is through Bainbridge (see *Discovery Walk 5*). No buses run to Semer Water.

Facilities en Route: telephone boxes in Countersett, Marsett and Stalling Busk.

Outline of the Walk: Semer Water Bridge – Countersett – Cam High Road – Carlows – Marsett – Stalling Busk – Semer Water Bridge.

Length: 8.3km (5.2 miles) for the full route, or 7.8km (4.8 miles) for the shorter alternative.

Ordnance Survey Map: 1:25,000 Outdoor Leisure 30 1:50,000 Landranger 98.

Introduction

The Yorkshire Dales are not exactly brimfull of lakes but, where in England is apart from the Lake District? Malham Tarn aside, there is only one other large lake within the National Park and that is Semer Water.

These two lakes share a number of features. Both occupy a splendid setting nestling at the foot of hills and crags, though the underlying geology has made sure that the fells are very different in detail. The diversity of plant life around both has led to the designation of Sites of Special Scientific Interest (Marsett Rigg and Semer Water here), and of Nature Reserves. Both share a glacial origin, neither is deep, and both have seen considerable shrinkage since their creation. Last, but definitely not least, both are best appreciated on foot. The beauty of Semer Water is that it can be viewed from on high, unlike Malham Tarn (unless you go off rights of way).

Scenic and floral richness aside, Semer Water was, like the Tarn, the supporter of prehistoric communities: fish, water and fertile land were in abundance. Archaeological investigations – and chance discoveries – have unearthed artefacts and signs of usage from the Neolithic period onwards. Perhaps the most exciting finds were a superb spear head, dated to 1000 B.C. and a Bronze Age pile village, that is a wetland village in which the huts were constructed atop wooden platforms resting on posts driven into the mud.

Let us clear up any possible confusion in names. The lake is Semer Water, which you sometimes see written as Semerwater. The lake sits in a short valley that was called Semerdale in the past: there still is a Semerdale Hall on the west road from Bainbridge. Now, however, we should refer to the valley as Raydale. Etymologically this suggests a valley where roe buck abounded in the days when people referred to where they lived by some distinguishing feature. In the Dark Ages villages did not have place-names as such. Interestingly, herds of wild deer still roamed through Raydale (and Cotterdale, by the way) into the middle of the seventeenth century.

Raydale has three subsidiary, or feeder, dales in addition to numerous small side valleys, namely Bardale, upper Raydale and Cragdale.

Today's walk offers you an option early on. There is very little difference in distance: the contrast comes in the amount of climbing. In both cases you will end up on top of Carlows (500 metres) to the west, having started by the lakeside at 250 metres, but on the full route you have to go down to go back up again. There is a very good reason for this, naturally!

England's Shortest River

The River Bain is widely acknowledged to be England's shortest river. To me this sounds rather like the oft made claims to "England's smallest house" or "highest pub". Does it really matter? I am prepared to accept that the Bain is on the short side as far as rivers go. To save you measuring it, the length from source to mouth is a smidgen under 4 kilometres and, should you know of a shorter claimant, please do not write in.

Actually, the claim must be somewhat tongue in cheek because all the becks feeding into the lake are indirectly feeding the Bain so they are part of the same river system. Anyway . . .

Cross over the bridge (constructed about 1770) **for the short, sharp shock of a climb** that begins today's walk. Take heart from the brilliant summer display of roadside meadow cranesbill *(Geranium pratense)* and from the knowledge that there is a seat at the top of the rise . . . not to mention the view updale. You will be able to pick out Stalling Busk beyond the opposite (south-east) corner of the lake with the sweeping line of fells either side of Stake Pass. Considering the extent of those fells it is perhaps surprising there is no one recognisable name for the area. Instead different sections have been given very local names. The Landranger map plumps for Cragdale Moor, but that is but one part in a much wider expanse.

To the south-west lie the plantations of Raydale, over the top of which is Langstrothdale. I made mention in *The Southern Dales* of an old road over that top, whose existence has been totally lost on the ground.

To the right of Raydale are more vaguely named fells either side of Bardale, with the prominent scar of Wether Fell (614 metres) visible at the far right of the panorama.

When you have recovered from the climb – and rush not because another climb lies ahead – **turn right at the crossroads into the hamlet of Countersett.**

Countersett

Early Days

In the Middle Ages much of Wensleydale was set aside as a hunting forest (see *Discovery Walk 5*). Within any hunting ground were areas reserved for settlements and cultivation, called vaccaries. One such vaccary was established about 1250 by a Constance or Cousbance. Archaeological evidence supports this date. Four hundred years later settlements are listed for other parts of Raydale, at Marsett, Stalling Busk, Raydale and Tongue, in addition to Countersett. This last had 13 houses, so was quite a substantial village. Most of the houses would have been simple dwellings, probably of wood and thatch.

Each vaccary was bounded by a ditch or embankment, or both. Countersett's boundary can still be traced, for example, on the longer route below Hawes End.

Semer Water from the south-west

Countersett Hall

There are few buildings left in Countersett now but all are interesting in one way or another. To me Countersett Hall embodies the very best of vernacular architecture in the Dales.

It started off as just one of thirteen houses in the village, belonging to a family called Robinson. They were yeoman farmers and tenants of the City of London which owned the extensive manor of Bainbridge.

In 1650 Richard Robinson purchased his tenancy and set about rebuilding the house he lived in. Stand on the road and look down on the hall. Let's take it apart. The pre-1650 core of the building was a two-bay direct-entry house with access directly into one of the ground floor rooms. This was the left half of the building as you look at it, partly hidden by the porch and the other building facing it. In 1650 the house was extended to the right to form a three-bay structure: this is the middle part of the building. Richard also added the two-storey porch at this date with its upstairs window having three panes (or lights as they are properly called), the middle one being taller. This design, with its stepped hood-moulding, or label mould, is typical of mid-seventeenth century Dales styling.

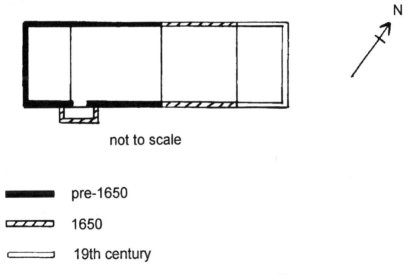

not to scale

▬▬▬▬ pre-1650

▱▱▱▱ 1650

▭▭▭ 19th century

Sketch plan of Countersett Hall

The bit on the far right – Elsie House – was tagged on in the nineteenth century.

Richard Robinson clearly had aspirations to bettering his yeoman status and entering the ranks of the gentry, as in fact his descendants did. A measure of his status and wealth is afforded by the Hearth Tax Returns for 1672. This tax had been raised by Charles II after the Restoration. Any property worth 20 shillings or more per year was to be taxed at two shillings per hearth paid in instalments. Countersett Hall had five hearths, putting Robinson well up the list of tax payers. Like so many taxes this one was exceedingly unpopular and was eventually repealed in 1689, as a gesture of goodwill when William and Mary came to the throne.

It is a common misconception that "big" houses in the past were furnished and decked out like a palace. This was far from so. Most yeoman families kept very simple homes. Robert Southey, who we have met already in *Discovery Walk 1*, describes a yeoman's home elsewhere in the Dales in the mid eighteenth century. Downstairs kitchen and parlour housed two oak benches, a wicker chair, two wooden chests, a huge oak table, a few pewter dishes on a shelf, silver goblets in a display case and a few religious pictures on the walls. There were six "uncomfortable" chairs set against a wall . . . and a back scratcher. And that was it: rather different from our homes today.

Quaker Connections

Richard Robinson heard Fox preach on his mission through the Dales in 1652 (see *Discovery Walks 2* and *11*) and became a staunch Quaker. He is believed to have been the first convert in Wensleydale and he became a preacher, spreading the word throughout the dale. Being such an influential person his preaching probably had a great effect on ordinary folk in isolated farms and villages.

Robinson fell foul of the law, in the form of his adversary Metcalfe of Nappa Hall (see *Discovery Walk 5*): he was jailed several times, fined, insulted, abused, but he maintained his faith, holding illegal meetings in Countersett Hall. This state of affairs persisted until William and Mary's Act of Toleration in 1689 (when Richard was 61) which permitted free worship in licensed chapels or meeting houses. By this time Countersett was but one of eight in Wensleydale.

In 1710 a purpose built Meeting House was built next to Countersett Hall, and it was rebuilt in its present form in 1778 (a very auspicious year in a way Quakers would frown upon – Boddington's first began brewing in that year!) You are welcome to enter the building whose interior is simplicity itself.

The small building by the road, above the entry gate to the Meeting House, was the Quaker school, built around 1772. On the lower floor was stabling for visiting Quakers. By 1874 the school had closed to be transferred to Stalling Busk.

Times change and people move on. The Quaker presence declined, particularly as Methodism grew in popularity. The last Robinson to live at

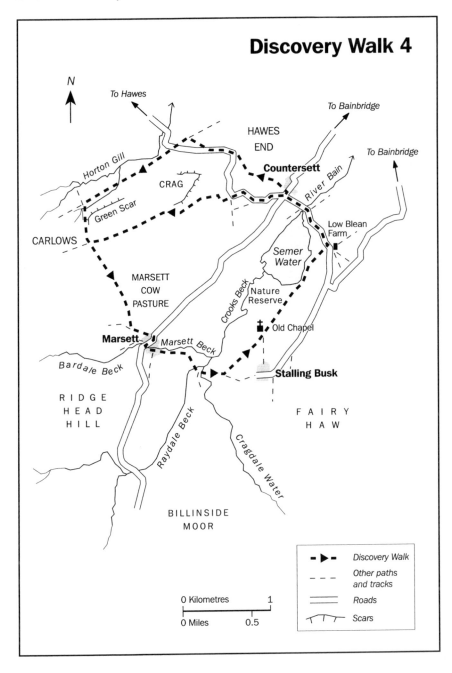

Discovery Walk 4

N

To Hawes

To Bainbridge

HAWES END

To Bainbridge

Horton Gill

CRAG

Countersett

River Bain

Green Scar

CARLOWS

Low Blean Farm

Semer Water

MARSETT COW PASTURE

Crooks Beck

Nature Reserve

Old Chapel

Marsett

Marsett Beck

Bardale Beck

Stalling Busk

RIDGE HEAD HILL

FAIRY HAW

Raydale Beck

Cragdale Water

BILLINSIDE MOOR

● ▶ ●	Discovery Walk
– – –	Other paths and tracks
══	Roads
⌐⊤⌐	Scars

0 Kilometres   1

0 Miles   0.5

the Hall died there in 1794, the family having moved up the social ladder and transferred to Bradford. They sold off their Semer Water estate in 1862.

Right! Time to get moving now . . .

– You have a choice of routes from Countersett –

. . . as I said earlier, so make the decision now. There is very little difference in total distance but the longer one has 30 metres more climbing with the possible irritation of having to descend only to come back up again later.

The Shorter Alternative

Return to the crossroads and turn right up the road to Burtersett on Crag Side Road. At the hairpin bend, above which the road becomes even steeper, go through the field gate on the left. The bridleway – yet another old route – is very clearly etched into the ground. It climbs relentlessly upwards below Crag. What an unimaginative name! Maybe in the distant past a group of elders sat around the fire trying to Name-that-Hill, with no agreement. Then, perhaps, one of their wives in a state of exasperation told them to stop arguing and just call it "Crag".

The climb becomes annoyingly steep above the wood but relief is in sight when you spot the next gate: the top lies just beyond. **The walking is now gentle and relaxed as you contour along the edge of the summit plateau, passing through one more gate on the way.**

It is not a common occurrence to come across tups (rams to you, perhaps) up on the fells. In fact I sometimes wonder where the farmers hide them. I suppose this is no bad thing as they can be grumpy and resentful at times, especially as they increasingly get in the mood as "tupping time" draws near. I came this way one day. It was a very warm day so I was day dreaming and dawdling, until half way between these two summit gates. Just over a slight rise on the track I came across not one Swaledale tup . . . but 12 of them. Needless to say, I started whistling and quickened my pace, expecting to be savaged and pummelled by a mass attack. I did not turn round till I was safely through the second gate . . . and they were still munching contentedly. I started singing to disguise my foolishness, and of course looked around in case anyone was watching!

Within a few minutes you reach a wall in an advanced state of dereliction.

– Rejoin the main route –

The Main Route: Hawes End

Turn down the road access to Countersett Hall but, rather than going behind the house with the Latin inscription, go through the gate on the left into the field.

This is an interesting house in its own right. It was rebuilt, as the datestone indicates, in 1667 as part of the great reconstruction in stone phase that followed the Restoration of the monarchy after the ill-fated Cromwellian interlude. The house belonged to Bartholomew and Isabell Harrison, Quakers and hosiers.

By the eighteenth century the house had become the Board Inn, later to be the Boar Inn until closure in 1920.

Note the inscription – was this the *board*, I wonder? How is your Latin? It reads:

NUNC MEA
MOXHVIVS
SED POSTEA
NESCIO CVIVS

and it means . . .

Now it's mine
Presently this man's
But after that
I know not whose.

Delightful.

The path is not really discernible on the ground as it swings uphill behind the houses towards an isolated barn. Pass to the *left* of the barn over the step-over stile in the hedgerow into the next field. Climb up the western side of this to just beyond the next barn where there is a squeeze stile in the wall. Cross the next field diagonally to the far side then go up the gully to the step stile in the headwall. Follow the left hand wall the length of this last field to meet the road at Hawes End. Walk right now as the road crosses the watershed between Ure and Bain.

As you look down the long slope from Hawes End you are seeing a coalesced series of drift tails (see *Discovery Walk 3*) running all the way to Bainbridge. Prior to the glacial phase the Bain only followed its present course as far as Semerdale Hall. It turned north-west here to enter the Ure at Cams Houses two kilometres west of Bainbridge. When the ice had gone the Bain found its old course completely blocked by morainic deposits, forcing it to flow north-north-east, and to carve itself a gorge below Gill Edge.

You then come to a stile on the right where the sign directs you to Horton Gill Bridge. At this point you are presented with a view up Wensleydale as far west as Cotterdale and the distant hills beyond Mallerstang. Downdale you should be able to pick out Askrigg over the Roman fort at Bainbridge and the prominent Ivy Scar near Carperby. I am sure you will have found this diversion out of Raydale worth the effort for the long-range views alone.

Drop down diagonally from the road, as if you were heading to the small, sad looking wood way below, and look for the small gate in the bottom wall. You are now on Cam High Road.

Cam High Road

A road as arrow straight as this can only be Roman in origin. It is almost stereotypically Roman. The fort at Bainbridge was an important centre for Roman military operations in the Dales, as we shall see on *Discovery Walk 5*, and it was the focus of routeways from at least three directions.

One Roman road passed through Raydale. You can follow one conjectured route on the Ordnance Survey map. It leaves Bainbridge as the tarred lane, passes through Out Brough as a field path, joins Blean Lane, cuts through Low Force as a field path again, then follows Stake Road and High Lane as far as Shaw Side where it becomes a green lane climbing straight over Stake Edge. From there it drops down as Gilbert Lane, Causeway and Buckden Rake to Wharfedale. This road linked Bainbridge to the Roman fort of Ilkley.

Cam High Road went over the Pennine watershed to Chapel-le-Dale and ultimately linked in with the road north from Ribchester to Carlisle.

Some say that the agger, the raised central part of a Roman road, can be made out on the part of Cam Road south of Four Lane Ends. I have my doubts, however. This road has had too much later use for us to say with certainly that this bit is a Roman surface. It is akin to saying the section of the M6 near Preston is the first motorway in England. The road might be, but how many times has the surface been dug up and relaid?

Cam High Road has definitely seen usage down through the ages. It might not be too fanciful to say continuous usage since Roman times. It served as an important cross-Pennine packhorse route and drove road. In 1751 it was created part of the Lancaster to Richmond turnpike road, though it was superseded in 1795 by the present tarred road through Widdale.

Cam High Road made a lasting impression on the Hon. John Byng, soon to be Viscount Torrington, when he journeyed through the Dales in 1792. He described the ascent from Bainbridge as "one of the longest, steepest and most stoney (sic) in great Britain . . . the first four (miles) are very steep".

Turn left up the old road to cross the tarred road at Four Lane Ends for two kilometres of following in Roman footsteps. After 200 metres or so the right hand wall does something that puzzles me. Why is such a large area leading down to Horton Gill enclosed within the confines of the old road? It cannot just be to allow access to the fields across the gill because the area is far too big. Was it, perhaps, designed like this to allow access to water for stock being driven along the road, its being the first water, rest and grazing on the four kilometres of climbing since Bainbridge?

From this point a ditch edges the left-hand side of the road. Soil and water conditions alongside are such that there is a wide species diversity compared to surrounding areas. It is a linear micro-habitat with a wealth of flowering species. A friend and I compiled a list one summer's day, to prove a point. I suppose that gems are to be found everywhere. Here goes:

valerian	*Valeriana sp.*
yarrow	*Achillea millefolium*
sneezewort	*Achillea ptarmica*
harebell	*Campanula rotundifolia*
greater stichwort	*Stellaria holostea*
germander speedwell	*Veronica chamaedrys*
tormentil	*Potentilla erecta*
eyebright	*Euphrasia spp.*
self-heal	*Prunella vulgaris*
common sorrel	*Rumex acetosa*
common horsetail	*Equisetum arvense*
common birdsfoot trefoil	*Lotus corniculatus*
fen bedstraw	*Galium uliginosum*
heath bedstraw	*Galium saxatile*
marsh willowherb	*Epilobium palustre*
crowberry	*Empetrum nigrum*

In the actual ditch, while poking about, we spotted beautiful chunks of crinoid fossils (long-stalked "sea lilies" anchored on the sea bed) and not so beautiful leeches, and in doing so were entertained by the antics of freshwater shrimps, pond skaters and caddis flies.

It is interludes and discoveries such as this bit of otherwise unspectacular ditch that make walking so pleasurable.

The road engineers were forced to momentarily divert from their ruler-straight line to cross the gill. Regular travellers west must have felt their spirits sink at this point, in their unsprung coaches, because the track surface deteriorates rapidly beyond New Bridge. I wonder if this is because the middle of the road is the parish boundary here. In the days when the upkeep of roads was a parish responsibility, who would have taken care of this kilometre long stretch? You can well imagine the arguments that must have raged: it's your responsibility ... oh, no it's not ... oh ...

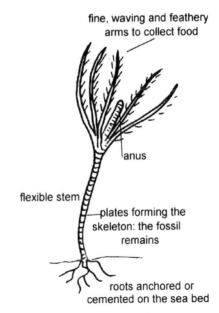

fine, waving and feathery arms to collect food

anus

flexible stem

plates forming the skeleton: the fossil remains

roots anchored or cemented on the sea bed

Crinoids grew in extensive 'forests' on the sea bed. They were animals, not plants.

Over the Top

You, at least, do not have far to go on the road. At the western end of Green Scar you come to a cross-roads where the old direct route from Marsett to Burtersett intersects Cam High Road. **You should turn left on the grassed track that climbs over the end of the Scar,** through the gate and the erosional gully that once carried a stream. **On the crest of Carlows there is another crossing of the ways** and one of those quaint Ancient Monument signposts. I cannot understand the logic of directing the way to the Roman road from this isolated point. Why is it not down in the valley or on the tarred road?

You will no doubt have noticed how fluted the limestone slabs are in the gully. These slabs are facing west so receive the full blast of the prevailing wind and rain, and the cracks in the rocks are gradually opened up and enlarged by chemical processes (see *The Southern Dales* for an explanation of the process of dissolution).

You should cross over, ignoring the broad bridleway,

– where, incidentally, the shorter route rejoins the main route –

There are distinct signs on this ridge top of man's activities. There is a large quarry just to your right below Carlows cairn, with a track zig-zagging down to Marsett, and there is another quarry at Crag End. In the eighteenth century local people prospected for lead on the ridge, as well as higher up on Dodd and Wether Fells. Plans were drawn up for a smelter on Horton Gill but the deposits proved not to be viable and the grand scheme fizzled out.

After the cross-roads head away from the derelict wall, but do not stray too far from it as the path is not clear on the ground. Very shortly the land begins to drop away, presenting you with a view downdale to Addlebrough and the fells south of Raydale.

Drop down to the ladder stile with its canine counterpart, go over the brow and back onto sandstone bedrock. Before you proceed, though, there is one of my obligatory view stops: you will stop and you will enjoy it! Down below, either side of Marsett, the flat land indicates the much greater extent of an immediately post-glacial lake that filled the whole valley. Since its formation behind a barrier of glacial moraine the lake has been continuously silting up at the inlet end, while the Bain is cutting ever deeper at the outlet, thus lowering the lake level. Lakes are ephemeral: they all silt up and drain away one day. Its eventual demise was hastened in 1936 when the local farmers (who own the lake bed) deliberately lowered the water level to aid draining of adjacent pastures. Nowhere now is the lake more than 10 metres in depth.

You can also see the length of Raydale from here. Indeed the view will be with you as you descend. Nestling in the dale bottom, below the plantation, lie Raydale House and Raydale Grange, the latter at least having monastic origins. There are also glacial features to be noted. I am referring to yet more drift tails. Three come down from Marsett Bardale: Long Ridge, Marsett Ridge and Faw Ridge, while another comes down between Raydale Beck and Cragdale Water to Duerley Barns.

Carry on downhill, steeper now, staying close to the wall, through several fields to join the road to Knight Close farm. Turn left to the junction with Marsett Lane, and then right over the bridge into the village.

Marsett and Stalling Busk

Countersett was originally the main settlement of Raydale and its demise led to the growth of Stalling Busk, which must lay claim to being one of our highest villages. Busk, as it is locally known, gained slight importance from its position at the foot of the Stake Pass road. Its inn was the first sign of warmth and cheer since Buckden or Cray in Wharfedale, by any yardstick a long and arduous journey. Busk had the dale's only church, built in 1909 to replace the old chapel by the lakeside, and the school.

Like Busk, Marsett was very much a self-contained farming community, on the lost Bainbridge to Langstrothdale road. Its Methodist chapel dates from the early nineteenth century.

The Ordnance Survey map does not indicate a right of way connecting Marsett with Stalling Busk. Fear not, however, as the "white road" from Marsett that becomes Busk Lane is still designated as a County Road, so you have the theoretical right to drive along it. (You can't get through by car, thank goodness!)

Walk round the village green on the road and along the stony track adjacent to the beck. Note the "Footpath" sign, technically incorrect. The early part of the track witnesses, it seems to me, a battle for dominance between the aromatic and pleasant looking sweet cicely *(Myrrhus odorata)* on the one hand, representing botanical order, and the somewhat untidy and unruly butterbur *(Petasites hybridus)* on the other, representing chaos.

Beyond the first footbridge the surrounding ground is wetter so meadowsweet *(Filipendula ulmaria)* is one of the dominant species, though that wretched yellow peril, the ragwort *(Senecio jacobea)*, is increasingly gaining a large foothold hereabouts. **The county road fords the next two watercourses but you should use the next footbridge,** thus forsaking the road for the footpath. **Cross two fields now, following the waymarks and walls, to an isolated and sturdily built field barn.** This is another crossing of the ways. Directly upslope is the path to Stalling Busk, but **you need to turn left through the gated stile by the barn.**

Follow the path through two more fields to a roofless barn. Note the number of barns in this area, each of which would have served a meadow in the days before "progress" changed the farming scene almost beyond recognition. **Carry on through the series of fields and stiles, sticking to single file in the large, sloping meadow, until you meet the track coming**

down from Stalling Busk 50 metres above you. The track was the route followed by the villagers to the now ruined Busk Chapel. The track is locally known as Donkey Trod. It probably felt like that after a long sermon!

Busk Chapel

The chapel was built in 1603 and rebuilt in 1722, though the basic form is seventeenth rather than eighteenth century. It remained in use until services were transferred to the new church in Busk itself.

The internal arrangement is unnatural and deceptive to the casual visitor. On entry you may well assume the stone slab at the far end was the altar and that the chapel was aligned that way. Not so. The slab was not the altar and the church was aligned at right angles to what the eye would expect. The arches cut across the alignment. It really is odd. If you stand, back to the doorway, the altar was set against the gable to your right.

Busk Chapel

Rowan or Mountain Ash
Sorbus aucuparia

Status: native to Britain.

Height: 15 to 20 metres.

Trunk: short with branching stems.

Bark: shiny, silver grey and smooth with thin brown lenticels (raised pores).

Crown: generally oval; arched upper branches; open canopy.

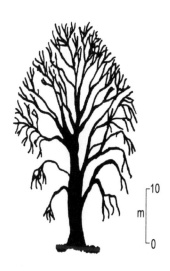

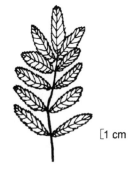

[1 cm

Fruit: bright red mass of fruits in autumn from a mass of white, scented flowers from May; fruits soon eaten up by birds.

Leaves: from 15 to 20cm; pinnate (leaflets paired on opposite sides of the leaf stalk); rounded base; slightly serrated with toothed edges; gains new leaves before most trees.

Uses: once planted in the north as protection against witchcraft; used in the past for tool handles and spinning wheel parts. The berries can be used for cooking and in herbal treatments.

Semer Water Nature Reserve

The footpath leads on from the chapel – which is built on a glacial drumlin – **past a small wood** planted in remembrance of somebody, **to enter Semer Water Nature Reserve,** maintained and conserved by the Yorkshire Wildlife Trust. This is an absolute gem. If you happen to be a member of the YWT, you can enjoy a pre-booked guided tour around the reserve. Otherwise you are restricted to its eastern edge where the right of way passes through.

The Reserve covers about one third of the lake and an area of marsh and wet pasture nearly as big as the lake. At times much of the marsh is under water so the plant community is quite different from that in the limestone area you will walk through.

Down on the flats the floral range is very impressive with a glorious seasonal display of pink ragged robin *(Lychnis flos-cuculi)* which can clearly be seen from the path. Other beauties include the pink and white bogbean *(Menyanthes trifoliata)*; the dark purple marsh cinquefoil *(Potentilla palustris)*; marsh orchids *(Dactylorhiza spp.)* . . . altogether around 130 flowering species can be seen on the reserve (out of a recorded total of 526 for all Wensleydale) including grasses, rushes, sedges and tree species. There are four species of willow, for example, including the basket osier *(Salix viminalis)*.

You can expect to see, close up, on the banking on either side of the path, the delicate blue harebell *(Campanula rotundifolia)*; masses of bluebells *(Hyacinthoides non-scripta)*; purplish devil's-bit scabious *(Succisa pratensis)*; orchids and the white, early flowering wood anemone *(Anemone nemorosa)*.

And what of birds? Over 100 species have been recorded here – residents, migrants and visitors. On one recent visit, sticking to the path and accessible lakeside I counted 17 species, excluding the various little jobs. You can expect to see large numbers of Canada geese, lapwing and oystercatcher, with wildfowl, waders, marsh and woodland species dotted about. The more time you are prepared to spend looking, the more you will see, as anywhere.

Beyond the far boundary fence of the Reserve, the route is clear and easy to follow, but, just when you think you can follow the lakeshore proper, the path heads uphill and away from the lake to Thwaite End House, just a barn in fact. The line of the path leads you through meadows to the road opposite Low Blean Farm. Please make sure you do not wander off the line of the path.

When you reach the road, turn left and walk back to wherever you started.

A final point. Have you noticed the huge rock sitting near the lakeshore in the general area where you can park? It is called the Carlow Stone and is an *erratic*, brought here by the glacier.

Place-name meanings

Addlebrough	ON	Authulf's (pers. name) fort
Bain	ON	straight river
Bardale	OE/ON	Bera's (pers. name) valley or
	ON	the valley with beavers
Burtersett	ON/ME	the shieling among the elder or alder trees
Cam	OE/ON	the ridge
Carlows	OE/ON	(possibly) the place occupied by free peasant farmers
Countersett	ON/OFr.	Constance's or Cousbance's shieling
Crooks Beck	ON	the stream with bends in its course
Hawes	OE/ON	the hill pass
Low Blean	ON	the low dark stream
Marsett	ON	Maurr's (pers. name) shieling
Raydale	OE/ON	the valley with roebuck
Semer Water	OE	the lake-pool or marshy pool
Stake Road	OE	the road with posts
Stalling Busk	ON/OFr.	the bushy place with stallions
Wether Fell	OE/ON	the hill with wethers (sheep)

Discovery Walk 5

Where Bain meets Ure: a walk in the Bainbridge and Askrigg area

Start and Finish: Bainbridge village green: grid reference SD 933 902.

Parking: there is normally room to park at the topside of the green.

Public Transport: Wensleydale is reasonably well supported with bus services. Askrigg, Bainbridge and Worton have links with Hawes, Leyburn, Northallerton, Richmond and Ripon (United 01325 468771); and even Leeds and Ingleton (Keighley & District 01535 603284). Postbus services also connect the three villages with Hawes and Leyburn (contact either post office or a tourist information point).

Facilities en Route: Bainbridge is well served: Rose and Crown Hotel, tea shops, village shop, post office, sweet shop across the Bain, toilets. Askrigg is also well served: post office, village shop, National Park Information Point, tea shops, restaurant and two pubs: The King's Arms Hotel and The Crown Inn. Worton has the Victoria Arms inn and a telephone box.

Outline of the Walk: Bainbridge – Grange – Askrigg – Newbiggin – Nappa Scar – Nappa Mill – Worton – Brough Scar – Bainbridge.

Length: 8.7km (5.4 miles) for the full route or 8.4 km (5.2 miles) for the shorter version.

Ordnance Survey Map: 1:25,000 Outdoor Leisure 30 1:50,000 Landranger 98.

Introduction

This section of Wensleydale comes as a total contrast to the dales previously visited on this collection of walks. Here the valley is broad, several kilometres from the northern tops to those on the south side of the dale. Everything is on a grander scale. The River Ure is already a force to be reckoned with, no longer like a beck, but wide, deep and very much a river as it twists and curls across its extensive flood plain.

The settlements, too, are bigger. Hawes is a fully fledged and very busy market town; Askrigg is more of a town than a village; and even Bainbridge spreads itself out from the village green to give the impression of greater size than most Dales' villages.

It is easy here to make sense of the underlying geology that makes the northern dales distinctive so this is one theme to be explored on this walk. Certain characters will pop up from the past: monks in a near-forgotten abbey, gentry of a prodigiously prolific local family, a famous architect, and our Roman ancestors . . . and we must not forget James Herriot, whose televised stories have done so much to raise the profile of the Yorkshire Dales.

The walk starts from Bainbridge as I feel it is the most accessible by public transport and has more parking space. I have included two routes, the shorter one cutting out some slight climbing but hardly shorter in distance. If time is limited you could start and finish in Askrigg making a circular walk out of two sections (so follow first the Long Route and then the Short Route of Askrigg to Nappa Scar). In fact, with judicious use of the Ordnance Survey map and the route description, you could make up a series of short circular walks out of *Discovery Walk 5*.

Bainbridge: Forest Headquarters

In the Middle Ages much of the northern dales and fells were incorporated into royal hunting forests or baronial chases. Considering the state of northern England in the Norman period, this comes as no surprise. The area was thinly peopled to start with and the local inhabitants – a mixture of Norse, Dane, Angles and descendants of the British natives, the Brigantes – were free-minded and in no mood to be suppressed by the Normans. The revolt of 1068 – 70 against the yoke has distinct shades of the Brigantian revolt against the Romans (see *The Southern Dales*), not only in the ferocity of the uprising but also in the callousness and venom of the official response.

It was said that the king and his barons "laid waste all the shire". An inspection of Domesday Book bears out the severity of the Harrying of the North. Almost every last village has the curt entry "*wasta est*". Mind you this does not necessarily mean the land was waste in the sense of unusable and despoiled. Rather it may well indicate that the land was not used because the villagers had fled or had been, let's say, liquidated.

The upper part of Wensleydale became the Forest of Wensleydale, though it was not royal. A new settlement was created in 1227 at Bainbridge to serve as the Forest headquarters. Eleven vaccaries were allowed, including Appersett and Burtersett, giving some idea of the extent of the hunting ground.

Twelve forest keeper supervised the running of life and work on behalf of the Lords of Middleham Castle. Each keeper had a house (a toft) in Bainbridge and a croft of 4 hectares for his own use. The stocks on the green are a reminder of medieval justice.

For a fuller discussion of the running of hunting grounds, see *The Southern Dales*.

The village grew in later centuries as a milling centre like most villages

Bainbridge village green and stocks

in the Dales. Its importance was enhanced by the construction of the turnpike road after the Act of 1751. Being at the foot of the long drag up Cam High Road, Bainbridge was an unavoidable night's halt. Some of this importance was lost, however, when the turnpike was re-routed through Hawes and Widdale in 1795, Hawes then becoming the main centre west of Leyburn.

Yore Bridge

Walk down past the village green. Behind the toilet block is Low Mill, a water-powered corn mill in the nineteenth century and a cheese plant in the 1920s. **Take the road to the east of the (probably eighteenth century) Rose and Crown, past the millstone and the Friends' Meeting House** exuding, like all such, piety and a no-frills approach to worship. This was built in 1836 to replace an older type of structure at the top end of the village. At the bottom of the slope, just before the river, is Yorebridge House. This, too, has had a religious past though now serves a much more mundane purpose housing National Park offices. The small outbuilding across the car park was the grammar school. The house itself was built around 1850 as the residence of the schoolmaster-curate. Why did the Established church feel it necessary to house its priests in such splendour?

In the field near the building is something called a *stackgarth* or stackyard.

There are 20 of them within one kilometre of the bridge, all thought to be late medieval in origin. The hay was stacked within these enclosures in the days before protective walls and barns. Do not bother trying to pick them out in the fieldscape: you need to have them pointed out specifically.

Cross the bridge – Yore, incidentally, is an old form of Ure. The bridge was designed by John Carr of York (1723 – 1807) in 1793 to replace an earlier bridge. Carr designed a number of great houses in Yorkshire, including Constable Burton Hall and Arncliffe Hall at Ingleby Arncliffe. By training he was a mason but rose to be the foremost northern exponent of the Palladian School of Architecture, Pevsner described Carr as "the most distinguished architect" in the county.

Take the footpath on the right, immediately at the end of the bridge. Cross the meadow diagonally and pass "under" the railway bridge then over the arched Hocket Bridge across Grange Beck. Cross the access track to a stile and pass behind the complex of Grange through a second field to meet the road again. Turn right along the road towards the low building that lies less than 100 metres ahead.

Grange and Fors Abbey

The name Grange should ring a bell in your historical mind. It normally signifies a monastic connection, as an outlying farm belonging to an abbey or priory. This grange was more than that, however. The fields to the right of the road, before and behind the low building, are the site of Fors Abbey, though no trace remains other than the inevitable humps and bumps.

Fors Abbey was established by a group of monks led by Peter de Quinciaco on land given by the relevant Norman overlord. The monks enjoyed the protection of the Earl of Richmond, lord of the manor in nearly 450 manors, and a vague relative of William the Conqueror (no wonder the local lord "gave" Peter the land). The abbey was established in 1145 and was one of 13 houses of the Savigny Order that itself was founded in 1112 and had Furness Abbey as its first English base. The Savignac monks were known as the Grey Monks, they followed the Cistercian way of life, believed in physical labour, and have been cited as the first people in Wensleydale to produce cheese using a recipe they brought from France. (Sorry – I refuse to accept that glorious, mellifluous Wensleydale cheese is French!)

The Order was too small to survive and, in 1147, it succumbed to a takeover bid by the Cistercians. Fors was abandoned in 1156 and its assets transferred to a new site that was to become Jervaulx Abbey. Poverty and lack of potential were given as the reasons. I suspect, however, that the new Cistercian management team, after the usual quiet period, decided to rationalise operations and close down unprofitable branches.

The site was not totally abandoned as a grange was maintained on the site, some of whose fourteenth century masonry survives in Abbey Cottage at Grange. There is another remnant, too, in the shape of Bow Bridge over

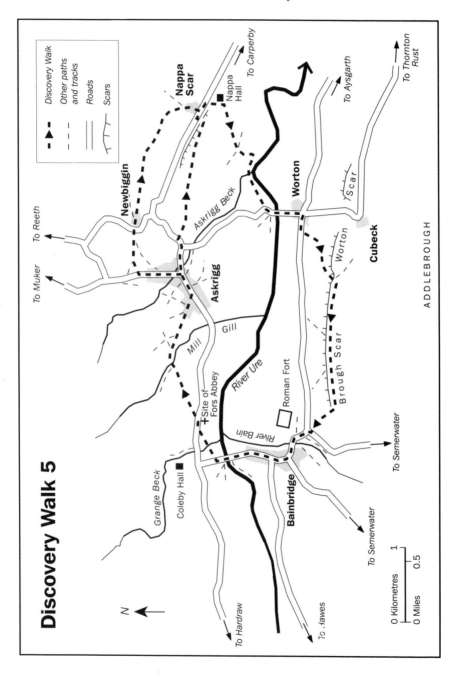

Discovery Walk 5

Grange Beck, immediately north of the road bridge. This is thought to have thirteenth century monastic origins.

Further up Grange Beck stands Colby Hall, built in 1633 but utilising an Elizabethan E-plan, that is having three wings projecting at right angles from the main body of the house. It is a fine building indeed.

The low building ahead on the road was built in 1807 as six almshouses for the aged of the parish by a philanthropist with local connections.

Lamb Hill and Mill Gill

Just before the almshouses there is a stile across the road. Take this path diagonally uphill towards the clump of ash trees and a gated stile. Cross the next meadow to another similar stile, then on to yet another.

As you rise over the flanks of Lamb Hill you are blessed with a view worth stopping to examine. More or less due south is Addlebrough (476 metres) with its flat summit; the entry to Raydale and Semerwater; the smaller flat-topped Yorburgh to the west of Raydale; while far to the east, downdale, is the bulk of Penhill (526 metres) also level on the top. There is nothing unusual about these tops: they merely represent particular bedding planes in the limestone.

Beneath your feet is something else worthy of more than a cursory glance: the various blue and purple hues of meadow cranesbill *(Geranium pratense)*, harebell *(Campanula rotundifolia)* and knapweed *(Centaurea nigra)*. Beyond the road, below, is an elongated hillock, large enough to show up clearly on the Ordnance Survey map. This is a drumlin, a depositional feature laid down under a moving glacier (see *The Southern Dales*).

From that gated stile swing across to the ungated stile in the next field boundary and proceed across two more meadows, heading half-left at the end to the line of trees. There is yet another gated stile. Beyond this you cross Mill Gill (which is worth exploring upstream someday to Whitfield Gill Force) **by the footbridge and turn right alongside the mini limestone gorge,** and the sweet smelling sweet cicely *(Myrrhis odorata)*. **Pass under the overhead leat that carried water to power the old mill.**

Mill Gill Mills

The gill does not seem much in times of normal water flow yet it supported three mills between the bridge you crossed over and the road. To alleviate problems of low flow a mill dam was constructed, from which the overhead leat fed water into West Mill, the uppermost of the three. This was a corn mill, having been the manorial soke mill in which peasants were obliged to have their corn ground. The mill ground corn and meal until the 1930s after which it became a saw mill.

Below West Mill, and now a private house, was the second, late eighteenth century mill which at various times has concentrated on cotton and flax;

and by the roadside stood Low Mill built in the early nineteenth century for carding wool. This is now an outdoor activity centre, offering facilities to disabled people.

From West Mill follow the paved sandstone causeway across the meadow to join Mill Lane into Askrigg.

Askrigg

Askrigg has enjoyed a prosperous past and possessed the entrepreneurial skills and courage to seek new ventures and capitalise on opportunities. One thing at a time . . .

Mill Lane becomes Church Street. Have a discreet look at the houses on the north side of the street. Two have late seventeenth century door lintels but West End House is reputed to have traceable origins two hundred years or more before that.

The church, along with Wensley Church an outstanding building, is worthy of inspection within and without. There are details inside telling the story of the church. Come out of the churchyard directly into the cobbled square. On the opposite side of the road is Cringley House, a residential home. It is better known to Herriot devotees as Skeldale House, home and surgery of the vets in the series. In fact it *is* now Skeldale House.

Opposite that there is a break in the line of buildings fronting the street. One house is set back from the rest. On this site stood a magnificent Elizabethan style hall, Askrigg Hall, that towered above the mainly Georgian frontages on Main Street. It was a sad loss when fire destroyed the hall in 1936. Outside, near the old village pump on the cobbles, is an iron ring. This was for tethering a bull when bull baiting was a popular "sport".

What else? The town's early affluence largely stemmed from being outside the Forest and having been granted a market charter in 1587. A cattle fair was also held north of the town in the field still called Fair Allotment. Askrigg also benefited from being at the junction of the Askrigg to Sedbergh and Richmond to Lancaster turnpike roads. This plus the droving trade led to the creation of new trades and industries. Our travelling friend, the Hon. John Byng, stayed at the King's Arms (then the King's Head). Though he moaned about the food and the service, he seemed impressed by the town's busy atmosphere.

So, what of its industry? Apart from the mills on Mill Gill, Askrigg has also been an important clock making centre, and a flourishing centre for the hosiery industry from the 1600s to the 1800s. Like Dent, Askrigg was stocking mad. Now, you may have read the rather distasteful recipe for tanning cattle hides in *The Southern Dales*. Can you stomach some more?

The final processes of making stockings went something like this: scour the garments in chamber lye (urine), then wash, then bleach in sulphur fumes. Finally lay them out on tenter frames to dry. Ugh!

There is so much to relate about Askrigg, but it is time you got going again.

Askrigg to Nappa Scar

– You have a choice of routes from Askrigg, one being shorter and involving no climbing worth mentioning –

The Short Route

Start from the village cross and walk down the narrow street by Skeldale House past another former mill. At the T-junction at the far end bear left on the gravel track below the new house. At the end of this track there is a stone squeeze stile. Go beyond this but look for a second stile on the right opposite a barn conversion. This track was Askrigg's back lane. Walk along the northern edge of the field, keeping close to the wall as far as a gated squeeze stile in this wall. Ignore the stile directly ahead. Drop down the sloping field, noting the medieval field system, to the bottom corner where a footbridge over Askrigg Beck gives access to the road.

Turn right along the road to the junction of Howgate and Low Gate. Gate is an old word meaning road so we have here the "low road" and the "road up the hill".

At the junction a gated squeeze stile leads into an L-shaped field. The way is clearly marked, not so much on the ground, but by the sequence of stiles in the walls separating the various meadows. As this is rich meadow land please observe the single-file convention. You will again note the early medieval cultivation terraces in two of the fields.

The views along this stretch include the prominent limestone crags of Ellerkin Scar to the north, with the less imposing but still impressive Worton Scar across the valley to the south, beyond the village of Worton. Addlebrough and Penhill dominate sections of the southern skyline, while far to the west you can make out Widdale Fell, Great Shunner Fell and the scars of Cotter End.

The field beyond the final stile of the sequence is rough pasture and here you **drop down half-left to ford Newbiggin Beck and clamber over the wall stile. Head up to the left of the isolated trio of sycamores towards the wooded scar.** This is Nappa Scar. **Do not go to the very end of this field: at an especially large ash tree turn up through the scar on the rough path to join the road. Turn right to the junction in the hamlet of Nappa Scar,**

– and rejoin the main route –

The Long Route

Walk all the way up Main Street to the junction at the top, next to the Crown Inn. Go along Moor Road, that eventually goes over the tops to Swaledale, as far as the small green. A finger post fastened to the far wall indicates the way from the green. Go between the houses and left through the hand gate at the end. **The path climbs up Stony Bank through four fields, passes close by a field barn, through a gated stile and joins a narrow walled lane which runs over Newbiggin Beck into Newbiggin,** one of several villages in the Pennines bearing that name. "New" of course, is only relative. At the time it was constructed the settlement was only new compared to whatever older one there may have been, in this case Askrigg.

On the far side of the green the right of way passes in front of the cottages and out through the metal gate into a field. I always feel slightly uneasy stomping past someone's front door, but I suppose it is no different from walking past the front door of garden-less terraced houses in towns. **In this first field two paths diverge,** though neither is apparent on the ground. **Stay close to the wall, on your right, then cross a number of fields using the field gates to pass from one to another.**

Notice the recesses set into the wall by the second field gate. It looks to be too neat and in good order to be old, and I have no clue as to its purpose. I do know, for someone of my height, it makes a perfectly proportioned armchair complete with footrest!

Carry on past the building and over the access track that leads up to Blea Busk house by the wood, through three more stiles in a more or less straight run, then veer slightly right up to a roofless barn. The path follows the top wall of the next field, past a second barn into a large meadow. A linear wet patch – you cannot grace it with the name "stream" – runs down the line of the path. The comparative wetness here has enabled water loving plants to gain more than a foothold. The white flowered watercress *(Rorippa nasturtium-aquaticum)* sticks to the wettest parts while the reddish water avens *(Geum rivale)* have spread about in some profusion. In mid-summer it makes a delightful spectacle.

Go through the stile and down the bottom end of the last field to join Harr Gill Lane into the farming hamlet of Nappa Scar.

Walk down to the main road and turn left

– thus joining up with the short route –

Pele Towers

Carry on along the main Askrigg to Carperby road for a little over 100 metres, and turn down the access road to Nappa Hall. In no time at all you are confronted with this historic edifice. To me the sense of something out of the ordinary is confirmed by the enormous sycamores that grow out of the scar itself.

Nappa Hall is a fine example of a pele tower. It is not open to public view and please do not enter the courtyard regardless of how much your curiosity pushes you.

The old counties of Cumberland, Westmorland, Northumberland and the

North Riding formed a broad and unstable frontier zone between England and Scotland. Intermittent warfare between the two kingdoms punctuated spells of uneasy peace and reluctant co-existence. Clan rivalry along the borders was strong and often caused warring feuds, cattle raids and general mayhem. This situation lasted well into the fourteenth century, though the local feuding lasted until the Union of the Crowns in 1603.

It was the peace settlement between the two kingdoms in the fourteenth century that brought a measure of stability to the northern counties. Many local lords and gentry felt secure enough to build their homes anew, in a style whose grandeur proclaimed their status yet gave them a defensible stronghold should fractious warfare resume. Thus was born the pele tower that is such a common feature of the landscape of the Penrith area in particular.

Peles are basically the same, variations on a successful theme. They are normally oblong with the largest axis aligned east-west and had from two to four floors, depending on the needs and wealth of the owner. Wall thicknesses, too, vary from one to two metres. As life became more settled, and people's perceived needs for comfort grew, a hall or *solar* was often added to the tower, altogether less cramped, dank and draughty than the tower. In some instances a second tower was built at the opposite end of the solar for aesthetic reasons. During the Tudor period in particular a range of buildings was often erected to form an enclosed courtyard, or *barmkin*.

Nappa Hall has all these features. The original four-storey west tower was built in 1459 – 60, a solar was added to its east face with a later, smaller tower at the far end, containing kitchen and office accommodation. The barmkin is there, entered through an archway, though I think the "new" range was erected in the seventeenth century rather than in the Tudor period.

The estate was granted to James Metcalfe in 1415. He had fought valiantly alongside Lord Scrope of Bolton Castle at the battle of Agincourt, in which the English fairly decisively trounced the French. The pele was built by James and his son Thomas Metcalfe. Down through the generations successive Metcalfes held influential positions in the north. Two, for example, sat on Richard III's Council of the North. This was a judicial body that acted as a court of appeal and arbitration between disputants, and also heard petitions from poor men with a grievance. It is probable that Richard stayed at Nappa with Thomas in 1484 on his tour of the north. This Thomas served as Chancellor of the Duchy of Lancaster. Later still the head of the clan is said to have entertained Mary Queen of Scots during her period of imprisonment at Bolton Castle and also Lady Anne Clifford, a cousin, on her journey north from Skipton. One of the charges levelled against Richard by the country's ruling body was his seeming obsession with the Metcalfes. In fact no less than seven of them either held office or received annuities in his reign.

A glance in the local phone book will tell you how prolific the Metcalfes were, yet the chief male line came to an end in 1756. Our companion Byng noted that the hall was derelict in large parts and deserted save for one part being occupied by a farmer.

Across the Ure . . . again

The walk continues down the farm track from the pele tower. At the bottom end there are three field gates. Have a look over the left-hand gate: that field is absolutely plastered with humps and bumps and traces of the field systems associated with the tower in its early days.

Go through the right-hand gate, then diagonally across this gently sloping field, on an old green way through the medieval field system, to the gate on the far side by the wall junction. Head down the second field to exit by the barn, and turn left down Thwaite Holme Lane over the old railway track to Nappa Mill farm. This mill undoubtedly had its beginnings as the water-powered corn mill belonging to the lord of the manor. All inhabitants of the manor were duty bound to have their grain milled in the lord's mill – and, of course, he took his share.

Turn right as you enter the farm complex and over the stile into the field. In quick succession you cross two streams for the second time: first Newbiggin Beck and then Askrigg Beck. The next stretch of walking could not be easier and, I am sure, a hot day will have you sauntering along here and maybe sitting watching the antics of the local bird population in and around the river. Sand martin, dipper, pied and grey wagtail, grey heron and various species of gull, have all captivated my attention along here.

The diversity of bird life is matched by the variety of bankside trees: alder, willow, ash, hawthorn and sycamore co-exist happily.

There has recently been a return to the Ure of one mammal I have never seen, the otter. I do not know if they are on this particular stretch but it seems to me to be a suitable habitat for them to rest up or excavate their holts (dens) in. Let's hope!

In due course the idyll comes to a temporary end in the form of the road over the Ure to Worton. I think the designer of Worton Bridge was more preoccupied with functionality, and probably economics, than with pleasing the eye. The surviving pier of the earlier structure hints at something far more graceful. Even before that bridge was built the ford here was an important crossing point on the major north-south drove road.

Bid farewell to the Ure and take on the stiff ascent to Worton, a pretty and unspoiled village that receives little of the attention accorded its busy neighbours.

If you have time, seek out Worton Hall in the village, constructed in 1600, with beautiful examples of mullioned windows. Worton has a mining past. Between the village and tiny Cubeck to the south there are a number of shafts and levels from which lead and fluorite were obtained until 1883 when the mine seems to have folded.

Walk up to the road junction and turn right past the bus shelter, unless you are in need of the inn which lies at the east end of the village.

The Wensleydale Group of Rocks

On the other side of the road a finger post, half hidden in the bushes, indicates the way through a field gate, past the outbuilding and towards the wooded scar ahead. Firstly, though, it is up and over a drumlin, its slopes terraced by early farmers keen to maximise the potential of whatever crop land was theirs to use.

The route lies diagonally ahead, clipping both the corner of the fence and the end of the ruined wall to a squeeze stile under a large ash. A steep climb up through the wood takes you to the level top of Worton scar where you join the path coming in from Cubeck. For a little over one kilometre you will be walking on the scar top with the intensively grazed slopes of Addlebrough to your left and the thickly wooded scar to your right. Wensleydale is largely denied to you now as the wood is so dense. If you have chosen the right time of year, the flowers underfoot make up for the restricted views. Personally I like woodland walks, and the Dales is certainly lacking in decent woodland.

About half way along you pass beneath the uninhabited and aptly named Scar Top farm, and into meadows with more of a view. The wall, you will notice, is made up of friable limestone. The original wallers knew this was Hobson's choice as far as obtaining stone was concerned, but they also knew that sandstone throughs would hold it all together.

Perhaps this is a suitable point to briefly describe the geology of Wensleydale. You have seen on today's walk a number of prominent geological features – Addlebrough, Ellerkin Scar, the gorge of Mill Gill, the scar you are standing on now.

The southern Dales are dominated by the massive Great Scar limestone, and the rocks of the Wensleydale Group (or Yoredale Series) only appear on the higher ground. In Wensleydale the picture is quite different. The Great Scar Limestone dips down to the north and only appears at the surface in a few locations. The gorge just above West Mill at Askrigg is cut into this rock, but everything else you see is younger.

The Wensleydale Group – let's call them Yoredales for convenience – consists of a repeated series of sandstones and limestones with shale bands between certain layers. In all there are 13 limestone layers and probably fourteen sandstone bands. The accompanying section through Addlebrough puts the various layers into perspective.

The prominent scars on both sides of Wensleydale represent specific layers of limestone more resistant to erosion than the sandstones and shales.

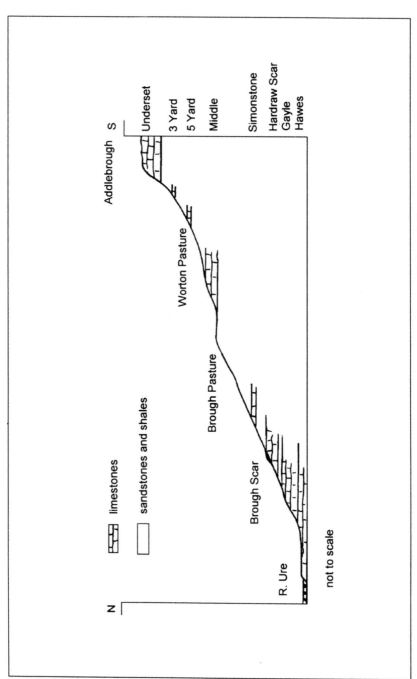

Geological sketch-section from the Ure to Addlebrough Top

The flat top of Addlebrough is the exposed surface of the Underset Limestone which corresponds with Ivy Scar above Carperby. The higher fells you can see to the north, forming the watershed between Wensleydale and Swaledale, are capped with Millstone Grit, younger than the Yoredales.

As you walk along the top of Brough Scar the wood peters out and you have the first glimpse of the Roman fort on Brough Hill.

The Impact of Rome

As discussed in *The Southern Dales* the Romans met stiff opposition from the Brigantes, the confederation of Celtic peoples that occupied most of the Pennines and adjacent areas. They were the last native tribe in "England" to be subdued and were not finally pacified until the AD 70s. Many were enslaved and either sent away to other parts of the Empire, or used in lead mines and road building within our general area.

To contain the Celts and to maintain Roman control, a series of forts and roads were built. Bainbridge, or *Virosidum*, was built in or around AD 80 of turf, though it was later rebuilt more substantially in stone with strong earthwork defences facing north and west. Covering a hectare, the fort could accommodate 500 soldiers.

It appears that the fort was abandoned between the years 120 and 160 but the cause of this is unknown. Some have suggested that there was a serious uprising among the Brigantes but there is no conclusive evidence for this. In any case this would not account for the fort being given up: rather it could account for its being re-occupied after 160. There is a problem here, however. The villa at Gargrave, probably owned by a Romanised native, was built around 160 which would suggest peace and harmony in the region.

There is evidence of the fort having been destroyed in the closing decade of the second century, along with the forts at Bowes and Ilkley. There is also archaeological evidence of industry being carried on within the confines of the fort in its later years. Does this imply a blurring of the distinction between the local military and civil population? Did this mean the local folk had come to accept the Roman presence and to make the most of what Romanisation offered? Or did it mean that the Roman veneer was so thin that life went on despite a Roman presence in the garrison? Whichever is the reality of that situation, the fort was abandoned permanently by 400 but I feel sure it had lost its strategic importance long before then.

After the Roman departure, life soon reverted to what it had been before. I am almost tempted to say it reverted to normal . . . *veni, vidi, vici . . . cucurri* and close the door behind you. *Gratia et vale.*[1]

1
   I came, I saw, I conquered . . . I ran away . . . thankyou and goodbye.

Back to Bainbridge

At the far end of the large meadow, when it seems you can proceed no further, there is a squeeze stile. Drop down the scar and the ensuing odd shaped field, then diagonally across the next, large pasture. You can now see the earthworks of the fort clearly on the flat top of Brough Hill: the short lengths of stone wall cut through its western end.

Your path ends at the junction of the main valley road and the road up to Raydale. Head down the road, over the River Bain, on the bridge widened by Carr in 1785, **and into the village.** The large mill by the bridge, High Mill, was a corn mill and I am told the grinding stones are still there. Down a ginnel between it and the shop is the village's old pinfold, the enclosure for "imprisoning" stray stock until collected and bailed out by the rightful owner. Behind the post office is Bainbridge's old dame-school – there is a plaque on the wall.

Roman fort from Brough Scar

Sessile or Durmast Oak
Quercus petraea

Status: native to Britain; more common than the English oak in the north.

Crown: noticeably domed but reaching tall; open canopy.

Height: up to 30 metres on average, but can be taller.

Trunk: long, reaching high into the crown with sub boles and branches radiating upwards and outwards.

Bark: greyish; very thick; finely fissured vertically.

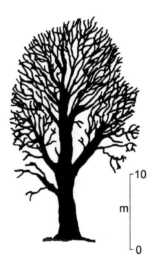

[1 cm

Fruit: acorns occur in groups of 4 to 6; up to 3cm long thus longer than on the English oak; acorns have no or only very short stems (sessile means stalkless) unlike English oaks.

Leaves: cuneate (wedge shaped at the base); up to 12cm long; with a long stalk, unlike the English oak; dark green; tough, leathery surface; not subject to attack to the same extent as leaves on English oaks.

Uses: a prized timber for joinery and ship building in the past; used for gate posts, panelling and high quality furniture nowadays; used to be coppiced and pollarded for tannin, fencing and building timber.

Place-name meanings

Addlebrough	OE/ON	Authulf's (pers. name) camp
Askrigg	ON	the ash ridge
Bain	ON	straight river
Brough	OE	the camp or earthwork
Ellerkin Scar	OE	Eller is alder
Fors	ON	waterfall
Harr Gill	ON	the high ravine or
	OE	the ravine with hares
Metcalfe		either the meadow croft dweller or the "mad calf" (a nickname)
Nappa	OE	(probably) the bowl-shaped enclosure
Newbiggin	ME	the new buildings
Penhill	Brit.	hill
Thwaite Holme	ON	the meadow in the clearing
Ure/Yore	Brit	strong river
Worton	OE	the village with vegetable gardens

Discovery Walk 6

A Parkland Landscape: Castle Bolton and Carperby

Start and Finish: Castle Bolton village (Grid reference SE 033 918).

Parking: there is a car park currently with an honesty box, just west of the castle. There is a pay and display car park at Aysgarth Falls for anyone doing a part of this walk.

Public Transport: Castle Bolton and Carperby are on the Postbus route from Hawes to Northallerton (phone a main post office for details). Carperby is also on a bus route from Hawes to Ripon, operated by United (01325 468771).

Facilities en Route: Castle Bolton has a post office that sells chocolate bars, cans and such like; a public telelphone and toilets. The castle has a shop and tea room. Carperby has The Wheatsheaf Inn, a tea room at Terrace House and a public telephone. The National Park Centre at Aysgarth Falls has a cafe and toilets.

Outline of the Walk: Castle Bolton – Bolton Parks – Low Gate – Carperby – Freeholders' Wood – Thoresby – Castle Bolton.

Length: 11.1km (6.9 miles) for the full route; 8.8km (5.5 miles) for the shorter version.

Ordnance Survey Map: 1:25,000 Outdoor Leisure 30 1:50,000 Landranger 98.

Introduction

Bolton Castle dominates Wensleydale not only physically but perhaps also psychologically. The sheer size and bulk and the elevated position make it impossible to ignore the castle's presence. For much of today's walk the fortress will be in sight from the most imposing western or southern facades. For the early part of the walk you will be walking through what was parkland, a hunting ground that is, belonging to the lords of the castle.

The quiet and unspoiled village of Carperby, with its real James Herriot associations (he honeymooned here), lies about half way along the full route. Beyond that lies a fossilised farming landscape and one of the very few surviving ancient coppice woodlands in the Pennines.

Elsewhere today there are signs of Norse settlers, place-name evidence reflecting the personal names of the founders. There are lost medieval villages and an almost lost road.

You have a number of options on *Discovery Walk 6*. There is, obviously, the full route. From Carperby you have the choice of shortening the walk by heading back to Castle Bolton through West Bolton. Another possibility would be to use the car park at the National Park Centre, or indeed at the castle, to make a route out of the shorter alternative in reverse and then the full route from Carperby onwards.

For the shorter route read up to and including "Through West Bolton". For the full route read all sections except that one.

Castle Bolton and Bolton Castle

The Village

It has often been written that the village of Castle Bolton is contemporary with the building of the castle, or earlier. The village plan as we see it now is in fact the result of deliberate redesigning and rebuilding after the civil war.

In the medieval period there were two villages called Bolton: West Bolton, now surviving as a single farm, and East or High Bolton that we now know as Castle Bolton.

Bolton Castle from the north-west

The village is one of the finest examples in the Dales of a *street-green* settlement. House plots (or tofts) face each other across the village green and their crofts run north and south from the tofts. The walled crofts south of the village street are contemporary with the laying out of the village.

The church of St Oswald is first documented in 1399, corresponding to the building of the castle.

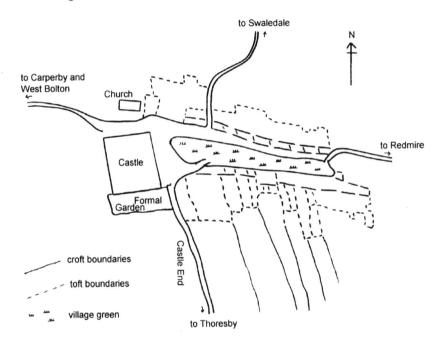

Sketch plan of 'medieval' Castle Bolton village

The footpath that links Carperby, West Bolton and the castle was part of the medieval High Road running along the north side of the dale. Another road ran from East Bolton southwards to the villages of Bishopdale. You can trace part of this on the ground: from the castle it ran south, not as the present tarred road, but as the bridleway called Scrogs Lane, just west of the present road. It then crossed fields past Thoresby – another lost village – and headed down to the Wharfe. The present bridleway, Watery Lane, is the line of this early medieval road that forded the river at Slapestone Wath, having passed through another lost settlement, then continued as Stony Stoop Lane and entered Bishopdale.

This road must be part of the one described in a document in 1173 as the "road going from Richmond to Bolton". As early as 1314 the road was diverted to its present course when the land hereabouts was emparked by the lord of the manor.

The Scropes

The manor of Wensley was purchased at the start of the fourteenth century by an old Norman family called Scrope (pronounced Skroop). In 1315 they persuaded Rievaulx Abbey to give back the Scropes' lands at Bolton in exchange for land elsewhere. The then lord was Sir Henry Scrope who had risen to a powerful position in the country being Chief Justice and Chief-Baron (i.e. president) of the Exchequer. It was he who emparked the land, including one of East Bolton's open-fields, whose cultivation terraces can be seen on today's walk.

Later Scropes also achieved high offices. Sir Richard (1327 – 1403) was created 1st Baron Scrope of Bolton in 1371 when the ill-fated Richard II appointed him Treasurer and Keeper of the Great Seal. In 1378 he was promoted to Chancellor though Richard II sacked him four years later. It was the 1st Baron who built the castle.

His son and heir, William, was created Earl of Wiltshire in 1397 – I am sure father was more proud than jealous – but he came to a sticky end two years later. The new king, the usurper Henry IV, had him executed for his support of King Richard. Another Scrope of the time, who was Archbishop of York, was also done away with by Henry, provoking an outcry and parallels with the murder of Becket two centuries earlier (see *Discovery Walk 2*).

Richard, 1st Baron, was thus succeeded to the title by another son, Roger, and his descendants held the estates and castle until the extinction of the title upon the death of the 11th Baron (also Earl of Sunderland) in 1630. One Lord Scrope, John, was a close companion of Richard III. John was one of his trusted leaders in the military campaigns that dogged his reign, as well as in Richard's final battle at Bosworth in 1485. The estates then passed to the Earl's son-in-law, Lord Bolton after 1630. A later Lord Bolton built Bolton Hall, near Wensley, in 1678 though the house was destroyed by fire and replaced by the present building in 1902.

Despite the high offices to which several Scropes rose, they were regarded as only belonging to the second tier of the aristocracy in the north of England, below the Cliffords, Percys and Nevilles.

The Castle

Sir Richard Scrope was granted a licence in 1379 "to crenellate his manor with a wall of stone and lime", though he had started building at least two years earlier. Whether the authorities had intended him to erect a castle on this scale, or a a lowly crenellated house, is not known.

He hired the services of a master mason called John Lewyn, who had just completed Raby Castle in Durham for the Nevilles, and was engaged on rebuilding Dunstanburgh Castle in Northumberland for John of Gaunt. The contract between Sir Richard and John survives.

Stone was quarried from within the general area north of Bolton and construction took 18 years. At today's values the cost was £1.5 million, no mean sum. The great timbers, incidentally, came by ox-waggon from the Penrith area.

According to Pevsner, Castle Bolton represents "a climax of English military architecture" combining the demands of secure defence with comfort, convenience and style. One notable feature of the structure is the enormous size of the storerooms and cellars. Not only could the garrison stock up in times of strife, but the castle could also use these storerooms, and the alehouse and brewhouse, to serve the travelling and local community, and thus make a tidy annual profit. There is nothing new in Bolton Castle serving food and drink to the public.

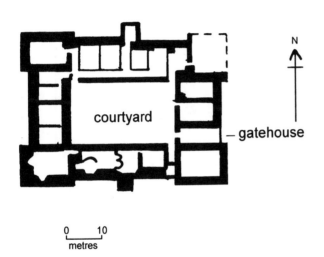

Sketch plan of Bolton Castle

Can I bring the story up to date? In 1990 a five year archaeological survey began, carried out by Lancaster University Archaeological Unit. The interior was filled with scaffolding and a most detailed, stone by stone survey was made over much of the castle. Advanced techniques were used as well as basic measuring and photography, to build up a full picture of the fabric of the castle. This was the first stage in a huge conservation programme.

I have no intention of describing the layout or function of Castle Bolton. Instead I would thoroughly recommend you go in and look around for yourself. I went in during 1995, not having done so for at least eight years. I was amazed at how much work has been completed. It is well worth the entry fee, if I may venture to say so.

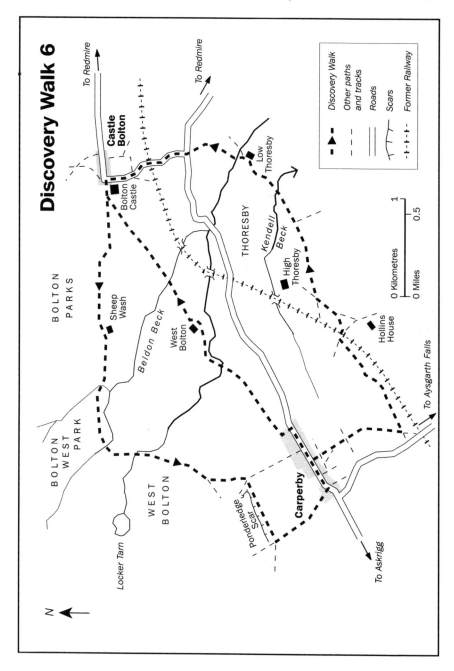

Discovery Walk 6

To Redmire

To Redmire

Castle Bolton

Bolton Castle

Low Thoresby

THORESBY

Kendell Beck

High Thoresby

Hollins House

Sheep Wash

Beldon Beck

West Bolton

BOLTON PARKS

BOLTON WEST PARK

WEST BOLTON

Ponderledge Scar

Carperby

Locker Tarn

To Aysgarth Falls

To Askrigg

N

Discovery Walk
Other paths and tracks
Roads
Scars
Former Railway

1
0.5
0 Kilometres
0 Miles

The Medieval Park

From the car park a broad track runs westward, slicing through the small sycamore wood called Cow Pasture Plantation. The Ordnance Survey map depicts it as a "white road" rather than a right of way. Fear not, though, as it enjoys County Road status to the parish boundary.

As the track swings slightly and rises a little look to the left where the lynchets, or medieval cultivation terraces, cascade downslope. Only grass grows round here nowadays but at one time, in the days of the castle and before, these terraces fed not only the cottagers, serfs and villeins of the township, but also the entire garrison of the castle. When his nibs was in residence the retinue would have been magnified umpteen fold, all of them needing to be well fed.

Away to the north, just to the right of the wood, is a spoil heap, an outpost of the Bolton Park lead mines.

The track passes through a series of gates then changes direction as it circumvents the agricultural buildings of Sheep Wash and a second, mainly sycamore, wood. Everything to the north of the track was parkland in medieval times. A glance at the Outdoor Leisure map reveals clues: between Apedale Beck in the east and the western parish boundary the map indicates seven names that include the word "park". The meaning and origin of most of them are obvious . . . but who was Anderson, I wonder?

The Medieval Park

All great houses and many castles had an extensive area of parkland attached to them. They were parks in one sense, there for the relaxation and enjoyment of the owner, family, friends and political clients. They differ from our modern conception of a park as a place of lawns, shrubberies and walkways. The medieval park was essentially a hunting ground stocked with deer to provide the wherewithal for "harmless" fun. (Better than hunting the peasants, I suppose.)

Bolton West Park

Some distance beyond Sheep Wash the track crosses Beldon Beck at the head of an ash wood. Now these were probably not planted, unlike the sycamores. The ash is native to the Pennines and one of the earliest species to colonise the fells following the most recent release of the ice sheets.

Beyond the next gate the track is transformed from being more like a road to being soft and green. At first you may even wonder where it goes. **Stick to the wall until it turns away south, then maintain the same line beyond that point. Cross the stream** – West Gill that rises high up on Green Hill to the north-west – and **pass through the gate** into Carperby-cum-Thoresby parish, an enormous parish.

Southwards to Carperby

The County Road is now a bridleway. I cannot understand why, as so often happens, one route can have different designations in different parishes. Were the decision makers of yore so insular in their attitude and actions? At least irregularities are now slowly being ironed out but why has it taken the Park authorities 40 years to address these issues? I am quite sure they have a reason and an answer to that question.

The track, soft and green, heads roughly due south and affords what I call mobile views. I can put my legs into autopilot mode because there is nothing to trip over or fall into, and thus concentrate my senses on what is around me. Soaring skylarks, haunting curlew calls and the vocal antics of bothersome lapwings engage my aural senses. The views, though, command my full attention. On my right, a kilometre to the west, is Wegber Scar (that has been in view from the beginning almost) with Blue Scar and Swinehaw Hill stretching beyond.

Across the valley to the south is the flat top of Penhill (526 metres) with Bishopdale and Waldendale reaching to the head of those fells separating Ure from Wharfe. Closer at hand the mind's eye notes the hawthorn bushes dotted about West Bolton. Are these the remnants of a continuous and extensive wood? More than likely.

Wegber and West Bolton

At the south end of West Bolton is Low Gate and a parting of the
bridleways. The medieval Oxclose Road connecting Castle Bolton with
Askrigg continues directly ahead. Long after the creation of the Richmond
to Lancaster turnpike road passing through Carperby village, Oxclose Road
was still used by drovers and others. By staying on this road between Askrigg
and Redmire they avoided three toll gates and saved a substantial amount
of money. This road is not for you, though. Your bridleway veers off slightly
to the left and follows the wall. Notice how the material that makes up the
wall is now totally limestone instead of the sandstones that have dominated
the route so far.

As the track surmounts a slight rise you will see the roofs of Carperby
down below, and Aysgarth across the Ure. The broadness and open aspect
of Wensleydale is apparent from here, giving the dale its distinctive character, so very different from all the other main dales.

The bridleway drops down into a narrowing valley, actually a meltwater
channel carved out by water escaping from the ice sheet that covered the
fells. In no time at all you arrive at a major track junction.

One very wide lane – Hargill, also still a County Road – drops straight
down to Carperby's East End; the road continues north through the gorge as
Peatmoor Lane. This old road connected the various lead mines on Carperby
Moor (Brock Holes, High Greenhaw and Brownfield mines) with Carperby.
As the name suggests the road was also the township's access to its supplies
of peat fuel. In addition it connected the township's flagstone quarries on
Wegber Scar with the valley. Carperby's quarries supplied stone for roofing
and flooring to much of central Wensleydale. The fourth road link (yours)
is the one going west along the top of Ponderledge Scar.

Your lane passes through a gate and parallels the wall topping the scar.
Note the boulder set into the wall a few metres beyond the gate, the one
which is made up of nodules of something set in a matrix, or natural cement,
of limestone.

Below the lane are the many small and irregularly shaped fields of
Carperby's inbye land; above it are the larger and more rectangular fields of
the New Pasture outbye (see *Discovery Walk 11* for a discussion of the
Enclosure Movement and *Discovery Walk 12* for a discussion of the wall
systems). Notice also the small gullies coming downslope, all being water-
carved.

Very shortly you arrive at another, staggered cross-roads. Turn right
downhill: is it a broad track or just two narrow fields? About half way down
the second field look for a squeeze stile in the left-hand wall. Cross the
adjacent field diagonally to the opposite side to a second squeeze stile,
down another narrow field to a step stile at the bottom. Cross over the
access to West End Farm and walk down the grassed way to the modern
house. A gate lets you out between the houses onto the village green.

Carperby

Carperby is a quiet village, overshadowed somewhat by the honeypot of Aysgarth Falls to the south. It is but a shadow of its former self, having once been a market town. Its charter was granted in 1305 but, like Wensley down dale, Carperby never really prospered. It was eclipsed first by Askrigg and later by Hawes and Leyburn.

Quarrying and lead mining above Ivy and Wegber Scars provided some prosperity but essentially Carperby remained an agricultural village.

There are a few points worth looking at as you walk through the village, especially towards West End. The Friends' Meeting House, built in 1864, is a very fine structure, looking somewhat out of place in a small village. Nearby are the old village school and the Methodist chapel, built in 1820. Perhaps the finest structure is the market cross. Notice the weathered faces on the sides of the cross, the letters RB on the western side and the date 1674 on the opposite side. This cross presumably replaced an older cross.

Through West Bolton

– If you now wish to return directly to the castle –

walk right through the village to East End Farm. At the far side of the farm complex there is a gap stile on the road edge, with a waymarked path leading alongside the farm and upslope. The track passes through a messy field full of yellow ragwort – a noxious and vigorous weed – **through a meadow with a barn and along the top side of a larger meadow. Drop down next by a small pond, cross the stream and go round the top of West Bolton Plantation. The way leads across to West Bolton farm,** all that remains of a medieval settlement. Angelhaw Hill nearby is neatly terraced into the arable strips of the lost village.

Walk through the farmyard and around the front of the house. From there head across the field to the gate and stile ahead. Follow the fence through the next field, a view of the castle's western range lying directly ahead. **You then reach a squeeze stile** (with a viciously sprung lambing gate) **cross the footbridge over Beldon Beck and climb up to the next stile.**

Look carefully at the surface of this next field. You can see a whole mass of strip lynchets – terraced fields – climbing up to Ellerlands Edge but in this first field the pattern is different: here ridge and furrow, running downslope, is the dominant medieval form. Remember that, to visualise the medieval landscape, you must mentally remove all the walls and envisage huge open fields divided up into strips. Each villager, of whatever status, had some land in different fields for he and his family to subsist on.

The way makes a beeline for the castle, climbing up the lynchet staircase to Cow Pasture Plantation. The path cuts through the lower end of this and rejoins the lane near the car park.

Freeholders' Wood

– Read on from here for the full route of today's walk –

Go through the gate directly opposite the entrance to the pub car park, into the field alongside the farm. Look for the stile in the right hand wall by the large tree, then head southwards through two narrow and ancient fields to join Low Lane. Almost directly opposite is another stile into another narrow field. Note on the Ordnance Survey map how narrow all these fields are, a sure sign of medieval open field strips having been enclosed at an early date.

Walk along the wallside and through the squeeze stile where wall meets hedgerow. Go diagonally through a series of small fields and squeeze stiles to enter the wood. If you require the facilities of the National Park Centre, turn right to the road and then left under the railway bridge.

If not, turn left and follow the broad path through the wood. This is part of the 12 hectare Freeholders' Wood detached from the bulk of the wood by the railway. Freeholders' Wood is a rare example in the north of England of a coppiced wood in sound condition. Mind you it was under threat through neglect, until the National Park purchased it and reintroduced coppice management.

It is called Freeholders' Wood because the citizens of Carperby had rights within the wood. Coppicing involves felling the trees close to the ground. New shoots spring up in a cluster from the stool, to be harvested on a 7 to 15 year cycle. Because the old growth is being repeatedly cut back, the individual trees retain a youthful vigour and, given sound management, can be harvested almost to infinity, so to speak. In any coppiced woodland some larger tree specimens, called *standards*, are allowed to grow to maturity.

Hurry not through the wood, particularly as this top section is peaceful. It does not attract the milling throng walking down the river to the falls on the Ure. Keep an eye out for roe deer, secretive but sometimes seen here. Keep an eye and an ear primed, too, for the birdlife of the wood: apart from the usual woodland species you would expect to find, various warblers and the nuthatch can be found here in summer.

Well over 100 flowering species have been recorded in Freeholders' Wood, far too many to single out any here.

The main coppice tree is hazel. One might, therefore, wonder if the hazel dormouse is resident here. An alternative name for this tiny mammal is the common dormouse. It emphatically is not common, and is on a serious decline in England and Wales and probably no longer occurs in the north. There is a national decrease in the area under hazel coppice, hence the wane in dormouse numbers. Do not turn your nose up, please, as the dormouse is one of the nicer members of the order *Rodentia*.

Just before you reach the gap that was a railway bridge, turn left to the step-over stile by the field gate, out of the wood.

An Ambitious Plan?

Follow the old railway course to the next railway bridge. Turn left here up the track by the fence to the top of the rise. At the fence corner a fingerpost sends you across the field, past a holly clump, to a gated stile. Beyond this follow the fence to join the access track to Hollins House. Cross the old railway bed here.

The Wensleydale Railway was constructed by the North-Eastern Railway Company in the late 1870s. It linked Hawes to the main east coast line at Northallerton and, as we have seen in *Discovery Walk 3*, it was linked into the Settle-Carlisle system. The line closed to passenger traffic in 1954 and to freight ten years later, though the track and lines still exist as far updale as Redmire.

There is now a Wensleydale Railway Association which is campaigning and fundraising to have the 30 or so missing kilometres relaid from Redmire to Garsdale station. There are clearly sound reasons for reinstating the line to serve locals and visitors, and to relieve pressure on the roads. Maybe I am being a jeremiad but I do not see how they can succeed. There are so many missing bridges, eroded embankments and all manner of obstructions – including the plantation in front of you now – that the task seems to be insurmountable. However I do wish them luck, and would be delighted to ride on the line.

Thoresby

Immediately beyond the railway bed turn left and walk round the two sides of this hay meadow, noting the old ditch and bank boundary on the second side. **You reach a gated step stile through the wall and follow the path through this meadow, heading for the north-east corner. Here the paths diverge. Ignore the gated stile on the High Thoresby path but climb the step-over stile to follow the wall on its south side.**

You are now back on Low Lane, a County Road from here to its junction with the tarred road by Carperby. The line of the old road follows the curving field wall to the west, under the railway line to become a proper road by the footpath junction at Grid Reference 017 897. Unfortunately it is badly obstructed either side of the railway bridge: County Highways Department please note.

Two more stiles follow and then you find yourself on the north side of the wall. At the far end of this field the path becomes a walled – and later hedged – lane. This is Thoresby Lane proper, past the junction with Watery Lane that leads down to Slapestone Wath. Thoresby Lane was an important link in the local late medieval transport network, linking Redmire, Carperby and Bishopdale via Stony Stoop Lane, and replacing the earlier road through Thoresby village.

The botanical diversity along the lane is rich, indicating great age (the

Common Hazel or Cobnut
Corylus avellana

Status: native to Britain; very tolerant of different soil and climate conditions.

Crown: more of a bush than a tree; broad and open, but tangled, canopy.

Height: few exceed 7 metres though some may grow into a small tree.

Trunk: the bole is very short and soon 7 splits into a confusion of upspreading branches and twigs.

Bark: smooth and grey brown, even verging on pink, in young specimens with small and horizontal curls or lenticels.

⌈1 m

⌈1cm

Fruit: male catkins are brown then pale yellow in autumn, 5cm long; female catkins are tiny; the fruits open in October.

Leaves: large for the size of the +&{! tree, up to 10 x 10cm; obovate (egg shaped but broader above the middle); hairy and dark green above; soft below with whitish veins.

Uses: coppiced in the past for many uses. It was a rural staple: firewood, fencing posts, hurdles, traps and cages, charcoal, wattle for building walls, walking sticks . . . and the nuts are edible. It is used in craft trades nowadays.

greater the variety of woody species, the older a hedgerow is). Some of the plants along the lane inspire me and give me good cheer: meadow cranesbill *(Geranium pratense)*, meadowsweet *(Filipendula ulmaria)* and bell flower *(Campanula latifolia)*, for example. There are others you can keep, thank you: nettles, overgrown hawthorn and hogweed *(Heracleum sphondylium)* in particular. Be careful where Kendell Beck crosses.

After a kilometre or so the lane passes by Low Thoresby, now just a farm, and fords Beldon Beck. Leave the lane here in favour of the steps on the left. You negotiate two stiles (the third is for private use only), **turn right and head upfield to a small decaying building. There is a gated stile just to its right, followed by a long wall up the east side of the field.**

A glance on the map will confirm that you are again in a fossilised field landscape: small and irregularly shaped fields like these must be, at the latest, late medieval.

At the far end of the field – another meadow so stick to the edge – is the last stile of the day. Cross the road and climb up Scallow Bank Lane to Castle Bolton. As you do so, spare a thought for any foot soldiers who were ordered to attack the castle from the south. The castle is not sited there by accident!

You re-cross the old railway which bisects what would have been a large open field in medieval times. You can see the ridge and furrow both above and below the railway cutting. Imagine, also, the labour of the oxen and ploughmen toiling up and down this slope. You pass the junction with the delightfully named and early medieval Scrogs Lane (heading both east and south) and complete the ascent up Castle End.

"A State Guest under House Arrest"

As you toil up the road think of the unfortunate Mary Queen of Scots who was brought here from Carlisle Castle in July 1568 to begin a 19 year incarceration in a succession of castles, a victim of Tudor politics and of her own failings: ambition, narcissism, folly and haste. She is often portrayed as a martyr but she was no feminine white knight. She took gambles in life and politics and made unwise alliances, not least in her marriages.

The problem was she was Catholic and was seen as the focus of anti-Elizabethan feelings and thus a threat to the country's stability. Much of the north was more Catholic than Protestant, the gentry certainly had Catholic sympathies, and the populace at large still remembered the brutality of the suppression of the Pilgrimage of Grace by Henry VIII, Elizabeth's father.

Mary was forced to abdicate the Scottish throne in 1567 in favour of her 13 month old son James VI (and later I of England). She did not lie down easily and was captured and imprisoned in Scotland. She soon escaped and fled to England, seeking protection from Elizabeth, thus beginning what was described as 19 years as "a state guest under house arrest".

Elizabeth sent her vice chamberlain, Sir Francis Knollys, to inspect Bolton

Castle to ascertain its state and suitability. He reported back, having found it to be "very strong, very fair and very stately after the old manner of building. It is the highest walled house that I have seen."

Thus came Mary and her retinue for a six month stay – in comfort and splendour, not in the dungeons – before being taken further south out of harm's way when an ill-fated revolt broke out in 1569 led by the Earls of Northumberland and Westmorland.

Ultimately Mary was found guilty of treason and was executed in 1587, proclaiming her Catholic faith on the scaffold.

Place-name meanings

Beldon (Beck)	OE	(possibly) beacon hill
Bolton	OE	the village with an enclosure
Carperby	OIN	Cairpre's (pers. name) village
Ellerlands (Edge)	OE/ON	the land with alder trees
Ivy Scar		as it sounds. There is still some ivy *(Hedera helix)* growing on the scar, a vestige of the mass that used to cover the rock.
Redmire	OE	the reed swamp
Scrogs Lane	ON/ME	the lane through brushwood
Slapestone Wath	OE	the slippery, stony ford
Thoresby	ON	Thor's (pers. name) farm

Discovery Walk 7

A Walk in Bishopdale Chase

Start and Finish: West Burton village green for the full route (Grid Reference SE 017 866), or Thoralby for the western loop (Grid Reference SE 001 867).

Parking: there is ample roadside parking within the village of West Burton. If you are only walking the western loop, park sensitively in Thoralby.

Public Transport: West Burton and Thoralby are served by a postbus service linking Northallerton and Hawes; and by postbus services and United (01325 468771) between Richmond and Hawes. West Burton also lies on a bus route from Leeds to Ingleton via Grassington and Hawes (phone Keighley and District on 01535 603284).

Facilities en Route: West Burton has a useful range of services: the Fox and Hounds inn, village store, craft pottery, post office and telephone box. Thoralby also has a post office, village store, the George Inn, a National Park Information Point and a telephone box. Newbiggin has a telephone box, and the nearby Street Head inn.

Outline of the Walk: West Burton – Newbiggin – Thoralby – Brown-a-haw – Folly Lane – Tomgill Bridge – Eshington Bridge – West Burton.

Length: 14 km (8.7 miles) for the entire route; 6km (3.7 miles) just for the western loop; and 8km (5 miles) for the eastern loop alone.

Ordnance Survey Maps: 1:25,000 Outdoor Leisure 30 1:50,000 Landranger 98

Introduction

Of the dales that branch off to the south from Wensleydale, Bishopdale is perhaps the most beautiful and full of character. The dale is long (about 10 kilometres) and narrow throughout. In parts it is well-wooded, in others open moorland: in parts it is almost tame and well tended, yet elsewhere it is wild and really quite forbidding. The road over the top to Wharfedale is to be avoided if snow threatens, as I found to my cost one day some years ago, even with a four-wheel drive vehicle.

West Burton lies at the junction of Bishopdale and Walden, though the confluence of the two main becks lies some distance to the north. In the Middle Ages much of the twin dales formed the baronial hunting ground of Bishopdale Chase. The lords of Middleham Castle, the Nevilles, held sway hereabouts from the middle of the fifteenth century, exploiting the land for venison and food crops.

Even before this, from at least a century earlier, wool combing and dyeing were carried on in the dale, and coal was won up on the fells.

Those fells to the east of West Burton, rising up to the flat-topped Penhill, are still part of a large estate based on Swinithwaite Hall. In the medieval period, from 1160, much of these lands was held by the Knights Templar based at the preceptory (estate) chapel first by Temple Farm and, from 1202, higher up at Layrus. Their estate boundary survives still, in part, as earth banks sometimes adjacent to later enclosure walls. There is an enormous amount of medieval ridge and furrow all over the lower part of Bishopdale. Higher up, incidentally, towards Dove Scars are signs of co-axial field systems attributed to the Bronze Age (see *Discovery Walk 12*).

What of today's walk? I have arranged the route into a pick-n-mix selection. You could take on the entire route, for which you would require a full day, starting and finishing at West Burton. Alternatively you could walk only the western loop using Thoralby as a base. In that case the section "The Western Loop" is for you, in addition to the interpretative sections.

There again you could opt for the eastern section using either West Burton or Thoralby as your base. If this is your choice, read everything *except* "The Western Loop".

Both loops would make self-contained and enjoyable walks in their own right . . . two for the price of one!

West Burton

The Yorkshire Dales possess some outstanding villages but West Burton is surely near the top in terms of gasp-ability value. The many who race up and down the main valley road probably have no idea what lies hidden behind the roadside buildings. It is beyond doubt a village that was very carefully planned and laid out, but the question that remains to be answered is when? Along with East Witton, it must receive the prize for best designed medieval village.

In times past West Burton has been known as Burton-in-Bishopdale and Burton-cum-Walden. Both are equally fitting and the latter is of course still the name of the parish. It was clearly a substantial settlement in the Middle Ages as four open-fields have been identified from early seventeenth century documentary evidence.

Many of the houses you see today owe their existence to industry rather than to farming. Many villagers laboured in stone quarries below Dove Scars, or in lead mines on Wasset Fell or Harland Hill. Indeed the remains of the Burton smelt mill can be traced at the confluence of Thupton Gill and Walden Beck.

As you walk round the village look out for the stocks; the former squatters' cottages on the green (see *The Southern Dales*); the obelisk, erected in 1820 – it is not a market cross replacement; and see if you can identify the building that was once The Black Bull. What you will not find in the village is an Anglican church, I shall return to this later.

West Burton to Newbiggin

You could lead off from West Burton in any one of thirteen directions, excluding the main road, but **the way you need today continues from the very top of the village green. A lane from there goes through Town Head farmyard onto a stony track, signposted to Newbiggin and Cross. Pass through the field gate ahead and ever south-westwards across a series of small fields. Little Beck is on your left throughout.** As you wander along take in the long-range views across Wensleydale with the sweep of hills: Redmire Scar in the east to Ellerkin Scar above Askrigg in the west. You should be able to pick out Bolton Castle against that backdrop.

There is a path junction by the particularly tall roofless barn. (Incidentally, it is known from archaeological evidence that many of the barns we see in today's landscape, themselves historic features, are built on much earlier sites.) The path to the left climbs over the watershed into Waldendale to Cross Farm: **your path continues straight ahead through a further series of stiles.** You will now be able to see Thoralby on the north side of Bishopdale

The village green, West Burton

with historic Heaning Hall, above the village to the north, sheltering beneath the wood.

After the second roofless barn and nearby stile head diagonally down the next field to a squeeze stile in the corner, and then along the top side of one of the few remaining meadows in this area. You have to walk right through the middle of the second meadow and then across a series of fields, maintaining the same direction . . . and keeping your eyes fixed on the view towards Kidstones pass at the head of the dale.

The route finally descends to a five-way path junction at the stony lane called Ox Pasture Lane.

– You have a choice of routes now: you can either go by the lane or through the fields –

If you choose the latter, cross the lane to the bridle gate and drop down through the small fields to the main road, turn left (having hacked your way through the butterbur by the stile), **and then right at Cross Lanes. Alternatively follow the lane to the left into Newbiggin, turning right there down the road to Cross Lanes.**

Newbiggin

Newbiggin, when founded, may have been new relative to either Thoralby or West Burton. As settlements go, it is a newcomer to the historic scene. The village has several very handsome seventeenth century houses, and traces (hard to find) of a medieval corn mill. Even in the eighteenth century documentary evidence tells of arable farming around the village.

The road into Newbiggin goes nowhere today, except up to the old mines on Wasset Fell. This was not always the case, though. Until the early part of the eighteenth century the road up Bishopdale passed through the village. It is now lost as a routeway but you can work out its general course from the Outdoor Leisure map. A major wall contours up the dale from just beyond Hargarth Farm, generally following the 240 metre contour, to the vicinity of Dale Foot where (I believe) it made for higher ground below the rectangular woods and on up to Dale Head.

The valley road, the B6160, was surveyed and constructed to replace the old road through Newbiggin. A short distance updale from Cross Lanes is the Street Head inn, built in 1730 to serve the new road. It was to become an important coaching inn in due course.

Thoralby

Follow the road downhill from Cross Lanes and over Mill Bridge. Just on the right at Machell Hill, at Chapel House, is the site of a chantry chapel established in 1316 by Lady Mary Neville. It was in use until at least 1546.

Climb uphill past the former mill to Thoralby village green. Note the

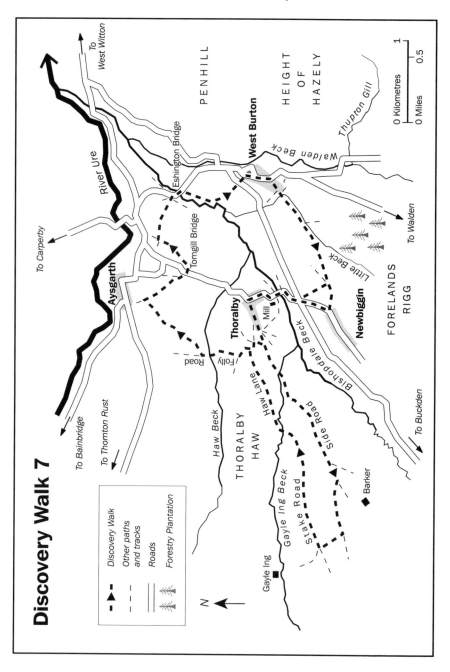

Discovery Walk 7

stately seventeenth century farmhouse at the top of the hill as you enter the village. The fine hood moulding over the ground floor windows was an architectural embellishment typical of that period.

The village is somewhat straggling but has some good examples of vernacular architecture.

A Lost Village

From the village green walk along the road to the west past the building with the interesting double storey porch, inscribed 1704, and the older house on the right with surviving stone mullions and a date of 1653. At the end of the village is a five-way junction, and in the apex of the two lanes is an old stone finger post indicating the way to Littleburn, down Westfield Lane. The name Westfield probably perpetuates the name of one of Thoralby's open-fields.

This lane continues up the dale to join the modern road at Har Gill Bridge. Part way along the lane is Crooksby Barn – it is shown on the Ordnance Survey map. This single barn name is actually perpetuating the name of a long-deserted village. Crocsbi village and manor were abandoned by the thirteenth century. I do not imagine we will ever discover the reason for this particular desertion but it could have something to do with major reorganisation of the manors within Bishopdale. A study of the map tells us that the surviving villages – West Burton, Newbiggin and Thoralby – have all been carefully planned. They have not just evolved from a farmstead like some villages. Was a decision made, at some point in history, by the lord and keeper to relocate Crocsbi and its hapless inhabitants?

All that remains are the humps and bumps of the village and the manor house . . . and the name.

Stay on the main lane at the junction with Westfield Lane and head up to Old Hall Farm. Shortly before the first corner, under an ash tree, is a spring that was walled in to provide drinking water to passing folk and stock. The first farm building on the left is a barn, whose gable end warrants close inspection. The roof line has been altered at some point in its life. The original pitch is very steep: this was a cruck-framed barn, the roof being supported on massive A-frame trusses. Some kind of thatch, quite possibly heather, covered the framework. When the decision was made to roof the barn in stone, the pitch had to be lowered to support the weight of stone. I would imagine this alteration to be contemporary with the rebuilding of Old Hall in 1641. Houses like this are a common sight throughout the Dales and most of them are architectural variations on a common theme. Presumably itinerant architects and craftsmen operated in the area carrying their ideas and visualisations around with them: a kind of early modern peripatetic design school.

Old Hall Barn

– To come back to earth, this is the parting of the ways for you, depending on whether it is your intention to complete the entire walk or just the eastern loop. If, however, you are only walking the western loop, you need to follow the description of the full route, using Thoralby as your starting point –

The Eastern Loop: Part 1

– Read on here if you are omitting the western loop –

Turn sharp right and head uphill at the cruck-framed barn on the stony lane past Top Cottage. Turn left at the first junction and follow this lane uphill. At the second junction you should go straight ahead through the gate.

– At this point the western loop and full route join the eastern loop –

The Western Loop

Side Road

Continue on the lane past Old Hall, gaining height gradually. Very soon views of the entire dale open up, as well as across the subsidiary and little frequented Waldendale to Penhill (526 metres) and Harland Hill (535 metres). Between the two dales is the long ridge that stretches from West Burton to Buckden Pike with Naughtberry Hill (573 metres) in between. The section you might be looking at now, above Newbiggin, is called Wasset Fell. You can probably make out a road climbing from the village towards the summit plateau. It once served as a mine road for lead workings and more latterly as access to grouse moors.

Your road, Side Road – and what an unimaginative name that is – **cuts through the upper part of Swinacote Gill wood and crosses Hacker Gill Beck.** Notice the extent of past coppicing in the wood (see *Discovery Walk 6*), and the two stone sheep pens near the stream. Maybe the stream here was used as a sheepwash in the days before chemical dips and pills. Sheep were "tubbed" in becks throughout the Dales at specific times in the year. They were collected from the fells, driven down to the nearest sheepwash, and then "heeafed" again, that is sent back up to their ancestral grazing grounds.

The road creeps ever higher, climbing a spur between the main dale and the parallel valley of Skellicks Beck. **Eventually the track forks,** the left turn being the access to the two houses down below (Blind Syke and Cote Bottom), **and the main track suddenly becomes "green" and less conspicuous. Pass through a gateway, and half way across the next pasture there is a second junction.** The way straight on is, unbelievably, the access to the still inhabited Barker.

You turn right to the gate at the foot of the slope and follow the dying wall to the point where it turns southwards, and then cut across the pasture on a very faint path to a cast-iron gate in the last wall. Considering this is a bridleway, it is not at all clear beyond that gate. Maintain the same line as before for 100 metres and turn north (i.e. to the right) on another bridleway, all trace of which seems to have vanished. Stay parallel to the wall you have just come through as you go beyond the hill crest of Brown-a-haw to join a more prominent track. This is Stake Road, once a major artery though today you may well have it to yourself.

Stake Road

The views into the distance are quite something from up here. If you look south-westwards, beyond the head of Bishopdale with Kidstones Scar and Dale Head Scar framing the panorama, you see several areas of upland. The furthest backdrop is Out Moor and Old Cote Moor, that separate Littondale

Looking up Bishopdale towards Kidstone Scar

from Upper Wharfedale. The rounded fell to the east of that, and nearer to you, is Buckden Pike (702 metres) with the ridge dipping to Naughtberry Hill and Wasset Fell. On your side of the dale, and again away to the south-west, High Scar stands proud despite the mess of lead mining activity above it in the shape of Thoralby mine.

Turn round and look north. Across the broad valley, nestling against the wood is Gayle Ing, one of the more remote farms in the Dales. It is no longer an active farm but is still occupied. I fancy the house and its situation but not the long, bumpy track down to civilisation.

Head eastwards along Stake Road. As you progress, with only sheep and birds for company, **Stake Road becomes walled on both sides** and changes its identity to Haw Lane. **Cross Hacker Gill Beck** (for the second time) **and carry on to the T-junction at Keld Gill.**

For the most of this western loop there has been a dearth of interesting botany, if I may arrogantly dismiss grasses and rushes as less than captivating for me. Towards the end of Haw Lane, however, the flora comes alive. I jotted the following down while drinking a cup of tea here one day:

wild thyme	*Thymus polytrichus*
lady's bedstraw	*Galium verum*
harebell	*Campanula rotundifolia*
yarrow	*Achillea millefolium*
vetch	*Vicea sp.*
tormentil	*Potentilla erecta*

– The western loop joins the eastern loop at this junction. If you are only walking the former, turn right and drop down to Thoralby, keeping left at the next junction. Otherwise, turn left through the gate and go uphill –

The Eastern Loop: Part II

At the top of the crest, through the top gate, a path to Thornton Rust bears left while your bridleway bears right diagonally across what was two fields. At the far corner, near the dying oak tree at the north end of the line, you pass through a gate onto Folly Lane. Ford Haw Beck and look for the stile on the right just before Folly House barn. The path, not distinct on the ground, heads up the first field then cuts across several more to a barn to the right of which is a gate and awkward "stile". I mentioned earlier the lack of a church in West Burton. Much of Wensleydale, its tributary dales and the adjacent fells, was contained within the ancient parish of Aysgarth, claimed to have been England's most extensive parish. The only actual church was at Aysgarth, near the falls. To get to church – and you had to attend – the only way was to walk. The path you are on now makes a beeline for the church, thus this may have been a church path, a kirkgate, though some disagree.

A further series of small fields follows, all meadows and all having clear crossing points in the dividing walls. Use Bolton Castle as a sighting point, if you need to. Note the strip lynchets hereabouts and how the path has worn a groove through them. Soon after this you meet a north-south farm track. Turn right here past the barn with the "interesting" roof line and head south-east along the edge of the ensuing fields. The area enclosed by the walls is known as Poor's Land.

As the land begins to fall away in front of you another view opens up. Straight ahead is Harland Hill with Height of Hazely (553 metres) and Penhill to the east. Penhill is part of the extensive Swinithwaite Hall Estate. As I explained earlier the owners commissioned a full archaeological survey of the whole estate, on a field by field basis. The very comprehensive report details 219 different sites and 32 separate routeways of historic significance. A veritable mass of medieval sites were identified and, in the Penhill area in particular, a lot of pre-Roman sites. From hereabouts you can also pick out strange objects just across the beck in the dale bottom, above Sorrelsykes Park. They are follies.

A Geomorphological Diversion

The Geology of Penhill

If you stand and look out towards Penhill and Height of Hazely, you will notice that the slopes are stepped. The general curvature of the hill, steep though the curve may be, is punctuated by a series of scars. The top of Penhill, from this distance and vantage point, seems unduly flat. I discussed in the previous walk how the Wensleydale Group of rocks – the Yoredale Series – consists of a repeated sequence of limestones, sandstones and shales.

Let's start at the top, with the youngest rocks, and work our way down to the valley bottom. Bear in mind that all the Yoredales were deposited in marine conditions around 300 million years ago, in the late Carboniferous period (see *The Southern Dales*).

The summit plateau of the hill is underlain by Millstone Grit, not part of the Yoredales. The grits were laid down after, in deltaic conditions similar to the delta of the Mississippi or Rhone today: this is made up of sandstones mainly, as are Penhill Crags round to the east. Dovescar Plain overlies cherts (Richmond Cherts) which were originally limestones very rich in silica making the cherts very hard indeed. (Chert is the limestone equivalent of flint in chalk.)

Below that are High Dove and Low Dove Scars formed, respectively, of Main and Underset Limestones, separated by shales and a thin sandstone bed. Morpeth Scar, lower still, consists of Middle Limestone, the thickest of the exposed limestone beds and possibly the most fossil rich, though all the Yoredale limestones and shales provide fertile ground for fossil fanatics.

Further lower and smaller scars have formed in the Simonstone and Hardraw Scar Limestone beds, while the falls on Walden Beck in West Burton are in the Hawes and Gayle Limestones.

The Glacial Impact

Ice has had a great impact on the local landscape. Bishopdale is a typical, text-book, glaciated U-shaped valley with steep sides and a flat bottom. Because this dale was over-deepened by glacial scouring more so than Wensleydale, the post-glacial situation found the Ure having to cut deeper to reach the new level of its tributary. Furthermore Bishopdale contained lakes in the post-glacial period: one updale from Newbiggin and the other from Thoralby downstream to Sorrelsyke. The lower of these two, at least, was moraine dammed. All such lakes have a relatively short life as the morainic dam is eventually breached to drain the lake. This extra volume of water enhanced the downcutting of the Ure downstream of Froddle Dub. What I am getting at is that the Ure upstream of the Dub had renewed energy and increased incentive to cut down rapidly to reach the new, lower level downstream. This is why the falls exist at Aysgarth: the Ure is pushing this new level back upstream.

In other walks in this collection (*Walks 3 and 4*) I have mentioned drift tails. The largest one in the whole of Wensleydale, as far as I can see anyway, has been on today's walk. Remember that very long, gradual descent down Stake Road and Haw Lane: that was a drift tail *par excellence*.

Tomgill Bridge

Drop down the final slope to join the road above Tomgill Bridge. Opposite the stile is a very interesting stone marker post. Do take the time to examine it and to try and decipher its partly weathered inscriptions:

Facing you:

HERE ENDS
AYSGARTH
ROAD
1833

On the opposite, rear face:

129?
RICH
MOND

On the lefthand face:

AS
KRIGG

On the righthand face:

MIDL
HAM

It was a boundary stone to delimit the point where road maintenance responsibility changed.

Having given up trying to decipher it all **climb over the stile and walk to the left of the small oak copse, contouring along into a shallow dry valley. At the far end of the very narrow field there is a four way crossing. Turn right uphill but soon to the left through a gated stile. Carry on past the top of the wood and diagonally down the next, larger field to the gateway. Head on down the field beyond the gateway passing to the west of Brant Lea barn. Continue down the steep banking and through the last field to join Eastfield Lane.**

Medieval Fields and Climate Change

A bit more medieval history now . . . Earlier today you encountered Westfield Lane, and now Eastfield Lane. In medieval days, long before individual fields were enclosed by walling or hedging, the community practised the open-field system. A village would have had from two to four huge fields divided up into individual strips. Depending on the nature of the terrain these strips would either have been in the form of lynchets (terraces) or ridge and furrow. In this case the strips – called *lands* – ran up and downslope to assist drainage and leave the ridges dry enough for crop growth. Groups of lands were termed *furlongs*. Earlier on, on the Poor's Land, you passed one furlong. Here we have another one. In other parts of the country furlongs have been dated, by documentary evidence or excavation of overlying features, to as early as the eleventh century.

Groups of furlongs were blocked together to form what was then called a *field*: the exact meaning of this word has thus changed through the centuries. The fields – hence the term open-field system – were farmed in rotation. A village with three fields practised a three year rotation, changing the use of each field annually to sustain fertility and productivity. Very often the open-fields were simply given names of the cardinal points of the compass. Thus, around Thoralby, we have the names of the two lands possibly perpetuating the two open-fields in the valley bottom. Was there also a North Field above Keld Gill? Possibly?

To confuse the issue here the slopes you are now on, around Brant Lea, are the site of another lost medieval village, called Ecington – the name is preserved as Eshington. If Eastfield Lane led to Thoralby's East Field, presumably Ecington must have been abandoned, or forcibly relocated, before the growth of the open-field here. Maybe the cottagers and villeins of Ecington moved to Thoralby. There are so many unanswered questions, and so much potential for archaeological research.

Village abandonment in the Middle Ages may also have been a response to climatic change. It is actually amazing how regularly and dramatically the climate did change. As I have said elsewhere, there is nothing novel in the concept of global warming – or cooling. Changes in the medieval and later periods can be summarised thus:

Years	Climatic summary
1150 – 1250	warm and dry
1250 – 1450	cooling and becoming wetter
1530 – 1700	cold and very damp
1700 – 1730	warming up again
1730 – 1900	stable
1900 –	warming up again

Clearly the prevailing climate pattern determined how high the limit of cultivation could be pushed, how successful valley bottom farming was, and thus how much food was available to sustain the populace. The deterioration from 1250 led to the abandonment of many marginal settlements in the Pennine chain. Matters were made infinitely worse by catastrophic crop failures and sheep and cattle plague in the years 1315 to 1322. Life then must have been purgatory.

Across the Floodplain

Time to move on now. **Cross over Eshington Bridge, spanning Bishopdale Beck, and take the field path to the right upstream. This was the church path from West Burton.**

Sycamore or Great Maple
Acer pseudoplatanus

Status: introduced into Britain before the Middle Ages. Naturalised in all parts of the country now.

Crown: very pronounced dome; broad throughout; closed and dense when in full leaf; often seems as broad as it is tall.

Height: average 35 metres.

Trunk: main bole is strong and straight, spreading into very strong looking branches.

Bark: smooth and grey in young trees; cracked and scaled and looking pink brown on older specimens.

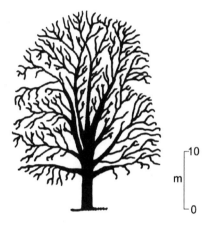

Fruit: occurs in bunches; green to red on the wings which are set opposite each other on a short stalk.

Leaves: set on long, reddish stalks; leaves up to 18cm long with lobes; unevenly and roughly toothed on the edges; dark and quite leathery to the touch; prone to fungal attack.

Uses: widely used traditionally for spoons, yokes, carvings and for storing food or for uses involving food, eg. chopping boards; nowadays for plywood, veneers and food treatment items. Sometimes grown on plantations as it is very fast growing when young.

The path crosses four fields on the flat and damp floodplain before reaching the main valley road. Cross straight over and climb up the steps to return to the village.

If you have time to spare, do have a look at Burton Force at the lower end of the village.

Place-name meanings

Aysgarth	ON	the open place with oaks
Bishopdale	OE	Bisceop's (pers. name) valley
Brant Lea	OE	the steep wood
Brown-a-haw	ON	haw is a hill
Crooksby	ON	Krok's (pers. name) farm or village
Eshington	OE	the village near the meadow with ash trees
Gayle Ing	ON/OWSc	the meadow near the ravine
Hacker Gill	ON	Hacker is a surname meaning cutter of wood
Harland Hill	OE	the hill with heaps of stones
Height of Hazely	–	hazel (?) hill
Keld Gill	ON	the ravine near the spring
Kidstones	OE	? stones
Naughtberry Hill	ME	Cloudberry Hill
Penhill	Brit	hill (hill)
Stake Road	OE	the road with marker posts
Swinacote (Gill)	OE/ON	the cottage where (wild) pigs feed
Swinithwaite	ON	the place cleared by burning
Thoralby	ON	Thorald's (pers. name) farm or village
Waldendale	OE/ON	(poss.) the valley settled by a foreigner (a Celt?)
West Burton	OE	the west village near the fort or the west, fortified village

Discovery Walk 8

A Medieval Miscellany: Coverdale and Middleham

Start and Finish: Middleham market place (Grid Reference SE 127 877).

Parking: there is ample parking within the town on most days. During the season Sunday Markets make parking difficult.

Public Transport: Middleham lies on bus routes from Hawes to Ripon, and Leyburn to Thornton Steward, operated by United. Coverham is on a route from Middleham up Coverdale to Woodale, again operated by United (01325 468771).

Facilities en Route: as one would expect for a small town Middleham has a range of shops, pubs and eating places, as well as gift shops, toilets and a filling station. There are no services en route.

Outline of the Walk: Middleham – Cover Banks – Braithwaite Hall – Coverham – Middleham Low Moor – Middleham.

Length: 12.5km (7.8 miles) for the long route or 9km (5.6 miles) for the basic route without the extra options.

Ordnance Survey Map: 1:25,000 Outdoor Leisure 30 1:50,000 Landranger 99

Introduction

Coverdale is a dale of extremes. The upper dale is one of the bleakest and wildest in the whole National Park with only one farm, Coverhead, in a distance of five kilometres. The lower dale is quite different being broader and more open, more akin to the lowland Vale of Mowbray east of the Dales than to the Pennine Dales themselves. Indeed, as Coverdale fans out to slowly merge into the eastern extremity of Wensleydale, it is not easy to decide where the dale has its bounds.

Here, between Middleham and East Witton, the farming scene is transformed in a rather abrupt way. To the west sheep dominate the fells and upper dales while cattle and grass crops prevail in the dale bottom. To the east, however, cereal crops are able to ripen in the sunnier, warmer and drier micro-climate in the lee of the Pennine chain. This is the only part of the Dales where you can expect to see wheat and barley rustling in the breeze.

Wensleydale and Coverdale were well protected by the great castle at Middleham, stronghold of the all-powerful Neville family in the Middle Ages, home of Richard III, and centre of the huge Honour of Middleham. The main route from north to south, from London to Richmond, passed from Skipton to Kettlewell, over the top of Hunters Sleets and down the full extent of Coverdale. The castle acted like an early form of customs post, tax collection centre and controller of traffic either way.

In the shadow of the castle, and within its protective bosom, there developed two monastic foundations: Jervaulx Abbey just outside our area, and Coverham Abbey. Both abbey and castle feature on this walk, as does Middleham's past and present importance for the training of race horses. You will also see, beyond Coverham, how the "other half" lives.

I have arranged *Discovery Walk 8* in a flexible way. There are several junctures at which you can extend the basic route by completing short diversions to points of specific interest. It would be quite possible for motorists with limited time to begin at Coverham church, to follow the back lane to Braithwaite Hall, and then to slot into the narrative at that point back to Coverham. It would also be feasible to limit yourself to the early section from Middleham to Braithwaite, returning the same way. Either of these short options would make up a gentle and easy half-day's walk. This is not to imply that the full route is not also gentle. There are no fells or high sections except in long-distance views.

Braithwaite Hall is open to the public by arrangement, and at a very modest charge, free to National Trust members. You must make a telephone booking in advance (01969 640287).

Middleham Town

Settlement at Middleham stretches way back to the very beginnings of history. A few hundred metres east of the castle, excavations revealed the remains of a domestic Roman building, probably a villa, sited here to develop the considerable agricultural potential of the area.

In the Anglo-Saxon period a village was established here – the middle homestead, as the name implies. The question is middle between what? Almost certainly in relation to Leyburn to the north, as 'ham' and 'burn' are both early place-name elements in the Anglican diaspora northwards. The other settlement may have been Coverham. It could not have been East Witton because 'ton' suffixes are associated with a later phase of Anglian settlement.

The church has Saxon origins but that would have been a very simple affair, nothing like the church we see today.

The town's importance was very closely tied in with the fortunes of the castle. The town is very much in the shadow of the fortress, in every sense of the word. Even now, of course, the one still depends on the other for drawing in tourists who boost the local economy in no small way.

A market charter was granted to the town in 1388 or 1389 (renewed and ratified in 1479). Trade grew from this, the economic activities of the two nearby abbeys boosted local prosperity, and Middleham developed into an important stock trading centre (see later) in much the same way as Great Close and Boss Moor near Malham (see *The Southern Dales*).

The church was granted collegiate status in 1477, as part of the town's rejuvenation under Richard, Duke of Gloucester and later king, and it was one of the few in the land to escape the suppression of chantries and colleges in the Tudor period. The church remained a collegiate foundation for another three hundred years. One of the last honorary canons, as a point of interest, was Charles Kingsley, author of *The Water Babies*, whom we have met before at Malham Tarn.

Do take the time to walk round the town, to visit the church, and to note the Georgian style of architecture around the market place and along the main street. Note too, the number of inns, and buildings that proclaim "I also used to be an inn".

Another of our old friends, the Hon. John Byng, stayed at the White Swan inn on his mammoth horseback tour of the North two hundred years ago. His comment here is more charitable than the one he made in Askrigg. In Middleham he enjoyed "a better dinner and better dress'd, I never sat down to . . ." and for only six pence!

I shall discuss the castle later.

At the top end of the main street – or top of the market square, if you like – stands a cross. Called Swine Cross, this is dated to 1479 and commemorates the confirmation by the future Richard III of a fair and market to be held at Whitsuntide and on the Feast of St. Simon and St. Jude (28th October).

The Nevilles

For many years the Nevilles held Middleham Castle and vast estates in the eastern Dales, as well as in other parts of the country.

At the time of the Norman Conquest the land was held by a Danish lord but the king gave Middleham to the Earl of Richmond. It was soon transferred to his younger brother Ribald (no laughter please) and his descendants. The male line eventually died out and the manors and estates passed by marriage to the Nevilles of Raby Castle, created Earls of Westmorland by Richard II.

The Nevilles were one of the most powerful families in the North Parts (as we up here were called then) throughout the medieval period, and they were either at the current king's right hand, or in disgrace depending on how the political wheel of fortune turned. Middleham remained Neville property until the death of Richard III, after which the Crown seized the whole lot.

From the Swine Cross make for the castle entrance and follow the broad track along the east side of the castle, past the remains of the original gatehouse which linked the castle to an eastern enclosure. Note the dry moat

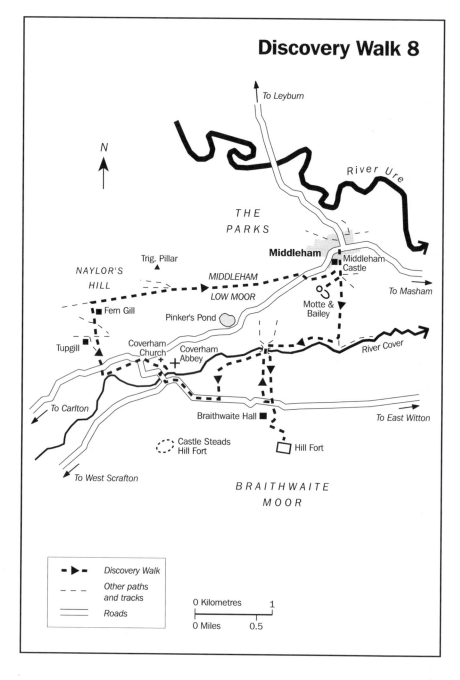

Discovery Walk 8

To Leyburn

N

River Ure

THE
PARKS

Middleham

NAYLOR'S
HILL

Trig. Pillar

MIDDLEHAM

Middleham
Castle

To Masham

LOW MOOR

Fern Gill

Pinker's Pond

Motte &
Bailey

Tupgill

Coverham
Church

Coverham
Abbey

River Cover

To Carlton

Braithwaite Hall

To East Witton

Castle Steads
Hill Fort

Hill Fort

To West Scrafton

BRAITHWAITE
MOOR

- ▶ -   Discovery Walk

- - -   Other paths
        and tracks

——   Roads

0 Kilometres   1

0 Miles   0.5

as you leave the castle behind, **go past the modern bungalow and through the gate ahead.**

– I would recommend a diversion now, to William's Hill –

Turn right immediately, through the gate into the field and cross over to the motte and bailey.

Middleham Castles

The Motte and Bailey

Ribald began construction of his new castle after he came into the ownership of the lands in 1069. This first fortress was far removed from the stone structure of the later castle.

Ribald chose high ground on William's Hill, which was more easily defensible than the site of the later stone castle. A high mound was thrown up on the crest of the hill to form the *motte* 12 metres high, surrounded by a ditch 6 metres deep and about the same in width. To the south-east of that an outer enclosure, the *bailey*, was built again surrounded by a ditch with a bank just over 4 metres high. To the south-east of the bailey, and some distance away, are three parallel banks forming an initial defence for entry to the courtyard.

Within the bailey there would have been thatched huts housing the

Middleham Castle

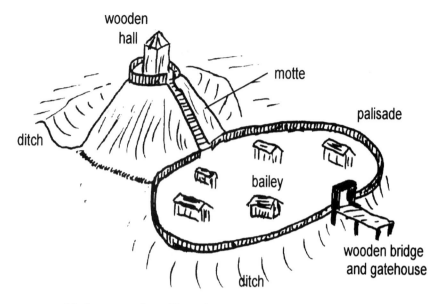

My interpretation of how the first castle may have looked

gagarrison, stables, stores and domestic buildings. The lord's residence, again of wood, stood atop the motte.

Such castles were purely defensive and were thrown up rapidly after the Norman Conquest. The Saxon peasantry was understandably hostile so the Norman masters needed protection from them. At the same time the lord wanted something that served the dual purpose of status symbol, proclaiming his power, and a base from which he could subdue and exert firm control over his estates. This was not a happy period for the peasants of Merrie England.

The Stone Keep

Mottes were not intended to be permanent. I suppose, if any individual Norman was cynical or pessimistic, he might have wondered how long he would be able to stay in England. Clearly they did subdue the peasantry, by incredibly brutal means, and they did stay. One by one the temporary wooden castles were abandoned in favour of stone keeps.

Look back now from the motte to the stone castle.

Ribald's grandson, Robert, built the first stone castle at Middleham in the 1170s. His castle was the keep – the central, higher part of the castle ruins you see to the north. Compared with other keeps of this era, Middleham was massive and palatial. Whatever wealth Ribald and his brother, the Earl of Richmond, may have brought with them from their estates in Normandy, it could have been nothing compared with the riches they amassed in their new lands. To have built a heap as grand and formidable as this today would need a roll-over lottery win.

The ranges of buildings surrounding the courtyard, together with the six towers, were erected in later centuries.

Middleham Castle has a long and fascinating story to tell, and much of interest to see. I would recommend a tour of the site as being a pre-requisite of a visit to the town. The new guide book, too, is excellent, so I need say no more here.

Before you leave William's Hill I would draw your attention to other points

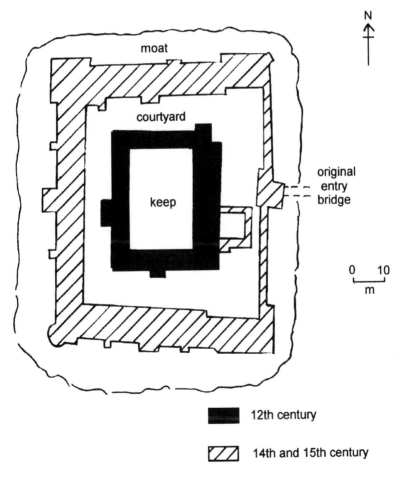

Sketch plan of Middleham Castle

of interest. Between the two castles you will note the medieval ridge and furrow features, once part of the great open-fields in which the peasantry cultivated their staple foods. Beyond Middleham you can perhaps see a church tower surrounded by woodland: that is in the village of Spennithorne. Harmby lies just to the left and, following the view round to the north-west, is the sprawling mass of Leyburn.

Return to the same gate, at what is amazingly a six-way junction, **and turn right, back on yourself.** Continue up the rise, passing through the outermost defences of the motte and bailey, **to the end of this part of Sunskew Park. Beyond the step-over stile you have the wall on your left side as the field gently dips towards the river.** Across the valley to the south you see the bulk of Braithwaite Moor (422 metres); on the skyline due west is the unmistakable shape of Penhill. Note the difference in land use: on this side of the river all the land is under grass, either as pasture or meadow, while the south side of the valley is mainly given over to the production of cereals. (This is the first encounter with true arable farming in any of these walks.)

At the top end of the wooded gully swing right across the field, then follow the fence along the side of Cover Banks woods. At the end of the woods the path cuts through the narrow belt of trees, via two ladder stiles. Drop down to the next fence and follow it above this stretch of excellent oak and beech wood. As you pass beneath the electricity cables look across the valley towards Braithwaite Hall. **Descend to the bridge over the River Cover, and cross over.**

– Decision time is upon you again. Either continue with the main route of this Walk (jump to "Bracken Parks") or divert to Braithwaite Hall –

The Braithwaite Diversion

From the bridge go straight upslope by the ash-hawthorn hedgerow on the path that is clearer on the map than on the ground. **Keep the hedgerow to your left till you reach the stile at the top end of the field. Cross the middle of the next field heading slightly to the right of the barns.**

In the lower half of this field you are walking parallel to the ridges and furrows of another farming system. **When you reach the end of the field use the gate to gain access to the lane.** Directly opposite is Braithwaite Hall.

Braithwaite Hall

Unless you have made prior arrangements to view the interior of the hall, there is no public access up the drive. You can, however, view it from the road or at closer quarters from the permissive path described in the next section.

Hullo Bridge

Braithwaite first appears in the written record as a grange of Jervaulx Abbey. The road, Braithwaite Lane, runs directly to East Witton and the abbey. After the Dissolution in 1536 the estates passed to the Crown, to be leased off five years later by one of the huge Metcalfe clan. From then it passed through several hands until hall and lands were bequeathed to the National Trust in 1940.

The building contains work from different periods of its history. What you see from the east or south, the frontage and the huge chimney stacks, date from a major rebuilding in 1667. Much of the interior has been preserved in a magnificent state. The highlights include an oak staircase, the drawing room with mid-seventeenth century oak panelling, and several fireplaces from the same period.

An Anonymous Earthwork

You may be feeling energetic, or curious in a historical way, and might relish the challenge of a climb up to the earthworks on Braithwaite Hill. The Ordnance Survey map labels it as 'fort', like Castle Steads to the west, but it has yet to be excavated. Nobody, least of all me, has any real idea of its age. It certainly was defensive, as evidenced by the network of ditches and banks, and the protected entrances. I am not even prepared to hazard a guess as to which period it belongs, but I will give you two conflicting clues to aid your own sleuthing. The National Trust has tentatively ascribed it to the Iron Age. However, Castle Steads is 2000 years older than that, and they could perhaps be broadly contemporary.

Should you wish to have a look at it, a permissive path starts at a stile a few metres east of the entrance to the drive to Braithwaite Hall. After the small tree planting cross the field to the head wall where there is another stile to the left of a large ash tree. Climb up the zig-zagging farm track towards the next wall. Choose the gate over to the left, which leads into a Countryside Stewardship Access Area (see *The Southern Dales*). Once through the gate you are inside the fort, though there are defensive earthworks before the wall as well.

You can work out the way the 'fort' was planned: the most impressive defences face south and west, uphill, which was obviously the site's Achilles Heel. The north is less strongly defended as only fools or desperate men attack uphill.

Even if the site does not overwhelm you, at least the view from up here should make the trudge worthwhile. On a clear day you can see across to the North York Moors, never mind to Leyburn, Bolton Castle and the hills bounding Wensleydale and Coverdale.

Retrace your steps to the road and

– either follow the lane westwards or go through the gate again on the other side of the lane –

This time follow the bridleway, the old way from the Hall to Middleham, past the former shaft of an old lead mine and **down to the river again at the bridge.** In the castle's days timber was extracted from Braithwaite Hill and carted along this bridleway on its slow and creaking journey.

Bracken Parks

Parts of the south bank have been designated as Access Areas under the Countryside Stewardship scheme, including the entire last field leading to the bridge. **To the west of this field a permissive path leads along the edge of the wood to a step-over stile.** The wood beyond this is also an Access Area so there is no footpath as such. Go as you please and linger at will, and marvel at the size of some of the ash trees within the wood.

At the western end you emerge into daylight again near another mine shaft. Swing up this meadow and the next field staying close to the hedgerow. When this turns sharp right head straight up the bank, through the gate and onto the road.

In the field opposite the gate – Hanghow Pastures – there is a plethora of mounds. It looks very similar to rabbit warrens I have seen elsewhere and I wonder if this was one. In the days before beef found its way into the English diet, rabbit was a major source of meat. For the ordinary folk it was probably poached: the monied and the privileged classes had access to specially constructed and managed warrens, where rabbits were farmed and bred like . . . well, rabbits. They are now a universal agricultural pest because of escapees from these medieval warrens.

Turn west along the road. This is Hanghow Lane (or Braithwaite Lane further east) and it has origins and importance at least in the medieval period. It was the main highway connecting the two abbeys of Coverham and Jervaulx, via East Witton. It is still the most direct route by foot or vehicle. Further along, as it begins to descend to the Cover, it is very much a sunken lane, a holloway, suggesting centuries of use.

At the bottom of the hill turn right over the picturesque bridge, and immediately right again. Ahead lie the remains of the early sixteenth century gatehouse of Coverham Abbey. Until recently there was a plant nursery through the old gateway that could be used as a pretext for having a sly look at the abbey ruins from within. The only legal way now is to follow the roads on a circuitous route to pick up a right of way from the north.

Coverham Abbey

You can buy a guidebook to Middleham and Bolton castles, as with most ancient ruins, but I have yet to see a guide to Coverham Abbey. (No doubt I will now receive letters telling me . . .)

Eight monastic houses held vast swathes of land in the Dales, only three of which were actually situated in or next to the area, namely Bolton Priory, Jervaulx Abbey and Coverham Abbey. Jervaulx held lands in most of Wensleydale to the west of Askrigg while Coverham had most of Coverdale, the area around Kettlewell and lands in the vicinity of Sedbergh. The idea was, if you were a medieval lord or lady heiress, that you made grants of land to a monastic foundation and in return the monks would pray for your soul for evermore. It was a kind of insurance policy against eternal damnation. Mind you, considering how mean and callous many of those lords were, they needed a foolproof policy to keep them from Hades.

Coverham was founded after a grant of land by the descendants of our friend Ribald, and it belonged to the Premonstratensian Order of White Canons. This relatively small order had been founded in France in 1120, spread rapidly on the continent, and founded its first English house in 1143. They believed in physical labour, in the simple life and in taking their preaching into the wider community. The canons had "care of souls" in parish churches.

The first house in our vicinity was established in 1190 at Swainby but was transferred to Coverham either in 1202 or 1212 (the authorities cannot agree). The abbey suffered on several occasions from the marauding Scots and was probably virtually destroyed by them in 1332. It was obviously rebuilt, and continued to serve the community until it was suppressed by

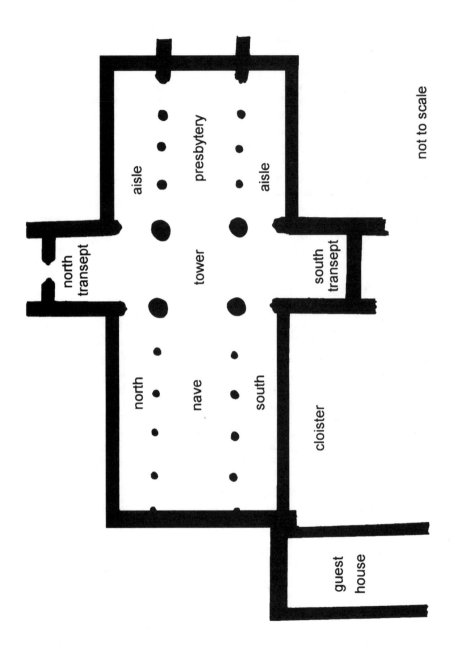

Sketch plan of Coverham Abbey Church

Henry VIII in 1536, its few treasures plundered by the state, its canons and *conversi* dispersed, and its lands sold off by the Crown.

Not a lot remains of the abbey as it ended up as a very useful quarry for local buildings, including those actually built into the ruins. Much presumably lies below ground, waiting to be excavated. The main upstanding remains are what is left of the gatehouse, and a double arch that formed part of the divide between nave and south aisle, dated to the mid-fourteenth century. Apart from these there are other odd bits scattered about, either just lying on the ground or built into later walls.

Let me stress again, please, that the grounds are private, apart from the right of way that cuts through the north side of the site. I had the privilege of being allowed a good look round quite some years ago, which is how I know it.

A surviving fragment of Coverham Abbey

There is another important religious aspect to Coverdale in the form of one Miles Coverdale (1488-1568). I do not know where in the dale he was born but I do know something of him. He was eventually to become Bishop of Exeter but had to flee into exile during the reign of the Catholic Mary Tudor. His fame lies in his translation of the Bible into English in 1535, thus bringing the Book within reach of ordinary folk for the first time. Four years later he was commissioned by Henry VIII to organise the production of the "Great Bible", the first Authorised Version of the bible.

Holy Trinity Church

Between Garth Cottage and the new gate across the track there is a small metal gate up steps by the small stream. **Follow the path up the beck into the churchyard of the redundant Holy Trinity, once the parish church for the entire dale.** Now, churchyards are not designated rights of way. You have the right of access if you intend to have a look at this thirteenth century church. If not, then follow the road round to the lych gate.

Holy Trinity, alas, went out of use as a church in 1985. There simply was no congregation any longer. It seems odd to me, in an illogical way, that churches should be subject to the laws of supply and demand. At least, thank goodness, this one is being preserved by the Redundant Churches Fund and saved from a terrible fate as a house or an art gallery or whatever else some old churches have become. Despite some hideous Victorian restoration (desecration?), the interior is worth a few moments, if only for the reflective mood ancient churches seem to inspire. The churchyard, too, is of interest: there was a lot of brass about in Coverdale judging by the size of some of the tombs.

Leave the church along the avenue of trees – sycamore, ash, pine and common lime – **and through the lych gate onto Coverham Lane by the road junction. Head west along the road but only to the first corner.**

A Surfeit of Gills

Where the road swings to the right, cross the footbridge over the sike, hack your way through the butterbur *(Petasites hybridus)* **and climb over the stile. The way turns right to follow the edge of a fairly recently planted wood,** thankfully hiding the somewhat unaesthetic dereliction of the former factory, a dairy I think it was.

At the end of the wood carry straight on to a field gate onto Bird Ridding Lane, a County Road. Turn right to Coverham Lane and right again as far as the granite gates near the post box.

You now enter an almost surreal world. I have to confess I find myself, nay cannot prevent myself, touching my forelocks on this estate. Fear not, though. This splendid tarred drive is a bridleway throughout.

At the first junction stay right as you pass by, at a suitably discreet distance, **the first of several splendid residences** all bearing the name gill. **At the cross roads go through the equally grand gates on the gravel track past the ornamental ponds, up alongside the wood, past the house, and out through the gateway in the high estate boundary wall – and relax!**

You are now on Naylor's Hill, whoever he (or she?) was, and no longer in the National Park.

Foals and Fillies

Naylor's Hill is but one small part of an extensive tract of common land called Middleham Low Moor. It was up here where Middleham's annual cattle and sheep fair was held in late October. You can imagine the hordes of drovers and Scotsmen converging from the north, buyers and other drovers coming up from all places south to drive their purchases to the towns of the Midlands, and all manner of traders, pedlars and chapmen, performing artists and, of course, a discreet smattering of conmen, pickpockets and other undesirables.

I know when the horse traders stopped coming to Bentham in Craven five or six years ago, as an adjunct to the great annual horse fair in Appleby, the community heaved a communal sigh of relief. Did the same happen in Middleham when its October fair ceased, sometime in the late nineteenth century?

The track across Low Moor is part of the medieval road connecting the castle with the Nevilles' hunting grounds in Bishopdale Chase. You can still follow it now via Common Lane, High Lane and Morpeth Gate.

Also up here, from 1676 to 1873, was a race course of the horse variety. I do not know whether Middleham became one of England's main training centres (which it still is) because of the race course, or whether the race course came second.

Theoretically Low Moor is crossed by three rights of way coming from the west and merging near the trigonometrical column on Cross Bank (the site of a medieval waymarker cross). **In reality you make your own path.** At certain times of the day when the stables call is "one out, all out", you may well find yourself dodging the seemingly endless procession of equines galloping, trotting, cavorting, snorting or just sedately walking on their exercise and training sessions. In theory horses give way to walkers on bridleways. Tell that to a galloping steed.

If the coast is clear, stop and look back up towards the head of the dale, to Little and Great Whernside (604 and 704 metres) – secure habitat for the golden plover, dunlin and curlew – and to the pass over to Scale Park above Kettlewell, once a deer park belonging to the Nevilles. To the north-west you should be able to see up Wensleydale from Askrigg round to the Leyburn area; and east across the Vale of Mowbray.

Nearer at hand, over the still high wall, is Cotescue Park. This name might suggest a place where battle had been engaged with a Scottish raiding party. To the east of the Park, and leading down to the sometimes dry Pinker's Pond, is Ever Bank. That name has something to do with wild boar. Personally, given the choice of meeting a Scots raider or a wild boar face to face, I think I would take my chances with the former. No doubt the Lords of Middleham Castle enjoyed chasing both.

After two kilometres of featureless "moor" you begin to sense a pincer attack on your wide open spaces, by a wall to your left and the road to your right. **Stay on the green to the bitter end and, just where the road is hemmed in by walls, escape through the gap stile on the south side of the road. A thoughtfully placed path along the edge of the fields allows you to forego the hazards and the fumes of the road. Cut across the third field to a step-over stile in the fence, then cross the moat to rejoin the lane at a bridle gate below the south-east tower of the castle.**

Place-name meanings

Agglethorpe	OE/OD	Aculf's (pers. name) settlement
Bird Ridding	OE	the clearing with birds
Braithwaite	ON	the broad clearing
Cotescue	ON	to do with shooting or
	OE	connected with a Scots skirmish
Coverdale	Brit/ON	the hollow valley
Coverham	OE	the homestead on the River Cover
Ever Bank	OE	the bank with wild boar
Hanghow	OE	the steep hill
Leyburn	OE	the stream by the forest clearing
Middleham	OE	the middle homestead
Sunskew	ON	the sunny forest clearing

Common or European Lime
Tilia vulgaris or Tilia europaea

Status: a hybrid that may be native or a very early introduction.

Crown: very tall looking crown, rising low from the ground with many arching branches; very dense canopy with a billowing appearance.

Height: out tallest deciduous tree, reaching 40 metres.

Trunk: main bole is long and straight with large branches reaching upwards; festooned with suckers and sprouting shoots that make limes distinctive.

Bark: smooth and grey in young trees; fissured and ridged in older specimens.

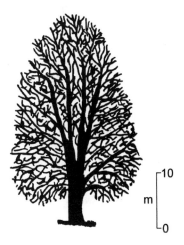

m

⌐10

∟0

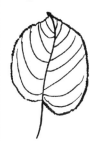

[1cm

Fruit: very small; round to oval; green and very hairy.

Leaves: broad and almost heart shaped with one lobe flattened; edges serrated; brightish green above; quite shiny below; often coated in honey dew from the tree's large aphid population; 6 to 10cm long but very large on suckers.

Uses: frequently planted in parks, streets and churchyards for ornament and shade, and because it grows readily in such conditions. Sometimes pollarded. Not normally found among native woodlands.

Discovery Walk 9

A Walk around Kisdon in Upper Swaledale

Start and Finish: Muker (Grid Reference SD 911 978) or Keld (Grid Reference NY 892 012)

Parking: there is a pay and display car park by the road bridge in Muker. Also at the bottom end of Keld there is a small car park.

Public Transport: Keld and Muker are on a bus route from Richmond operated by United (01325 468771).

Facilities en Route: Muker caters for the visitor with The Farmers Arms offering bar meals, a tearoom and a licensed restaurant, a village store, post office, a shop selling locally made woollens, toilets, telephone and National Park Information Point. Keld has toilets and a telephone.

Outline of the Walk: Muker – Ramps Holme Bridge – Arn Gill – Fair Yew End – Swinner Gill – Crackpot Hall – Keld – Kisdon Road – Muker.

Length: 10.5km (6.5 miles) for the full route or 9.5km (5.9 miles) missing out Swinner Gill.

Ordnance Survey Map: 1:25,000 Outdoor Leisure 30 1:50,000 Landranger 91 and 98

Introduction

Swaledale shares a west-east alignment with Wensleydale but beyond that any similarity between the two dales ends. Swaledale is narrow, much more hemmed in, with the fells rising steeply from the narrow valley floor. While Wensleydale has half a dozen tributary valleys, each one a dale in its own right, Swaledale has only one real sub-dale, Arkengarthdale. True, there are tributary valleys like Gunnerside and Summer Lodge, but these do not really qualify as dales.

There is another contrast, too. There are no towns on the Swale west of Richmond, only villages and most of them small. One such village is Muker, nestling at the foot of Kisdon Hill.

To the casual, but inquisitive and aware, visitor Kisdon itself raises many an eyebrow. Why is such a large hill completely surrounded by large valleys? Why does the valley on its western and southern flanks only contain small becks? Why is there such a clustering of waterfalls in the vicinity of Keld? We shall be exploring, and hopefully answering, these thoughts on today's walk.

As everywhere in the Dales, we shall touch on the visible remains of the past, particularly north of Kisdon, once an extensive mining area.

No excursion in Upper Swaledale can ignore the floral richness of the valley bottoms: this is definitely a walk to be best completed between the blossoming of spring and the onset of haytiming.

I have used Muker as the starting point today largely because of its car park and ease of access. You could just as easily use Keld as a base, if that happens to be more convenient, and follow the narrative accordingly.

Shorter walks could be created out of the larger whole. You could start at Keld and stick to the northern sections of the route by following "Bracken Hill" in reverse and then the sections from "Swinner Gill" to "Keld". There again, if time is limited or commitments pressing, you could follow the route from Muker to Keld as described, and return on the eastern slopes of Kisdon. I have indicated this within the text.

Also indicated in the text are short extra diversions to Keld from the main route, and to Kisdon Force, a splendid and hidden cascade on the Swale.

Muker

Like many of the settlements in Swaledale, Muker is a Norse foundation that began to prosper in a small way after the lands were granted in 1241 to Rievaulx Abbey. After the Dissolution the lands were sold to Lord Wharton whose family we shall meet again (see *Discovery Walk 11*). Muker's boom time was in the lead mining era when it must have resembled somewhere in the Klondyke. The population then was far greater than now. In the 1881 census, for example, 2002 people were registered in Muker. Ten years later the terminal decline of the lead industry had reduced that to only 1215. Now, one hundred years later, the total population of the whole vast parish (stretching from Nine Standards Rigg to Gunnerside, from Tan Hill to Abbotside tops) hovers around the 500 mark.

The small but interesting Literary Institute of 1868 was built for the betterment of the miners, its one-time three pubs for drowning their sorrows perhaps! Very popular with them and their families too, was Muker's annual fair and its Wednesday produce market held on the Green opposite the church entrance. Vegetables, meat and clothes were the main items on offer, much like any market. Both are long gone.

The church itself dates from 1580, in the Elizabethan period, not noted for the founding of new churches. In this sense, but certainly not architecturally, St Mary's is unusual.

Muker has always been a close knit community, despite the influx and exodus of lead miners and the more recent ingress of *offcumdens*. Family names illustrate this. In 1538 the township housed 21 Aldersons, 8 Milners, 7 Metcalfes, 6 Harkers and 5 Coates, 47 out of a total of 55 heads of family tenanting the lands. In 1832 there were 14 Aldersons, 3 Metcalfes, 2 Harkers and 1 Coates and Milner. And now? Check the phone book!

Hay-meadows

Leave the riverside road by going up into the village centre, past the Literary Institute and the village hall, with the church tucked away behind it. **Pass to the right of the post office and walk ahead on the track by the fingerpost indicating Gunnerside and Keld. This soon ends at a squeeze stile through which a sandstone flagged path heads across the meadow to another such stile.** These flagstone causeways, as they are called, were sometimes laid so that the nailed boots of miners tramping to and fro did not harm the precious grass crop. **Carry on past the shippon and through the Carrs, a series of meadows, on a well-surfaced path.**

Muker in particular – and Swaledale in general – are renowned for traditional herb-rich hay meadows. In summer these are an absolute riot of colour covering almost the entire spectrum, and supporting a diverse range of species. There are far too many to list (and I have done so already in *The Southern Dales*) but the most dominant numerically, out of the 70 or more possible species, are perhaps worth mentioning: the mauve wood cranesbill *(Geranium sylvaticum)*, white, delicate pignut *(Conopodium majus)*, and meadow and bulbous buttercup *(Ranunculus spp.)*.

The richness of the meadow's biodiversity has led to their being afforded protection by a series of tiered designations. Many of them form individual pieces of the mosaic that is the Muker Meadows Site of Special Scientific Interest (SSSI), and the area is also part of the Swaledale Environmentally Sensitive Area (ESA). One particular field, Yellands Meadow just down the road to Satron, was taken into the care of the Yorkshire Wildlife Trust in 1982 in recognition of its diversity of plant growth.

In 1995 the best meadows were submitted to the authorities for possible designation as one of the county's first batch of Special Areas of Conservation (SAC), the dreamchild of Eurocrats. Not another tier, do I hear you groan? I can see some sense in it as SACs will be recognised as having value on a European scale, but I do wish the whole gamut of designations could be simplified.

Altogether 21 hay meadows in the Dales, as well as Ingleborough and Malham Moor, have been submitted. At the time of writing no decision has been announced. The idea is to create across the European Union the concept of *Natura 2000* with the new SACs alongside Special Protection Areas (SPA). I am sure it will all make sense in the end.

It is important, also, to remember that the hay meadows owe their continued existence to the willingness of farmers to pursue practices that will not reduce diversity, by not hay-timing until the flowers have seeded,

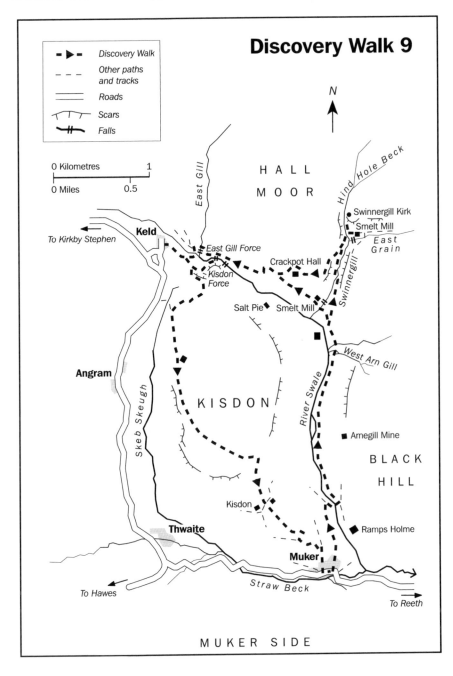

Discovery Walk 9

Legend:
- Discovery Walk
- Other paths and tracks
- Roads
- Scars
- Falls

0 Kilometres 1
0 Miles 0.5

N

HALL MOOR

Hind Hole Beck

East Gill

To Kirkby Stephen

Keld

East Gill Force

Kisdon Force

Swinnergill Kirk
Smelt Mill
East Grain

Crackpot Hall

Swinnergill

Salt Pie   Smelt Mill

West Arn Gill

Angram

Skeb Skeugh

KISDON

River Swale

Arnegill Mine

BLACK HILL

Kisdon

Ramps Holme

Thwaite

Muker

To Hawes

Straw Beck

To Reeth

MUKER SIDE

by not adding chemicals or nitrate-rich slurry. Given that the UK has lost a frightening 97 per cent of its traditional hay meadows since 1945, we should be more than grateful to nature conscious farmers.

Another feature of Swaledale, as of many of the dales, is the large number of field barns, relics of past agricultural needs. Look high up on your left and you will see a number of what seem from down here to be steep slopes. Each of those fields was originally a meadow, some smallholders' guarantee of winter survival for his cow or two. This is not to say, however, that each field belonged to a different farmer.

Towards the end of this run of meadows is an especially well-built barn. Note the five parallel layers of *throughs*, long stones that project beyond the wall's face to give stability to the whole structure. Sandstone like that used in this barn makes for sound and relatively easy walling stone.

Many barns, as we have observed elsewhere, are crumbling through neglect. They are redundant and have no place in the modern farming scene. Before mechanised milking cows were over-wintered in the field barns, the hay fodder collected in summer being stored on the overhead baulks for winter use, the manure and slurry being spread across the surrounding meadow. Cattle were let into the fields once the hay had been gathered, and remained there until early the next spring. The cows were milked in the field barns and the milk was carried to the farmstead in 40 litre backcans. It was

Field barns north of Muker

a system that worked very well, except that the farmer had to spend time going from one barn to the next, and back to the farm with the milk. Modern methods save time, and therefore money, and certainly make life much easier.

Have you ever noticed that many farmers cut the hay or silage around the edges of meadows first, to return often in a day or so to cut the rest? I have never had a straight, convincing answer from farmers I have asked why. Is it perhaps a hangover from pre-tractor days when the field edges were hand scythed first because the horse-drawn reapers and sheaf-binders could not get close to the walls? Or is it to let the drying air in?

And . . . Kisdon hill was noted for the quality of its cheeses, on a par with Wensleydale apparently.

Walk past the barn to the last stile, onto the banks of the Swale, and turn right to Ramps Holme Bridge. The river here is one of many moods: now quiet and tame; now a violent torrent. The scale of the bank revetments and the wire gabions is testament to the power of the current.

Once over the bridge, turn left to walk further up the dale. As you go keep an eye open for pied and yellow wagtails, sandpipers and dippers in addition to the more common species.

Ivelet Side: Woodland Management

The next section of the walk is along a bridleway that once formed part of a road, still traceable throughout, connecting Gunnerside with Stonesdale and Whitsundale beyond Keld. It served as a through route as well as linking in with the various mines higher up the dale.

For the first kilometre or so the way spreads out between the foot of the slope and the river banks. The path parallels Ivelet Side and Ivelet Wood.

In the not too distant past much of these hill slopes was wooded: what you see above you now in Ivelet Wood is a mere fragment of the former extent of tree cover. The quality of the trees – height, girth, straightness – deteriorates both upslope and updale. Those trees on the upper fringes of the wood are really quite scrappy. Much of the wood consists of hawthorn and coppiced hazel with occasional *standards*, taller trees left to grow to maturity. These are birch and the odd ash.

The practice of coppicing is thought to have its origins back in the Neolithic period maybe 5000 years ago, in the time of the first cultivation and semi-permanent settlement in our land. It was definitely a widespread form of management in the Middle Ages. There were two types of woodland then, in terms of stewardship. Some areas were under *wood pasture*, woodlands open to common stock grazing. Ivelet Wood was one example of a wood pasture. The common place-name element *side* is indicative of a walled township wood pasture. Each time you see "side" on the Ordnance Survey map there should be a settlement, a former township, associated with it. A few examples in upper Swaledale are Muker with Muker Side, Ivelet with Ivelet Side, Kisdon with Kisdon Side. There are many such throughout Swaledale. Some are just isolated farms, or a cluster of farms, rather than a village, as the townships have contracted and declined. This form of management was dominant to the west of Reeth: see how many "sides" you can find downstream of Reeth. Not many.

The other form of management was *coppiced* woodland, and this was more common east of Reeth though obviously not exclusively so. Wood pastures could also be coppiced, as in Ivelet. Two other place-name elements hint at coppice management. One is *spring*: a wood called Springs Wood does not necessarily mean a wood with a spring in it. Rather it is likely to suggest a wood that was regularly harvested, and within which new shoots would spring forth. The other is *hagg* which my rather aged dictionary tells me means 'where brushwood is cut'! Several of them are marked on the Outdoor Leisure map.

The woods were coppiced to provide on a sustainable basis chopwood and charcoal. *Chopwood* was the green branches, up to 7 or 8 centimetres thick, stripped of bark and dried out in a crude kiln called an *elling hearth*. These were shallow, oval depressions, generally 3 to 5 metres across and less than 2 metres deep, stone lined, rather inefficient but adequate enough for their purpose. Great quantities of chopwood were used in the lead mining industry.

Charcoal was made by stacking up chopwood, covering the stack with turf, and letting it burn ever so slowly. The technology is much the same today except that large metal cauldrons have replaced the sod covering, but in much of the developing world the old methods are still very much in current use. The Ivelet Wood area has 50 or so charcoal making platforms cut into the slopes, and a number of early modern wood kilns, which can be readily identified if you know what you are looking for. Not that I am encouraging you to trespass, mind you: far from it.

A Geography Lesson

This part of Swaledale, sandwiched between Kisdon and Black Hill, is a superb outdoor classroom for the budding geomorphologist. A number of features resulting from either river or glacial action, or both, can be observed from the bridleway. The Swale is a forceful river hereabouts as it swings from one side of its narrow flood plain to the other, at times braided or split up into different channels between boulder islands. The size of the rocks within and even beyond its banks testifies to its potential at flood level to erode and transport material along its course.

You will also observe that the flood plain is stepped into a highly complex series of river terraces. The higher levels represent earlier, post-glacial flood plains into which the Swale has been actively incising for millenia. A river of this size could never have created a valley on such an enormous scale:

that came about owing to ice and glacial meltwater, but more on that later today.

Towards the northern end of Ivelet Wood the track crosses Arn Gill, higher up which are the remains of Arn Gill lead mine and Adelaide Level. Notice the falls on the gill, formed after the gill was left stranded as the main valley was rapidly lowered, and the *debris fan* of large boulders below it, material splayed out at the foot of the gill in the distant past.

At this point the river is split into two distinct channels either side of a grassed island. This might give the impression of comparative stability in the river but just one major flood could wipe it out and rewrite the geography of this locality. Once past the island, the path rises to a slightly higher level, another terrace, and down below you can see traces of abandoned channels on the lower terrace. The flood plain sediments from here northwards to Arngill Wood must be at least 20 metres thick, judging by map contours. All of it was laid down after the final retreat of the glaciers, and represents enormous rates of sediment transportation and deposition. Such deposits are very soft and loose, hence easily eroded by the river.

The Swale here illustrates the unpredictable and ephemeral nature of upland rivers and valley features.

Look across to the opposite bank of the channel. A layer of fine, dark silt overlies the rubble, though with varying thicknesses. At one time this silt covered the entire area, and suggests a distant period of stability when deposits had chance to build up to this depth.

Look upstream and the view is framed on the one side by Arn Gill Scar and on the other by North Gang Scar. In the centre distance of the picture stand the ruins of Crackpot Hall below massive mine spoil heaps, with the cleft of Swinner Gill right of centre.

Old Springs and Fair Yew End

In the middle ground of your live picture is Kisdon Side wood – a plantation but, to my eye at least, aesthetically pleasing with its mixture of coniferous and broadleaved trees. Evergreen spruce and seasonal larch, birch, rowan and ash, give the wood character, especially as the leaves change colour in autumn.

Stretching along the hillside to the south of the plantation is a relict wood, overgrazed, unprotected and not re-generating. It is called Old Springs, once again telling of former coppice management.

As you progress northwards the slopes below Arn Gill Scar are much disturbed. In the period after the retreat of the ice, when the land was still unvegetated and thus prone to erosion, the slopes failed in a series of massive landslips. If you are observant – and interested! – you will come across others today and elsewhere in Swaledale. I shall mention this again later.

Cross the twin streams of West Arn Gill (should it not be North Arn Gill?), the first of which is rapidly cutting into the soft sediments. A row of mature alders lines the gill down to the river plain with at least two of them, by the trackside, having been pollarded in the past. Judging by their girth in the lower bole they must be ancient. Pollarding was another form of woodland management. Instead of harvesting the shoots near ground level, pollards were cut at a height above the reach of grazing cattle. Swaledale probably has more pollards than the rest of the Dales, especially elms. In some cases pollards had individual ownership, much like fields and meadows.

The track climbs now, affording an almost aerial view of the deserted farm on the west bank with its deserted barns and meadows. This is Hartlakes though I believe it was called Boggle House, by the locals if not by the tenants. A boggle (or boggart) is a goblin or a ghost so Boggle House was (is?) a place to be avoided during the witching hours. You have been warned!

Next, you pass below Arngill Wood, very much decayed and past its prime, but at least fenced to hopefully save it for the next century.

Look updale and a very prominent gash – or nick – can be seen between the small, rounded Beldi Hill and the main fell. This is an example of a meltwater channel, carved out by centuries of fast-flowing glacial melt, probably underneath the mass of ice.

Stretching into the distance you will be able to see up the dale west of Keld.

– It is at Arngill Wood that you must decide which way to go. For the short route read on now: for the longer route read "Swinner Gill" –

– In any case, even on the long route, I would recommend you divert to where the track crosses the beck. It is only 200 metres each way –

Bracken Hill

Follow the main track from Arngill Wood as it curves gracefully down to ford Swinner Gill beck. The feature that the track is curving down to is a massive *debris fan*, a mass of post-glacial sediments from the fine to the very coarse brought down Swinner Gill and dumped at the confluence with the Swale.

Across the footbridge are the remains of Beldi Hill lead smelter. Not a bad spot to have spent one's working life, I suppose, given the view down to Muker, and the falls below Fair Yew End. This smelter was first built in 1770 and was extended in 1843 though it closed down some 40 years later. There is so much rubble within the walls that it is hard to make sense of what was there. Despite its small size the smelter contained three furnaces and a 8.5 metre diameter waterwheel, with a short flue leading north-west to the chimney.

The mine that bears the name Beldi Hill is higher up and will be met in due course but there is another level – Low Level – in the woods ahead. In that area, too, are remains of an ore crushing floor, four bouse teams, a wheel pit and settling pits. There is, however, no access to any of them.

Pass through the gate and head up the track through Hall Wood on the slopes of Bracken Hill. In the wood above the track there is ample evidence of hazel and alder coppicing, no doubt to feed the smelter below. It is nice here to see attempts being made to regenerate woodland.

As you near the top of the climb parts of Keld come into view: on the left is the Youth Hostel. In the far distance are the bleak and little known fells and moors of Blackburn.

In the valley bottom on your immediate left, sandwiched between the old walled lane and Rukin Wood is deserted Salt Pie House, Now that place-name tells a tale – or does it? Many place-names containing the element 'salt' do refer to the pre-modern packhorse trade in salt, carrying it from coastal salt pans or from the Cheshire mines. Salt Pie does not, however. In local dialect a salt pie was a lean-to shed or a building with an attached lean-to.

Follow the track, along the wall now, to meet another major track coming in from your right.

– You rejoin the main route here –

Swinner Gill

As I suggested earlier I think it is worthwhile making the short diversion to the beck and smelt mill along the main track, returning here to Arngill Wood.

According to the Outdoor Leisure map the path up the gill cuts through the corner of Arngill Wood. Carry on and be legal if you wish to negotiate the stile either end and the dense bracken in between. Otherwise let sense prevail and just **head uphill, steeply at first but less so as the path contours gently upstream.** Note the exposed bedding planes of the limestones of the Wensleydale Group on the far side of the gill, and the falls caused by the resistance of the lower, massive Main Limestone beds.

At the remnant of the wall the path clings somewhat tenaciously to the hillside with rather an exposed drop, so do take extra care in wet conditions. At the falls the acid in the water is dissolving away the weaker rock around the vertical joints to leave a mini limestone pavement. Above this the **path fords the beck and climbs steeply up the other side.** The mine adit is Parkes Level exploiting part of an extensive complex of lead veins. This was driven into the hillside from 1746 to 1749 at the behest of Lord Pomfret, owner of the land and mining rights. It soon flooded out, however, and was replaced by a higher level just three years later. And he, too, was flooded out – or flushed out perhaps – as we shall soon hear.

As you climb you pass from limestone to sandstone, to a narrow bed of limestone, and back onto sandstone as the gradient slackens. Ahead lies the ruin of Swinner Gill smelt mill: you can see the line of the flue running 20 metres up towards the heather moor.

Just before the stream confluence there are some easily missed stone structures, once part of the mine's surface workings, either side of the main beck. What a precarious footing on which to erect buildings! Between the two streams is a well-preserved mine entrance, Swinner Gill Main Level. I have said elsewhere in these books that I cannot resist a good hole. This one is no exception. If you poke your nose in, the first impression is perhaps one of disappointment as it seems to fizzle out after three metres or so. It does not. It twists to the left and cuts through bedrock as a dry, rock passage. The bad news is that the passage is no more than about 50 centimetres high, so progress is painful.

Let me emphasise again that old mine passages are potentially very dangerous and you should not enter except with someone who knows the ropes, and with the requisite gear.

You may care to spend half an hour or so in this vicinity. There is the ruin of the smelter, in operation from 1804 to 1819, for the lead-ophiles. The mill housed two hearths and a water wheel, nearly two metres in diameter less than at the earlier mill. The veins turned out to be less productive than was

Swinnergill lead mine

hoped or imagined, and Swinner Gill cannot be classed as a successful mine. And there is the Kirk.

Swinner Gill Kirk

– If you have time, you may care for an extra, short diversion from the mill. It is up Hind Hole Beck to Swinner Gill Kirk –

It is to be strictly avoided in wet weather, on safety grounds.

The easiest way to reach the Kirk is as I describe but it does involve a bit of a scramble. **Cross the footbridge and clamber up the spoil heap to follow the old mine path upstream.** If you look upslope on your right there are a number of gullies. I am not at all sure but they could be hushes (see *Discovery Walk 10*). **You come to a small stone structure** by the path and may wonder if they are bouse teams . . . but why here? Look to the left of the path and there lies the answer in the form of North Vein Level. I have always left this one alone as I am none too keen on getting wet in the first five minutes! **After this the path fizzles out as it clambers uphill. Forget that but drop down to the stream bed and follow it up to the waterfall.** In the corner by the fall is the entrance to a cave. It is dry and normally safe though does not go very far into the hillside.

It is the ampitheatre that bears the name Kirk. It is said that early Nonconformists came here to worship in peace in the days when it was forbidden, in other words in the reign of James II in the mid to late seventeenth century. I find it a hard concept to accept, that folk would trudge all this way just to worship, but that is what people say.

Return now to the footbridge by the smelt mill.

The rock strata here are dramatic, gently dipping in the upper gill, looking cheerful and white in bright sun but grey and forlorn in the clag. Someone once described limestone as being obdurate, that is stubborn in the sense that it resists the combined efforts of all the erosive powers. The same writer also used the word arcane (mysterious) in his description of the limestone underworld. I am in no way a poetic animal but I do think that, for this tiny part of the Dales, both words are apt, especially when the mists are hanging low.

Crackpot

Have a last, lingering look down the gill, through the window of the crags, at the river plain so far below. Have a look, too, to the east up East Grain and its valley. It is all grouse country up there on those featureless and pathless moors. For nearly 8 kilometres, north to south, there is but one right of way. It is a well-used path, as you can well imagine, and especially so since Wainwright's popular Coast to Coast walk (a walk well worth considering, by the way) comes this way on the stretch between Reeth and Keld.

Set off, when you are ready, **on the broad mine path that contours round the side of Buzzard Scar** (I have never seen one here). **When you reach the field gates,** cheek by jowl, **choose the lower one on the soft green track** with its grandstand view of the valley below Arn Gill Scar, of the area round Keld and of Birkdale far to the west, green and tame compared to the bleak fells rising from it towards Great Shunner Fell.

You come to a building, on its last legs. Inside is a large hearth still more or less intact. This was the smithy for Hall Out Pasture lead mine. **Divert from the track,** if you wish, to the far end of the huge area of still unvegetated spoil. Even after the passage of so many decades the ground can still not support plant life. Beyond the tip are an adit, Crackpot Hall Level (or Beldi Hill Top Level), and the row of bouse teams and associated ore crushing floors and wheel pit of the former mine. This level was in use from 1773 to 1880 and proved to be one of Swaledale's more productive operations. The mines here were developed in the Main Limestone which was known by the miners as the Twelve Fathom Limestone owing to its great thickness. On Kisdon and around Crackpot and Swinner Gill the strata reach a thickness of 40 metres, though its normal thickness is about 24 metres (= 12 fathoms).

Just down from here stand the crumbling ruins of a once substantial building. Crackpot Hall was first built as a shooting lodge for the gentry but, when the local deer population dwindled (poaching or disturbance by miners?) in the late eighteenth century, it became a farm. In those days even the gentry did not have the benefit of a geographical education. They were not taught the concept of slope dynamics. Had they been, they would have recognised the sheer folly of building something substantial on a landslide. The whole hillslope is moving, imperceptibly, down towards the valley. It has been doing so probably since the retreat of the glaciers and nothing will stop its relentless progress. I have seen two photos of the farm. One, taken in 1952, has curtained windows and smoke rising from the chimneys. The other, taken in 1978, shows dereliction, the house part having collapsed at the front.

An inspection of the upstanding remains shows something of the grandeur of this once proud residence.

Beldi Hill

Carry on along the main track

– to join the short route –

and cross Oldfield Gutter, the stream issuing from the meltwater channel behind Beldi Hill. The devastation up there is staggering: Beldi Hill mine was a prosperous venture. So prosperous, in fact, that a member of the late eighteenth century aristocracy came to grief here . . . in a bad way. Lord Pomfret was a major owner of land in upper Swaledale and, seeing a golden egg in the making, he laid claim to many of the mineral rights – and therefore profits – in this very area. The rightful owner objected, disputing his claim, and the matter went to court. The noble lord lost: the humble miners who had supported their rightful owner, won. Pomfret was not going to accept such a shockingly revolutionary outcome so he went to appeal . . . three times no less . . . and lost . . . three times. The whole rigmarole bankrupted the poor man and he ended up in the Tower. How the mighty fall!

The track passes through West Wood, dominated by two native species, ash and rowan. The river in the gorge below seems far away yet still somehow threatening. **Your partnership with the Coast to Coast walk ends at the footbridge. Turn left here and transfer to the Pennine Way and follow the path alongside East Gill with its cascades. At the bottom another bridge grants sole passage across the Swale.** The Pennine Way north from here, through East Stonesdale to Tan Hill, follows the exact line of an old coal road. Packhorse trains carried the coal from a complex of pits and adit mines all round Tan Hill to the smelters we have seen today, and down into Swaledale proper. The old road crossed the Swale on a packhorse bridge that was swept away, along with much more, in a disastrous flood one hundred years ago. The bridge you cross is its descendant.

Climb to the right from the bridge, through the gate and up the track to the junction at the top.

– If you wish to make another short diversion turn right: if not, turn left on the Pennine Way, and pick up the narrative under "Kisdon Force Woods" –

Keld

So, turn right and follow the walled track – Keld Lane – **into the village.** Like so many settlements in the Dales, Keld was basically a mining village. A quick meander highlights some of the features typical of mining villages. Keld boasts two chapels: the Congregational (now United Reform Church) built in 1840, and the Methodist chapel on the top road built a year later. The village had a school and an inevitable literary institute: the education and moral welfare of mining communities were not forgotten. There was also the Cat Hole Inn to cater for man's other main activity in those days. Since 1954 it has been a private house and stands next to the Youth Hostel. Some of Keld's cottages are really tiny – more like hovels in the past. At the height of the mining phase, in the middle of the nineteenth century, Keld housed no less than 40 families. You will be hard put to find 40 individuals now.

Return along Keld Lane to the earlier junction and continue ahead on the Pennine Way, through the gate ahead and into the woods.

Kisdon Force Woods

I am sure you will have noticed the information sign indicating that Kisdon Force Woods have been entered into and thus afforded the protection of an Environmentally Sensitive Area scheme (see *Discovery Walk 11*). The wood is also an SSSI, and rightly so.

At one time most of the Dales had a woodland cover much as you see here but many centuries of timber clearance and extraction, and sheep grazing, have changed the scene totally. Natural forests of oak and ash, alder, birch and hazel provided an endless habitat for the beasts and mini-beasts of the land, not to mention being a source of food and firewood for local people. To find semi-natural woodland now you have to seek out the inaccessible gorges and scars. An alarmingly small proportion of the National Park has broadleaved woodland today – only 0.7 per cent of the total. Any attempt to redress the imbalance, as here, must be welcomed. Think that our country has lost 45 per cent of its ancient woodland extent since 1945, and the gravity of the situation is perhaps illuminated more graphically. And we point an accusing finger at Brazil and Malaysia for doing the same.

These particular woods are exceptional in having hornbeam set amongst the other species. It is far from being a common tree in the Dales.

– To savour the experience I would strongly suggest another short diversion at this point –

Kisdon Force

Walk along the main track through the wood, beyond the gate I mentioned earlier, and into a limestone gorge. After 100 metres or so look for the small path branching off to the left (it is signposted) and pick your way with care around Birk Hill Scar. At the corner you pass by a huge slab of limestone that looks as if it has been prised away from the scar by some giant.

This is of interest to the geologist and geomorphologist. The technical term for the process is *block gliding*. The limestone strata here are resting on soft and friable shale beds. In the periglacial period immediately post-Ice Age, the slope failed and the block slipped over the shales. As both sets of rock are still there, relative to each other, it will come as no surprise to learn that the detached block is not stable: movement is still apparent from time to infrequent time. How often are we reminded how restless is the Earth and how powerful are its elemental forces?

From this point the path approaches the edge of the gorge above Kisdon Force, to me the most impressive of the six sets of falls in the Keld area. Its natural beauty and grandeur are enhanced for me by the relative lack of access. If you have the time scramble down to the river bank . . . or file it in the bank of places to return to.

To refer to the sequence of rock in the Wensleydale Group again, Kisdon

Force is in the Underset Limestone while those upstream are either in that band or in the Main Limestone. The question is why are there so many falls around Keld, and why does such an impressive gorge separate Kisdon from Beldi? To answer this we must return to the Ice Ages . . . but not just yet.

– You could return direct to Muker from the path junction at Birk Hill, if time is pressing –

If so, **turn left at the signpost and follow one of the two paths:** either the low-level riverside path past Salt Pie, or the high-level Pennine Way. Both are clear and you cannot go wrong.

Otherwise, return the same way (right) to the gate at the end of Keld Lane where it enters the wood and mentally prepare yourself for the climb that lies ahead.

Ice and Water

One hundred and twenty metres of height gain await you but they do not come all at once, so relax.

Next to the gate across the main track is another gate into the field containing a barn. **Enter the field and cross it below the barn to a squeeze stile in the far corner, and carry on to a second such stile in the second wall. Turn sharp right uphill to follow this wall to a gateway – *not* the gate next to the corner sheep fold but the one higher up. Through the gateway the path clings to the wall and is soon transformed into a walled green "lane". Keep straight on after the next gate which, annoyingly, begins to drop down again to join a stony lane climbing up to Scar Close. I am afraid that is the way you have to go.**

At least there is a new area to occupy the eye – and perhaps the mind. Down below is a broad, open valley yet you have to look hard to find the stream within it. Skeb Skeugh is there, flowing through Angram Bottoms (another SSSI) but there is no way such a puny stream could have created a valley on this scale.

These two posers – Skeb Skeugh's valley and Kisdon Force gorge – have a common solution, so let us digress back to the glacial epoch.

Imagine ice filling all the valleys and lower hills, some stagnant, some moving slowly towards the north-east and what is now the Stainmore Gap. Kisdon stands proud of the ice, a *nunatak*, too high to be ice covered. Beneath the ice friction with the ground surface causes meltwater to flow downslope, that is southwards down what was then the valley of the pre-glacial Swale but is now the valley occupied by Skeb Skeugh. As the ice flowed north-east, uphill over Hall Moor, much of it was diverted east round the top end of Kisdon. The effect of this was to concentrate erosion in that corridor and to deepen it, thus forming the gorge that contains Kisdon Force.

Fast-forward to the final melting of the glaciers and picture torrents of

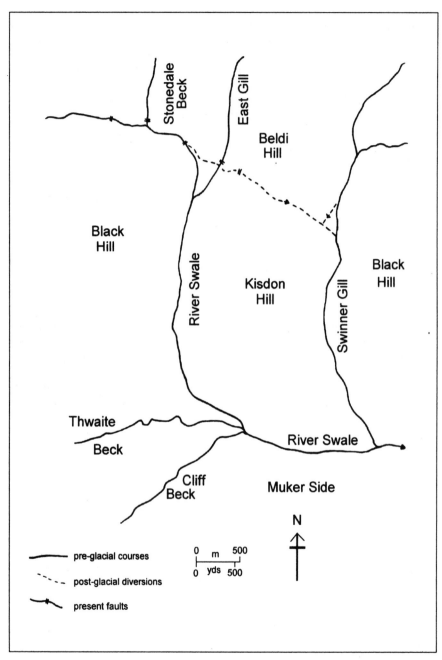

Pre-glacial drainage in upper Swaledale

meltwater taking the line of least resistance, through this newly carved corridor, deepening it even further. Wait for this torrent to subside, many centuries later. The Swale no longer flows to the west of Kisdon: it has now been diverted round to its present course, leaving its old valley high and comparatively dry.

East Gill, which used to flow south to join the Swale south of Keld has been diverted, too, and forced to cut down to reach the new lower Swale. Swinner Gill has had its pre-glacial course and valley east of Kisdon usurped by the new Swale, reducing it to the status of tributary and forcing it to cut down to join its mother river.

The forces of nature, the power of ice and water, reduce us to mere spectators and commentators. Will the ice ever return, though?

Kisdon Road

The stony lane you need to climb now is – or was – Kisdon Road. It was the only road from Keld and beyond to Muker and all places east. It appears on early road maps and in the records. In 1771, for example, the road is shown as passing over Kisdon *Island*. It was also part of the Corpse Road from Keld to Grinton in the days before a church was built at Muker, so that takes us back to the late medieval period at least. Imagine carrying the wicker casket from Keld all the way to Grinton – in winter. It was a journey of at least 16 kilometres and apparently took two days. Incidentally, if I may prolong this morbid thread, the registers for Muker for the period 1780 to 1804 relate the sad fact that one third of all burials within the parish were of children below the age of ten. Let's move on!

As you climb let your eyes wander to the west, starting in the far distance in the lonely spread of hills of Birk Dale and Blackburn, and the massive Mallerstang-Swale Head SSSI. The nearest fell, Black Hill, is scored by a whole series of gullies running roughly west to east. These are all meltwater channels cut under the ice sheet.

Down in the valley bottom, below the straggling hamlet of Angram, are mounds of a similar shape though dissimilar in size. These are *kames*, also of meltwater origin (see *The Southern Dales*).

I think "view stops" should be mandatory on steep climbs, particularly so if the view encompasses as much as this one. When you have done with kames and other ice "things", cast your eyes further north. You will see the road going up Stonesdale to Tan Hill and its lonely inn. West of that is Whitsun Dale and the tiny hamlet of Ravenseat, once an important night-halt on an old packhorse route.

Carry on uphill, onto more gentle ground once you pass the lonely house – amazingly not abandoned and derelict. You can be forgiven for wondering why anyone chose to settle up here in the first place. What I think could be the answer lies ahead. **The track is now a broad green sward that passes**

through the former farmstead's enclosures and eventually becomes a walled lane. Once again, you might wonder why this short section was walled, and why a vaulted tunnel was built under the lane. And where did that huge pile of rock come from – surely not just from that tunnel?

The answers to all these conundrums lie in the field to the right of the lane. There is an oil drum marking the entrance to a mine level with two shafts and shallow workings further up the vein. My interpretation is that the ore was brought from the level, possibly on wagon rails, under the track to avoid disturbance with passing travellers, and sorted where the dump is. The farmstead may well have belonged to the miner. It is guesswork but it sounds plausible enough for me. The mine worked Kisdon Vein, described by those who know these matters as a "weak" vein.

Beyond the "lane" you are onto more open moor, and doesn't the vegetation differ either side of the path? **The track takes you over the crest of Kisdon Hill and on the start of a long descent** . . . and yet another panoramic view. Ahead, to the east, stretch the managed grouse moors of another Black Hill with its obtrusive shooters' road. To the south-east is the main body of Swaledale and the subsidiary dale of Oxnop rising up to more grouse moors. To the south the ruler-straight Enclosure Walls, dating from 1828 to 1832, carve Muker Side up into regular shapes (see *Discovery Walk 11*).

Walk on down, onto a walled lane where the ground steepens, and cross the Pennine Way just by Kisdon Cottage. Below Kisdon Farm there is another massive periglacial landslip. Incalculable volumes of over-lubricated rock and smaller debris crashed down to block the valley at Usha Gap. **Carry straight on to join the surfaced track that connects Kisdon Farm with Muker.**

Down below you can see how flat the valley floor is around Muker. In the later stages of the most recent Ice Age there was a lake here between stagnant ice to the east and west. You may also be able to discern in the meadows between Ramps Holme and Muker, traces of long abandoned river channels. As I said earlier, the Swale up here is fickle.

Beyond the final hairpin bend you enter civilisation through Kisdon Gate, the locality of the township's pinfold and bull field. The poor old (or lucky?) communal bull earned his keep here by servicing the local cows in rotation. And that is the end of another very long and full day.

European Hornbeam
Carpinus betulus

Status: native to southern Britain; planted throughout the country in lowlands and valleys.

Crown: varied some have a conical appearance or are ovoid (egg shaped), but others can be very irregular. Pollards have no special shape.

Height: 20 to 25 metres typically, except in pollarded trees.

Trunk: anything but straight it may bend to one side or the other; tall with branches rising upwards, giving the tree a top heavy look.

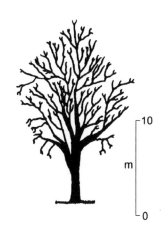

Bark: silver grey and rather smooth with stripes of grey or brown. As the tree ages the bark becomes vertically fissured and ridged.

Fruit: in clusters of 8 to 10 pairs; catkins up to 7cm long, opening out in spring; female flowers winged and tapered.

Leaves: very dark green above but lighter beneath; rather shiny on both sides; edges are saw toothed; up to 10cm long, tapering to a long point; leaves turn bright yellow in autumn.

Uses: very common pollarded or coppiced tree for chopwood, firewood or timber. Formerly used for skittles, mallets, piano innards, cog wheels and meat blocks. Nowadays it is favoured by craft producers.

Place-name meanings

Angram	OE	pasture land
Arn Gill	OE	the ravine with eagles
Birk Hill/Dale	OE/ON	birch hill/valley
Crackpot	ON	where crows abound
Hind Hole	OE	(as it sounds)
Ivelet	OE	Ifa's (pers. name) slope or hillside
Keld	ON	spring
Muker	ON	small area of cultivation or pasture
Oxnop	OE	the small valley with oxen
Ramps Holme	OE	? water meadow
Ravenseat	ON	the mountain pasture with ravens
Skeb Skeugh	ON	? forest clearing
Sled Dale	OE/ON	the valley (both words mean the same)
Swale	OE	swift river
Ravenseat	ON	the mountain pasture with ravens

Discovery Walk 10

Gunnerside Gill: a lead mining foray

Start and Finish: Gunnerside village (Grid Reference SD 950 982).

Parking: there is a small parking area by the beckside just north of the main road bridge within the village, next to the former Literary Institute.

Public Transport: Gunnerside lies on a bus route from Richmond to Keld operated by United (01325 468771).

Facilities en Route: Gunnerside has a shop and post office, a tearoom and licensed restaurant, telephone and toilets. The King's Head offers the usual facilities of a village inn and there is a National Park Information Point. There are no services on the walk itself.

Outline of the Walk: Gunnerside – Heights – Barf End – Winterings – Bunting Hush – Eweleap Scar – Gunnerside Beck – Gunnerside.

Length: 12.5km (7.8 miles) for the longest route; 8km (5 miles) for the shortest.

Ordnance Survey Map: 1:25,000 Outdoor Leisure 30 1:50,000 Landranger 98.

Introduction

We have come across evidence of lead mining in a number of Discovery Walks. So far the signs have been small-scale and dispersed across the landscape. Only around Swinner Gill and Beldi Hill has there been any hint of concentration of mining activity. Even that is of a minor significance compared with Gunnerside and the surrounding fells.

The mining area in Swaledale, the so-called North Swaledale Mineral Belt, stretches all the way from Great Sled Dale in the west to Marske in the east, a total distance of 30 kilometres. In this whole mining field Gunnerside Gill can surely lay claim to predominance. The entire landscape of valley and fell tops has been modified by the hand of man, in places altered beyond all recognition.

It is lead mining that provides the focus for today's walk, from beginning to end. The traces are everywhere: Gunnerside itself as a mining village, scattered miners' smallholdings on the fell sides, surface workings, building remains, tremendous man-made gashes in the landscape. All are there and demonstrably so.

How long this walk takes you will depend on how long you spend exploring the ruins or scouring the spoil heaps for mineral samples. There are both a-plenty. I shall also discuss certain social aspects of the mining scene. Without the people, the picture is incomplete.

The route basically heads north up one side of the gill and returns in the valley bottom. There is only one place where you can start, and that is the village of Gunnerside. The flexibility today comes towards the head of the gill. You will find indications in the text where the walk can be shortened.

Let me sound a word of caution. Any former mining area by definition is full of potential hazards. The area abounds with levels, shafts and loose rock slopes. If you stick to the paths all should be well.

Gunnerside

Of all the villages in Swaledale I feel it is Gunnerside that appears to grow out of the very landscape itself. Its huddled form, its greyness, its matter-of-factness, set the village apart in my mind.

Gunnerside has a long history. Indeed the name of its Norse founder is preserved in the name of the village. There is, of course, no trace of that wood and ling thatched settlement but we can perhaps suggest with some degree of conviction that it was sited on the east bank in the eastern part of the present village.

That part of Gunnerside east of the gill has grown out of the medieval village. The green is still there, but you would be hard pressed to play cricket on it. The area west of the gill is essentially an eighteenth century extension developed during the lead mining boom.

The medieval field system has been identified by scholars. The meadows that make up Gunnerside Bottoms were once the village water meadow, long since split up and enclosed into small and irregular plots. To the north of the medieval village, stretching uphill to Bents, Lodge Green and Heights, was the old common pasture on which all township folk could graze their stock. West of the gill, extending towards Ivelet, was the medieval open field that would have been divided up into tiny strips of crop land to sustain the local population.

Thus were the needs of the peasants met in the days when the land was their only provider, in the days before lead bestowed a temporary prosperity to the dales. By the time that relative well-being came to an end with the collapse of the lead industry, the land could no longer support the populace. As early as the 1830s there was large-scale emigration from Swaledale to the New World and, later that century, to the coal mines of Durham and the mill towns to the south. The population of Gunnerside crashed in common with most of Swaledale. What it is today is a mere shadow of its earlier self.

Heights and Barf End

Cross the beck and walk east through old Gunnerside past the pub to a road that rises steeply to the left. It has an "Unsuitable for motors" sign.

There are various ways up from here but we will opt for the longer but more gentle incline.

So, go through the gate and follow this road but only to the first hairpin bend where you take the stony track ahead by the barn, between wood and wall. You soon cross a small stream, come out of the wood into the open, and climb away from the wall to meet another wall on your left. Now comes a second stream, Staney Gill, in a sycamore wood, then a small barn. Carry on along the walled track, ignoring both gates and stile, past the ruins of buildings connected with a long defunct quarry, to the tiny hamlet of Heights.

The whole south-facing slopes of Swaledale, from Thwaite to Reeth, are peppered with isolated farmsteads or small clusters of houses, set in small enclosures. The majority of them were smallholdings of lead miners who added to their effective income and maintained their health by working the soil and pastures as well as toiling in the gloomy depths of the earth. Heights was one such hamlet.

In the first cottage above the track, which I believe is called Loaning House, the old roofline is clearly visible in the gable end. This building was originally thatched, possibly with ling. Near the house a spring feeds a water trough. Even at the height of the 1995 drought water still issued from the spring, cool and crystal clear. The builders of Heights chose this spot with good reason.

A number of paths and tracks converge here. You should climb up the grassed track above the two eastern cottages, called Heights House, where there are signs of holloways, tracks etched into the slopes by the passage of countless hooves. **Ignore all other tracks and carry on diagonally uphill.**

At the top of the climb you come off sandstone onto limestone, and the whole tone of the immediate landscape changes. **Do not pass through the gate in the wall but turn left to follow the broad, level track** which looks as though it should be a bridleway but is only a path. The limestone band is thin here and not far uphill it reverts to sandstone and grouse moorland.

I hope the day is clear for you because the views into the valley and up the dale are stunning. The early field patterns are clear to see with a patchwork quilt of fields near the foot of the north slopes. Houses and roads hug the valley sides, north and south, as does Gunnerside village built on an alluvial fan, a flattened conical mound of debris brought down the Gill by glacial meltwater. Its position on the fan kept the village above ground liable to flood.

In a few hundred metres you come to another parting of the ways where a wall comes up from the left near an old stone marker post. In the early eighteenth century stone *stoops* such as this were ordered to be erected as guide posts at remote road crossings for the benefit of travellers. **Turn right here, through Barf End Gate, then immediately left on the bridleway to the former hamlet of Barf End.** Here stand the ruins of early eighteenth century

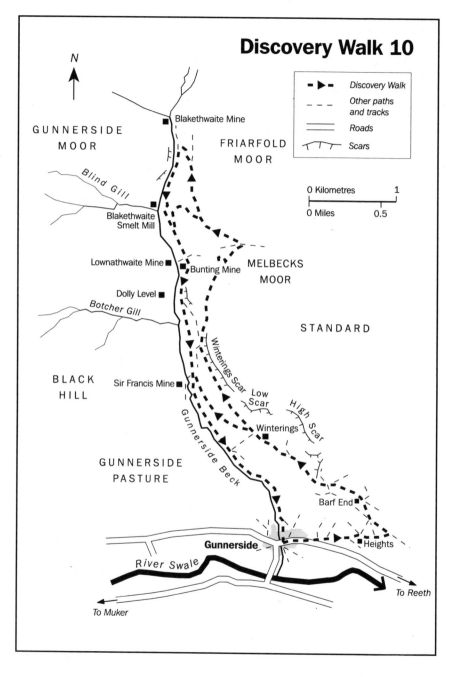

thatched cottages as well as a more recent house. The mine spoil in the vicinity accounts for the growth of a settlement at this altitude.

Again tracks converge at Barf End, as one would expect. **Yours is the broad track alongside the wall** that separates the improved inbye fields from the rough, open pastures of the moor above. **In no time at all you meet yet another major junction just above the farthest point of the tarred road. Carry straight ahead on the rough, stony track,** as it begins a long and gentle curve into Gunnerside Gill.

Winterings

The eastern slopes of the lower end of Gunnerside Gill display a hotch potch of small irregular fields with former farmsteads in close proximity. On the western slopes, however, there isn't even one farm or field – just open fell. This is partly a reflection of relief. On the eastern side there is an easing of the gradient between the 350 and 400 metre levels, sufficient for fields to have been carved out and improved. This is lacking across the valley.

Aspect is the other factor: this side of the valley faces south and receives sunlight for most of the day, while on the other side the shadows are long for the bulk of the day in the winter months.

I feel it is good to see houses being kept alive even if some of them are holiday or second homes. The occasional ruin is perhaps romantic, or indicative of the irrelevance of such places to modern farming. Too many domestic ruins, though, and romance is replaced by despair and by creeping forlornness. If one goes, others often follow on the road to decay: if one is saved, however, the opposite can happen. This seems to be the case here, except for Barf End which is the highest though not the most isolated.

The track contours along above the houses of Potting, passes by the restored Whin Hall and goes through a gate into the hamlet of Winterings. The Outdoor Leisure map shows a tight clustering of tiny and very irregularly shaped fields, former crofts, meadows and paddocks. The situation is ideal, given the altitude, as the settlement is well sheltered from the icy north-east blast by Low and High Scars. It is also a sun trap.

The other – and perhaps main – reason for the existence of Winterings was lead. Mining in these hills stretches back well before the early modern period. Up on Winterings Edge a kilometre further on there are signs of early smelting sites or bail hills. Bail, or bale, hills were bowl-shaped hollows, less than two metres across and barely 60 centimetres deep, lined with puddled clay and constructed of stone and turf.

The track skirts Hugill House. A couple of years ago I came up here to view what was then a sadly neglected house that happened to be for sale. I decided the task of restoration, and the track, were too much for me. I am delighted, however, to see that someone has not only bought it but has lavished loving care on the house.

The head of Gunnerside Gill

Just beyond the building the track splits: a path drops down to other houses in the hamlet while your **track climbs slightly uphill.** Above in the tiny enclosures there is the ruin of a house. Like Barf End this was thatched and is a good example of a simple longhouse, little altered in concept from the Norse longhouses of the early medieval period. At the west end was the living space while at the east end were the barn and byre, whose stone boskins are still standing.

In the past there was an inn at Winterings and I think this must be it. It was called "The Drovers". Do not bring to mind the image of a modern inn with beams or mock Tudor and soft comfy seats, a range of drinks and food. These early inns offered the most basic of "comforts". For most travellers a roof, a meal, a jug of ale and some straw to lie on more than sufficed, fleas and lice included in the price.

A clear track heads northwards through Winterings Pastures, the hamlet's outbye land. **It passes through an open gateway below Winterings Scar.** Just before the gateway look away to the right to the foot of the scree. This well preserved lime kiln once supplied the wherewithal to sweeten the acidic and sour sandstone pastures and meadows hereabouts. A short distance beyond the gateway is another feature once considered important in the farmscape. There is an L-shaped section of wall, free-standing. This is a bield. They come in all shapes and sizes – straight, criss-cross, curving – but all served the same purpose, to provide shelter for sheep from the prevailing wind of the day.

The Legacy of Lead

The major part of today's walk, from now onwards, is dominated by the lead industry, or rather by its impact on the landscape. Gunnerside Gill was one of the most productive mining fields in the Dales and contained a number of individual mines, operated by separate companies. As the rest of the walk unfolds I will attempt to guide you through the maze of remains and clues in the valley.

Hushing

The track begins to climb, very steeply at one point, and forks near a second lime kiln close by Winterings Scar.

– If time is short today you could take the path downhill from this point to meet the valley track below. Rejoin the narrative in "Sir Francis Level" –

Otherwise turn uphill on the path across Swina Bank, to enter an extensive mining area associated with Bunting Mine. After the initial climb the path broadly contours along, becoming more distinct further on. Beyond the ruinous wall the track meanders on an easy incline through a series of cairns to emerge on the plateau top, into a scene of utter devastation. I can find no more suitable word for this area than wrecked – wrecked beyond repair. Fingers are pointed nowadays at countries like Brazil and Malaysia for desecrating the environment through thoughtless mining practices, but what about this mess?

When you reach the most prominent cairn, turn left on the "motorway" track. Ignore the path at the finger post

– unless you choose to shorten the walk by dropping down to Blakethwaite (so move on to the "Bunting and Lownathwaite Mines" section) –

Otherwise stay on the main track past the top of the rocky gullies which are not natural but are the end result of the practice of *hushing*.

In many mining fields the mineral veins almost break the surface, particularly in deep valley topography such as this. The accident of geography made the task of winning the ore a relatively easy one, here as with the later coal mines in the Welsh valleys. An early method of extracting ore on steep slopes was by the use of water.

At the head of natural gullies or streams a stone dam was built to pond back the water. When the miners felt the time was ripe the dam was breached and the rush of water scoured the gully, increasing its dimensions and exposing the veins containing the mineral ore. Where the ore seemed to be plentiful the surface stone was picked and loosened after the visible ore had been removed, and the hushing process was repeated. Hushes as prominent as the ones in this vicinity were not created by a single release of water.

No one can say for certain when the technique was first introduced. The larger ones were used into the nineteenth century and they cannot possibly be dated. I am sure, however, that hushing first came about by accident as miners witnessed natural floods doing what they would later mimic.

Bunting (or Bunton) Hush has a bridleway cutting through it though the descent is awkward and entails picking one's way across very broken ground. Not for to-day.

I had a very unnerving experience up here just over ten years ago. I was back-packing the Coast to Coast route, looking forward to a night of luxury at Keld Youth Hostel, when I deliberately strayed off the main track. With horror I realised I was on a linear quaking bog that began heaving like slow motion waves. The weight of my rucksack was pushing me down into the bog. All I could do was loosen the waist band and throw myself to the side. As it was pouring down already, I could not get any wetter, but it was a while before I had regained my composure and felt ready to proceed.

Bunton hush and adit

Blakethwaite Mine

Follow the road northwards towards the head of the gill but do not day dream or you will miss the turn. Just where the left-hand drop from the road becomes particularly high and steep, slither down to the flat area below. It is supposed to be a bridleway but it must have forgotten itself. There is a faint path, if you have an imagination! **Contour along the flat bench, parallel to the road, and then descend towards the stream on a now clearer path.** In the distance you can see buildings that once served Blakethwaite Mine but you are not going that far.

As the path drops it joins the beckside bridleway, again not recognisable as more than a narrow path. **Follow this downstream, staying on the east bank, through the mini-gorge at Eweleap Scar.**

The geological structure of the Wensleydale Group is particularly apparent here. Limestone beds overlie darker and coarser sandstones which in turn overlie soft and friable shales. Each rock type has different characteristics and resists the vagaries of the weather in varying ways.

The track leads through a dressing floor and a second gorge to the confluence with Blind Gill, the focus of the industrial endeavours of Blakethwaite. The ore was mined around Blakethwaite Gill and brought by pack ponies to be smelted here. The smelt mill, whose remains nestle at the foot of the slope near the footbridge, worked from about 1820 to 1878. It not only processed ore from Blakethwaite but also from Lownathwaite and Swinner Gill mills once their own smelters had been closed down.

The building was divided into a number of rooms and contained two hearths and a furnace as well as a large water wheel. You can see the flue rising steeply to the chimney, an old lime kiln, an adit in Blind Gill and several stores in the vicinity. The coal for the smelter came from shaft and adit mines above Blakethwaite Gill. Altogether Blakethwaite was one of the most prosperous and profitable lead mines in the Dales. Operations ceased, not primarily owing to a fall in market prices or exhaustion of the ore body, but because of incessant drainage difficulties within the mine.

Across the slab bridge stands the peat store. This once had a roof carried on columns, but was open on the sides to allow air to dry out the peat sods for use in the smelter.

Bunting and Lownathwaite Mines

When you have "done" Blakethwaite **walk on downstream, again sticking to the east bank.** Note the shale beds in the stream, how very thin they are, and how intricate are the shapes they have been worn into.

When you are more or less opposite North Hush the terrain forces your path uphill, but do not go higher than the level of the buildings ahead. A small path turns towards the buildings of Bunting Mine which is your next stop.

– It is here where the track down Bunting Hush meets the valley bottom, and those of you who took the second short cut should take up the narrative from this point –

The extent of the spoil and remains at Bunting bear witness to the mine's productivity, though there was no smelt mill here. Perhaps the most impressive ruin is the long row of *bouse teams* or *bingsteads*. Each mining team had its ore tipped into these conical structures. Water was fed into the structure from a leat on the top to wash out any unwanted loose material. Inevitably some ore was flushed out as well so this was collected and sorted in a wooden contraption called a *hotching tub*. The technology was simple and much of it would have done Heath Robinson proud, but it worked very effectively.

The entrance to Bunting Level can clearly be identified as well as the pit for the water wheel with some timbers still *in situ*. There is also the large building I will return to soon.

Across the valley are the spoil heaps and remains of another very prosperous mine operation, between North Hush and Botcher Gill. Lownathwaite Mine was part of Lord Wharton's Swaledale interests (see *Discovery Walk 11)*, though it later passed to Lord Pomfret whom we have already encountered. The mine has an early origin though it is not possible to put a date or even a century to its inception. However, it has been estimated that the hush originated in the sixteenth century.

Lownathwaite smelt mill, just above Botcher Gill Gate, had a relatively short life (*circa* 1760 to 1830).

If you stand at Bunting and look up the hushes, you will notice several prominent scars standing proud of the general bouldery devastation. In Friarfold Hush in particular the sequence of the Wensleydale Group is clearly displayed up to the youngest gritstones at the top of the hush. The prominent scar about half way up is in Underset Limestone. The richest ore veins are associated with both the Underset and the Main Limestones.

Now, let me return to the large building at Bunting Mine.

Mine Shops

This building was the Mine Shop. In the smaller and less profitable mines the miners had to make do with a simple hut – a cabin as they called it – for shelter and warmth. In the larger mines, however, they enjoyed the relative comforts of the mine shop. This had nothing to do with buying goods or working. The shop was the rest house or bunkhouse. Some housed the smithy, whose warmth made the bunkhouse nicely warm; others contained stores or stables for the mine ponies; while some also housed the mine office.

To the miners the shop was a place to escape the cold and the damp, to change into dry clothing, to eat and drink and, likely as not, to smoke and chat with their fellow men. The shop also provided lodgings for the working week. The men walked up at the beginning of the week bringing with them a supply of food and a change of clothes in a kind of sack commonly called a *wallet*. As one shift ended the wet and dirty miners took up the space vacated by those going out for the next shift. Bunks were large, big enough for three or four men, probably with a boy laid across the bottom end of the men's feet.

Imagine a room, filled with sweaty and dirty men, bacon sizzling on the range, tea stewing on the cradle, damp clothes steaming on the racks, smoke filling the room, the flicker of candles and firelight . . . and you have the mine shop. Add the chronic coughing of those with lung complaints, the patter of tiny feet in the rafters, the bed bugs and lice, the stentorian snoring . . . and you are beginning to feel at home. Do not imagine a place of debauchery, though. Many miners were very religious, others passed the time playing dominoes or draughts, and many filled in spare moments with knitting.

Metallophytes and Minerals

The overall impression around here is of botanical scarcity. Much of Gunnerside Gill seems like a desert devoid of soil and plant growth. It is true that the majority of plants cannot tolerate the still high levels of lead residue in the soil and on the spoil heaps. Come at the right time of year, on the other hand, and the picture can be different as certain lead-tolerant species flower in May and June. These are the *metallophytes*, the lead lovers. They favour a bedrock with high calcium content so you will find them more readily near limestone than sandstone or shale.

The main species to be found within the North Swaledale Mineral Belt, as throughout the Pennine ore field, are all small and delicate but no less beautiful for that. The most common is spring sandwort, or leadwort *(Minuartia verna)* with tiny white, five-petalled flower heads, growing low to the ground with leaves narrow as needles. It is best admired through a hand lens.

Alpine pennycress *(Thlaspi caerulescens)* can be found alongside leadwort though to a lesser extent as it is quite rare. It grows taller than leadwort and has a head of tiny four-petalled flowers ranging from white to lilac or mauve. Scurvy-grass *(Cochlearia pyrenaica)* may also be located on damper patches amongst the workings. This is superficially similar to pennycress being similar in height and also having four-petalled flowers varying from white to lilac. The leaves, however, are quite distinctively heart-shaped, are much bigger than those of the pennycress and grow on straggling stems.

Minerals

The spoil heaps in Gunnerside are rich in ore specimens despite the thousands of people who have sifted through them over the decades in search of souvenirs. You will not find any large samples on or near the surface, and digging is forbidden, but a careful search over the surface should produce small samples. As with any activity it is the patient and persistent mineral hunter who finds the samples. Perhaps those of us who are mineral fiends should observe and handle them but not remove them. Leave the specimens for others to enjoy, perhaps.

Some minerals to be found in Gunnerside Gill

Mineral	Compound	Composition	Colour
baryte[1] (Heavy spar)	$BaSO_4$	barium sulphate	mainly white but colour tinged
barytocalcite	$Ba\,Ca(CO_3)_2$	barium calcium carbonate	white and colour tinged
calcite	$CaCO_3$	calcium carbonate	often white or transparent but can be one of several colours
dolomite	$CaMg\,(CO_3)_2$	calcium magnesium carbonate	white to brown, or yellow tinged
fluorite[2]	CaF_2	calcium fluoride	white, blue, purple, green or transparent
galena	PbS	lead sulphide	dark grey and shiny
pyromorphite	$Pb_5\,(PO_4)_3\,Cl$	chloro-phosphate of lead	bright green
quartz	SiO_2	silicon dioxide	transparent or white and glassy
sphalerite (zinc blende)	ZnS	zinc sulphide	dark brown to black
strontianite	$SrCO_3$	strontium carbonate	white to brown but often greenish
witherite	$BaCO_3$	barium carbonate	white to brown

1. barytes is the name of the commercial extract.
2. fluorspar is the commercial product derived from fluorite.

Sir Francis Level

Leave the Mine Shop at Bunting and follow the miners' track downstream, taking the right turn at the cairn opposite Dolly Level.

– If you had taken the first short-cut of the day, dropping down from Swina Bank, you should resume the narrative now –

Your path drops down towards the valley floor having passed just above a run of walled fields. Across the beck are the remains of the Sir Francis lead mine. If you wish to have a closer look, drop down to the gate and ford the beck, returning later the same way.

The Sir Francis level was cut as late as 1864 and was the last adit to be driven in Gunnerside Gill. Apparently it was possible to enter here and to travel underground by tunnels and connecting shafts all the way to the Arkengarthdale mines ten kilometres distant. Needless to say, you cannot now. The level entrance is visible as well as the compressor that fed the mine's hydraulic pumping engine, sited some 1600 metres into the mine, that in turn operated the ore hoist and water pump. This was, at that time, the application of modern technology. The compressor was installed in 1881 but it only operated for a year or so. The very next year the mine was flooded out and a collapse of the market price for lead ruled out any possibility of re-opening it. Cheap imports had killed off the domestic industry.

Birbeck Wood

Continue downstream on the path that at times hugs the banks, passing through dressing floors and bouse teams associated with Sir Francis.

Across the stream slope dynamics are in evidence in the form of recent landslips. The soil and shattered, weak shales become saturated, the natural balance is broken and the whole slope fails. Channel dynamics can also be observed along here in the storm banks of rocks and pebbles within the braided bed of the beck. The enormous quantity of rock debris in the channel owes its existence to a combination of factors. The narrow, V-shaped nature of Gunnerside Gill acts as a funnel for material from upstream, and there is also a high input of debris from the steep valley sides. In addition the hand of man cannot be underestimated. Hushing produced prodigious quantities of easily transported material.

Just beyond the barn the path enters Birbeck Wood for a delightful stretch of walking in total contrast to the rest of today's bleakness. Native species abound – rowan, ash, birch, hazel, alder being prominent – in this small but important woodland. **At first the path contours high above the beck but joins it further downstream, and passes through a gate for the final short stretch into the village.**

As you walk along this stretch: note the depth of glacial till exposed on the opposite bank in this final stretch, and then return to the village.

Place-name meanings

Barf End	OE/ON	hill end
Birbeck	OE/ON	the beck by the birch trees
Gunnerside	OE	Gunnar's (pers. name) shieling
Heights	OE	the high place
Loaning House	OE	house with a lane
Melbecks (Moor)	ON	the stream with sand banks
Swina Bank	OE/ON	the bank with (wild) pigs
Whin Hall	ON	the hall near the gorse

Silver Birch
Betula pendula

Status: native to Britain; very common on heaths, moors and as an invasive scrub tree.

Crown: very narrow, pointed and rather open canopy; has been described as being graceful.

Height: typically 20 to 30 metres.

Trunk: tall and slender with twig like and drooping branches.

Bark: starts off rather pink or brown, but soon turns silvery; becomes blotched grey black with age; smooth on young trees, distinctively peeling when mature to give a papery effect.

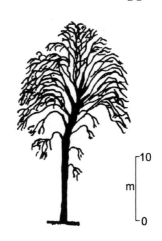

Fruit: enormous numbers on each tree; bears male and female catkins on the same plant, hanging down in a drooping fashion.

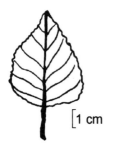

Leaves: from 4 to 7cm long; very easy to distinguish being almost triangular in shape, both truncate (having a straight base) and acuminate (pointed at the opposite end); rough, saw toothed edges but with irregular edges; shiny and bright green.

Uses: nowadays used for plywood and for tool handles and some kitchen items. Traditionally used by headmasters for whacking young boys; by witches for their broomsticks; by the Swiss for their alpenhorns; and a cousin by North American Indians for wigwam frames.

Discovery Walk 11

From Healaugh to Low Row: a walk in Mid Swaledale

Start and Finish: at Thwaites where the riverside path meets the B6270 (Grid Reference SE 012 985).

Parking: there is a large parking area at the start.

Public Transport: Healaugh and Low Row are on the bus route from Richmond to Keld, operated by United (01325 468771).

Facilities en Route: Low Row — Feetham has the Punch Bowl Inn which provides bar meals and has both tea shop and shop. The village also has a post office, telephone and public toilets. There are telephone boxes at Isles Bridge and Healaugh.

Outline of the Walk: Thwaites — Scabba Wath — Low Lane — Isles Bridge — Smarber — Blades — Gallows Top — Thiernswood Hall — Healaugh — Thwaites.

Length: 12km (7.5 miles) for the route as described; slightly less if the Low Row shortcut is taken.

Ordnance Survey Maps: 1:25,000 Outdoor Leisure 30 1:50,000 Landranger 98.

Introduction

Downstream of Gunnerside Swaledale has a more open aspect and one feels less hemmed in by the fells that bound the dale. The Swale is more of a river here as it sweeps across its flat floodplain, now abutting against the northern slopes, now against the southern. At the best of times it is a force to be reckoned with: in full spate it can be truly awesome. The early settlers made an apt choice when they christened it the swift or turbulent river.

This section of the dale still displays the clear contrast between northern and southern slopes. There is an almost unbroken line of hamlets, villages and farms facing south with only a few scattered farmsteads on the north-facing slopes. Life was hard enough without cutting yourself off from the sun.

Settlements hereabouts are small without exception. Healaugh and Low Row just about make village status. Feetham seems to have been subsumed in Low Row to form a long, discontinuous and straggling settlement. Else-

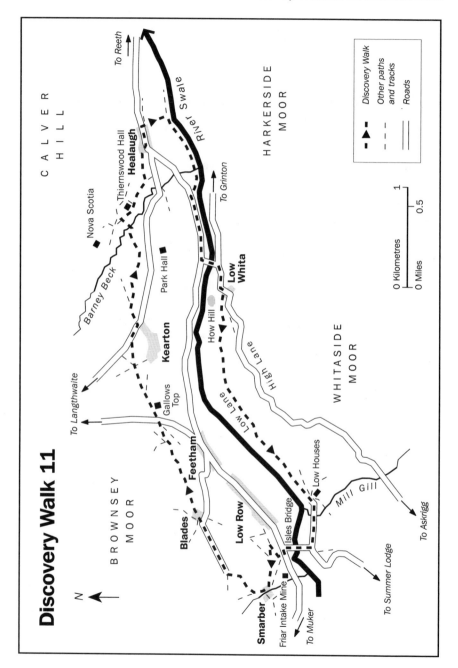

Discovery Walk 11

where there are tiny hamlets, once thriving and tightly knit communities, now just collections of houses: Low Houses, Smarber, Blades and Kearton have lost their former vibrancy. The decline of the lead industry is responsible for this, as around Gunnerside and Kisdon.

Apart from the ghosts of the "Old Man" (a miner's term for those who worked before him), we shall meet today a family of noble lords whose impact on life and work lasted for several centuries.

Having kept you in suspense until now as regards the Enclosure Movement, I shall use Whitaside to explain the whys and wherefores of that great parcelling up of the landscape. Just as that had a profound influence on the way the landscape looked and was utilised in the most recent centuries, so today another movement is gaining in importance. I refer to the Environmentally Sensitive Area (ESA) scheme. Whether this will still hold sway two hundred years from now, as the Enclosure Movement has for the last two hundred, will be judged in the fullness of time. In our time it is a significant input to the countryside in Swaledale, as elsewhere in the Dales.

Today's walk starts near Healaugh. Being realistic I have used a large parking area about a kilometre upstream of the village as the base. If you are using public transport then start in Healaugh and do the last bit first. Because the walk is circular – up one side of the dale and back down the other – I have not included options. You could, however, make your own alternative by following the road through Low Row and Feetham, to pick up the narrative again at Peat Gate. As with all the routes in this collection, I would urge you to complete the whole.

Along the Swale

The first steps today are up the road that runs alongside the river through Park Hall Meadows (an SSSI). We have discovered elsewhere that the Dales possess some superb examples of traditional hay meadows, especially in Swaledale. English Nature and the National Park have surveyed all the meadows in the Dales. To achieve the top Grade 4 rating, at lease ten species must be present from a special list of 47 characteristic traditional hay meadow plants. An estimate for the UK suggested that in 1985 only 3 per cent of such neutral grasslands remained unaffected by modern agricultural methods. A sample survey of 40 high grade sites within the Park showed that, for various reasons, one third of the area recorded as such in 1985 had been downgraded by 1991. The best grasslands can contain over 80 species, so the loss of even one meadow is unacceptable.

This area is the Swale's floodplain (and a former lake bed) and it lives up to its name. A stone bank separates river from road . . . until the river decides differently, as it did in the serious floods of early 1995. The protective bank was quite ineffective then. The plain was covered in gushing water, unable to pass through Scabba Wath bridge, and a whole section of meadowside wall was swept away, and the road liberally sprinkled with silt and sand.

When you reach the junction with the Askrigg road, turn left over the Swale. This is Scabba Wath, and wath means ford. Before the bridge was erected the river could only be forded here, or crossed at Grinton Bridge, a good way downstream. The drove road from the north and the Corpse Road I have mentioned elsewhere, connecting Reeth and the upper dale with the parish church at Grinton, ran from Feetham to the wath and thence through Harkerside. Even in times of low flow, the crossing must have been hazardous, and I am sure the pall bearers of old cursed the combination of death and wet weather, as the alternative route through Healaugh and Reeth is significantly longer. For the drovers time was money and they, too, must have cursed high flow.

On the other side of the bridge you should turn right along Low Lane as far as the bunkhouse barn at Low Whita. Here the tarred road, High Lane now, begins its long and tortuous climb over the watershed to Askrigg and Wensleydale. **Low Lane, your route, follows the foot of the valley slopes as an unmade track.** It is part of a once important south bank road that ran all the way from Grinton to Gunnerside. Low Lane still "enjoys" County Road status.

As you leave the tar for the quiet and secluded track, look to the right. There is a prominent hillock – a glacial mound – with prominent ditch and bank earthworks around it. The hillock is called How Hill, a topographical

River Swale at Low Whita bridge

name that often indicates antiquity. Without detailed excavation it is very difficult to ascribe a feature like this to a particular prehistoric period. It is Bronze Age or Iron Age . . . or? It may, however, be contemporary with Maiden Castle on Harkerside which is assumed to be Bronze Age, but any link between the two is pure conjecture.

You have a clear view of the northern slopes of Swaledale from down here, and particularly of the scattered hamlet of Kearton just to the north.

It is said you can date a hedgerow by counting the number of woody species per linear metre. If that be the case, this lane must have a long history. The floral count is impressive in summer not to mention the diversity of tree and shrub species: blackthorn, wild rose, hawthorn, holly, hazel, ash, elm, sycamore are but a few of the commoner species on Low Lane. The wych elm withstood the fatal ravages of Dutch elm disease for longer than the English elm, but it too has begun to give way under the onslaught. In parts of the country local authorities are choosing common lime as a replacement for stricken elms. I fervently hope the wych elms in the Dales are not to be afflicted by the disease.

As you walk on you begin to parallel the straggling village of Low Row and Feetham, more than a kilometre in length and barely more than one building deep. There was little choice, mind, as the lower land is liable to flood and the higher land too steep. The builders of Low Row built this way from necessity.

The difference between the two sides of Swaledale is marked. On the north-facing slopes there are only scattered farmsteads and few field barns. The pastures are sour and neglected and the whole impression is of decay. The warmer south-facing slopes provide a total contrast. Settlements are more in evidence, the pastures have been improved and maintained in sound condition. The feeling engendered here is of industry and prosperity. This same dichotomy is evident as far west as Thwaite. Like Dentdale, Swaledale has its "money side" and its "sunny side".

After two kilometres on the lane you pass the junction with Gale Lane and enter the hamlet of Low Houses. Across the valley bottom there is a large, three storied building with a walled garden, altogether an imposing structure. This is Paradise (dated 1663). This building was an industrial establishment connected with textile manufacture. On the top floor is the knitting room where yarn was spun for Haverdale Mill (see later) which belonged to the same Knowles family. Originally local farmers, they had interests in lead and coal mining in addition to textiles.

Low Lane is now finely cobbled and then hard-surfaced as it passes through Low Houses. **Simply follow the road west to the next junction.** This particular locality is called Haverdale and the textile industry was also in evidence here. An old corn mill below the falls was converted to manufacture worsteds, blankets, carpets and seamen's jerseys, and finished off garments hand-knitted in homes throughout Swaledale. Stockings and jerseys were always made ridiculously big, to be washed and shrunk to size at the mill. For many years water provided the motive power, but later on coal from Tan Hill. Operations ceased in the 1870s when the mill reverted to corn, but that too died out.

From Haverdale the road runs up to Summer Lodge, once an important lead mining centre. A place-name there, Bloody Vale, commemorates a bloody skirmish between local folk and Scots raiders after the Battle of Bannockburn in 1314. The Scots were wiped out, so the story goes.

An old drove road forded the Swale at Isles and at Rowleth Wath before heading over Summer Lodge to Askrigg.

At the junction you should re-cross the Swale on Isles Bridge. A glance upstream will confirm why "Isles". In a particularly broad, meandering sweep, the channel splits into two, separated by a huge and unstable shingle and rock island. **Carry on up the road, past the row of former miners' cottages at Isles to the junction.**

Low Row

– It is at this point that you need to decide whether to go through Low Row or to follow the main route –

If you are doing the latter, pick up the route description under "Smarber and the Whartons". If you want to shorten the route, read on here.

Walk east along the road through the straggling village of Low Row which becomes Feetham further on. As you walk you will notice the Methodist chapel. Wesley graced Low Row with his presence on one of his journeys spreading his message, leading to many conversions to his church. The chapel was built in 1769, a year after his visit.

Most of the rest of the upper village was connected with mining. Indeed the Punch Bowl Inn was once The Miners' Arms, though it featured in the drove trade from Barnard Castle via here to Askrigg. It was the only stop between Arkengarthdale and Summer Lodge.

Turn off the main road at the inn and climb up the steep Langthwaite road. Carry on past Peat Head Gate but only as far as the access track to Gallows Top.

– Rejoin the main route here –

So pick up the main narrative in the section "From Blades to Kearton".

Smarber and the Whartons

– Read on here if you are following the full route –

Turn left at the junction at Isles but do not get carried away as you are to turn off by the Low Row sign, hardly a few metres from the junction. There is a dense network of paths and tracks on this hillside, so do follow these directions carefully. **A rough path climbs up alongside the wall from the road through a scrubby wood. At the top end of the wood maintain your line along the wall.**

Where your path joins a major track, turn left uphill again. You should go through the gate, ignoring the cross tracks, on a broad, green track. This passes through disturbed mining ground, once part of the Friar Intake lead mine downhill from here. **The track ends at a field gate next to Smarber Cottage.**

Head up the concrete track through Smarber and follow it all the way till it joins the tarred road at the foot of Low Row Pasture.

You cannot go far in Swaledale without coming across one reminder or another of the Wharton family, so let me introduce them to you. Like so many aristocratic dynasties the Whartons came from nowhere, rose through military service into the ranks of the gentry and eventually reached the peak of nobility, only to collapse in disgrace and disappear from the scene, leaving only their story and tangible reminders in land and literature.

They can be traced in the records back to 1292 at their seat, Wharton Hall, south of Kirkby Stephen. They made their exit in the 1720s when the 6th Baron, 2nd Earl, 2nd Marquess and 1st Duke of Wharton (such was the speed of their rise) fell into disgrace, fled into exile and had the family's estates attainted.

How do they fit into Swaledale? The 1st Baron bought the manor of Muker in 1544, and came into the possession of half of the manor of Healaugh in 1556. His descendant, the 4th Baron, purchased the rest of Healaugh. Together with the lands they also gained all mining rights, a very lucrative proposition. They owned ten lead mines, including Swinnergill, Arngill and Lownathwaite (see *Discovery Walks 9 and 10*) and were very important in the development of the industry.

The 4th Baron, Philip, also left quite a different legacy. In 1690 he built Swaledale's first independent chapel, on the slopes below Smarber. The chapel has gone but the site is known and a plaque records its establishment, and a gravestone dated in the 1870s suggests a long use for the chapel. He chose a site in proximity to his shooting lodge at Smarber Hall. Philip was a prominent Dissenter and played a part in formulating William and Mary's Act of Toleration in 1689, which granted freedom of religious worship.

He also established a charitable trust to distribute free bibles to children in the Wharton estates in Yorkshire, Cumberland, Westmorland . . . and Buckinghamshire. Any child was eligible to receive a bible as long as he or she could recite seven prescribed Psalms and several Bible readings.

I shall make a further reference to the Whartons near the end of the walk.

Blades and Kearton

As you proceed eastwards along the road you will, I am sure, note that most of the houses and barns have similar kneelers on the gable roof ends. These were a decorative feature added to the coping stones to give the house that little extra something. Maybe around here it was a question of keeping up with the local equivalent of the Jones's. Or maybe they were all the work of one builder who "sold" his style to the farmers of the day. Or, again, maybe the landowner decreed thus.

There is a splendid view downdale. The northern part is filled by the bulk of Calver Hill (476 metres) and the humpbacked form of Fremington Edge. Over to the south is the massive fell called Gibbon Hill (543 metres) to the east and High Carl (565 metres) at the western end. Both are flat topped and display the same geological bedding structure as Calver.

The moorland on your left, Low Row Pasture, has a system of Bronze Age field boundaries, about the 400 metre contour, part of a sequence that continues eastwards through Calver to Marrick and Marske (see *Discovery Walk 12*).

The road brings you to the hamlet of Blades.

This was a former lead mining community with many of the menfolk tramping over the moors to work in Old Gang mine in Mill Gill to the north. The majority walked there daily, leaving in the dark and returning home late, knitting as they went. I find their endurance and acceptance of their difficult life both amazing and worthy of deep admiration. How many of us could do it today?

When Wesley was preaching in Swaledale in 1768 he used Blades as his base.

Several of the houses fell into disrepair, but you will see the amount of renovation and restoration that has gone on in recent years.

Leave the road here and turn into the hamlet, soon bearing right to walk between Simon's Garth and Pursglove Cottage on the path signposted to Kearton. Go through the gated squeeze stile, across the croft to a second such stile, and then on through two more stiles.

Pass through the gateway ahead, behind the field barn, to another squeeze stile set at the far end. Mind the strategically placed bog here! **Carry on in the same direction, passing above the former Bird's Nest farm, to join the tarred Peat Gate** connecting Low Row with Langthwaite.

– If you took the shortcut through Low Row, slot back into the narrative here –

Cross straight over and follow the gravelled track alongside Gallows Top until just before it dips through a normally dry stream bed. The right of way, to be precise, follows the wall to this point, rather than the track, but let sense prevail. **An unmarked path starts at this juncture and cuts across**

the moor towards the wall corner you will see, at which point no less than five paths converge. **Yours follows the headwall of the series of inbye fields of Kearton.** The difference in the vegetation either side of this wall is amazing.

Follow the wall up to the tarred Morley Gate and turn down it to Hill Top, a good example of a (stretched) Pennine long-house. Farms such as this, with living accommodation at one end, barns and byres at the other, are probably direct descendants of the much smaller Viking long-houses (see *The Southern Dales*).

Pass along the frontage of the building to a squeeze stile in the end wall, a stile that forces you to squeeze, its being so narrow. Before you head on, focus your eyes and look far down the dale. Can you make out a church tower? This is really all that remains of Marrick Priory. The Priory, founded in 1150, was a nunnery following the Benedictine Order. It seems sex discrimination was institutionalised in the medieval church because management of the priory was in the hands of a Master, and the prioress had to submit to the Archbishop of the day. Having said that, though, there was clearly a local women's movement as, barely a kilometre from that priory, stood a Cistercian nunnery, Ellerton Priory.

The Enclosure Movement

I have made numerous references in these two books to the Enclosure Movement. As you stand, or sit, by Hill Top, and look to the south to Whitaside, you have in view a classic example of parliamentary enclosure. Walls climb up the moor side, parcelling the land up into regular portions. Such walls provide a total contrast to the irregularly sized and shaped fields around most villages in the Dales.

In lowland Britain the Enclosure Movement generally refers to the dividing up of the old open-fields. In the Dales most of the lowland tracts had been carved up piecemeal from at least the late monastic period. Here the Movement was aimed at enclosing the vast common pastures on the fells.

Enclosure is specific to northern Europe. The same process occurred in Denmark and Sweden, but was rarely found on the Continent proper.

Pressure was applied on governments from the late sixteenth century to improve the agricultural state of the country, to carve up the unproductive open-fields, commons and "waste" and to place it all under private and therefore efficient forms of management. (Now what does that remind me of?) The first Act was passed as early as 1604, in the south, and the movement slowly spread northwards. Thousands of awards were gazetted in England and Wales with the bulk of the Acts being concentrated between the 1770s and the 1820s. Each township required its own Act.

It was this Enclosure Movement, as the process has come to be called, that created the landscape we see today. There is very little "natural" space left: it has almost all seen the hand of man. Once moors and fellsides had been enclosed, lime was added to neutralise the acid soils, drains were put in, and land management was introduced.

Each Award necessitated the appointment of commissioners to draw up the plans, to determine which exact line the new walls would follow and how large each field was to be. They stipulated the dimensions of the walls, where drains should be dug, where streams were to be diverted or culverted, how and where existing trackways should be realigned. Their decision carried the weight of the law.

The commissioners were also involved in the process of allocating enclosed land, or *allotting* it to the new owners, hence the common term "allotment" as a place-name element in the fieldscape.

Each Award created a local system of new Enclosure roads, variously called Occupation Roads or Accommodation Roads. Their function was to provide a walled route from the township or valley road, through the walled inbye to the edge of the open fell pastures, to prevent passing stock from grazing someone else's fields. Typically these roads were 12 metres wide to allow for on the hoof grazing and detours around mud wallows. Of the 24 walks in this collection only two do not include a section on Enclosure roads, such is their number.

The ESA Scheme

From Hill Top you should contour across the field to the wall. Just beyond the wall junction there is a stone stile set into the wall. Look out for it as it is easily missed, especially if your eye is drawn to the view across Swaledale. If you go too far down the field (as the O.S. map would wrongly have you do) you will have to retrace your steps as there is no way out at the bottom. **Through the stile, turn right and keep the wall close by as you follow it to the access track to Birk Park. Turn right here also, over the cattle grid, and immediately left into a large field,** once part of an extensive parkland.

The path is not evident on the ground but its line makes for the lime kiln and its feeder quarries, and then for the three lonely ash trees at the western end of an old boundary feature.

Down here the landscape is tame and verdant, disciplined and moulded by the hand of man. Beyond the wooded valley to the north, the slopes of Calver present a very different picture. Man tried to create fields out of the moor, and made an attempt to improve them for stock, but Nature is reclaiming what she considers hers. The house that stands alone and almost forlorn – Nova Scotia – bears witness to the futility of defying the forces of nature.

Very shortly after the three ash trees, swing north and drop down to a bridle gate into the wood. Now this is an absolute gem.

I have mentioned elsewhere in this book how deficient the Dales are in

Nova Scotia and Hawking Pots Wood

broad-leaved woodland. It is so refreshing to find woods as healthy and extensive as this, particularly when it is set amid such bleak moorland. I just wish there was much more of it. You will not be beneath the trees for long so do take your time and make the most of Hawking Pots Wood.

From the gate the path makes a broad sweep down to Barney Beck, and to a footbridge. Note the state of the beck here. If it is in full spate you will need to adjust the route from Healaugh, as I will point out when you get there.

There are many impressive and mature trees in the wood: pedunculate oak, sycamore, alder, rowan, horse chestnut, beech, Scots pines and various exotic conifers. Here, too, is a species you see very little of in these parts, the sweet chestnut, with its very long and bright green saw-toothed leaves and bright green sea urchin-like seed pods.

A short path climbs from the footbridge to join a bridleway, an old and once busy miners' track leading up to the mines and smelters of Old Gang. Turn right on the track past Thiernswood Hall. If you happen to be here in autumn – a delightful time for woodland walking, I am sure you will agree – your boots will be crunching beech mast and conkers as much as gravel.

Some way down the drive there is a small field barn and a squeeze stile on the left. Cross the field to a gated stile, cut across the corner of the next, and then follow the north side of the third field to a stone step stile hiding in the corner under a sycamore. Follow the lane now into Healaugh.

I have discussed elsewhere various countryside schemes, such as the Countryside Stewardship Scheme set up by the Countryside Commission but transferred to MAFF (the Ministry of Agriculture) in April 1996; and the Woodland Guardianship Scheme. I have mentioned in passing MAFF's Environmentally Sensitive Area (ESA) scheme.

The ESA scheme was introduced in 1987 to give protection to five areas of national importance seen to be under threat from modern, intensive farming methods. The following year five more were added, including the Pennine Dales. The whole of Arkengarthdale and Swaledale, upstream from Reeth, are within this ESA.

The main aim in the Pennine Dales is to conserve those traditional hay meadows whose floristic integrity has been damaged by the use of modern methods such as re-seeding, the use of slurry or inorganic fertilisers. Farmers who elect to enter the scheme, for a period of ten years, are given financial compensation for adopting methods in tune with overall conservation philosophy. They must not apply any chemicals, must limit the use of organic fertilisers, must remove stock in the spring to allow full floral growth, must not cut silage, and must not cut hay before July. The stricter the controls, the higher are the payments.

Farmers also receive assistance in the management and, if necessary, regeneration of broad-leaved woodland; and in the maintenance of stone walls and field barns. In short, birdlife and small mammal populations benefit, floral diversity is maintained or enhanced, the beauty and aesthetic value of the landscape are ensured, and the farmer does not suffer financial loss.

The scheme has been an outstanding success. The take-up rate within the Pennine Dales has been impressive with more than two-thirds of eligible land entered into the scheme. Indeed Brussels has decreed that all member states must introduce a similar scheme. The ESA scheme is complementary to Countryside Stewardship, which is open to farmers outside designated ESAs, and we are fortunate to have such policies in place. It was MAFF's intention to spend £100 million on environmental conservation programmes in 1996. To set that figure into context, however, this represents less than two per cent of its annual budget for agriculture. Let us be thankful for small mercies.

Healaugh

As a settlement Healaugh dates from the twelfth century, relatively late in the peopling of the Dales. It was established as a village stronghold in a clearing in the hunting forest that stretched over much of Swaledale. It was the property of the de Gaunt family, kinsmen of William the Conqueror, who held manorial and hunting rights in Swaledale through several generations.

Sweet or Spanish Chestnut

Castanea sativa

Status: introduced by the Romans; naturalised in the south east; planted in the north.

Crown: tall main dome with lower subsidiary domes.

Height: typically 30 metres.

Trunk: tall and straight with huge spreading branches and strong twigs.

Bark: grey to brown and deeply fissured vertically, or even spirally, in mature specimens.

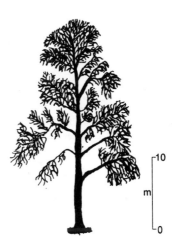

[1 cm

Fruit: bears huge, long yellow male catkins in summer; female catkins produce the chestnuts in October in their distinctive bright green and strongly spined husks.

Leaves: very long indeed, up to 20 or even 25cm; very bright green; strongly toothed around the edges; turning pale yellow in autumn.

Uses: formerly a popular coppice tree for fencing posts, pit props, ships' timbers and fuelwood; nowadays used for chestnut palings, rustic furniture and fuel for wood burning stoves.

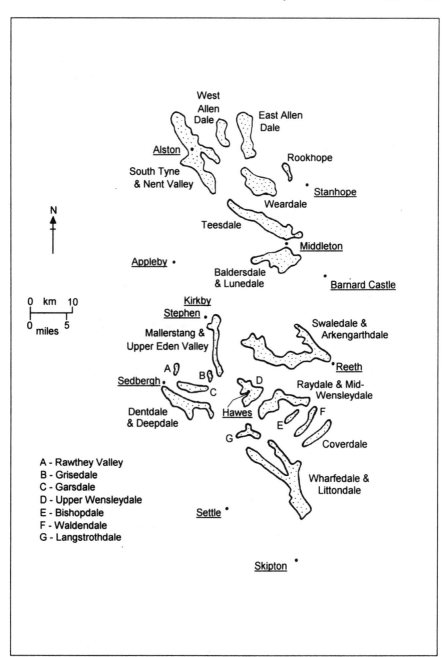

The Pennine Dales Environmentally Sensitive Area

– If Barney Beck was high where I asked you to take note earlier, I would advise you to return to the start by road. The beck has to be forded if you follow the remainder of today's route –

Make your way to the eastern end of the village, to Manor House Farm, and down the short walled lane alongside the farm. Two paths diverge here so ensure you do drop down to a field gate into a large meadow. The right of way follows the boundary wall all the way to the river bank.

Turn upstream and follow the flood defence bank, passing a number of impressive stiles as you go. **About two thirds of the way you have to ford Barney Beck,** hence my earlier caution. In normal conditions the crossing presents no real problems.

Keep an eye and an ear open for reed buntings which have recently begun to nest in the area. The male is easy to recognise. He is slightly larger than a sparrow and has distinctive white collar, cheek flash and unders with a brown streaked back. The female, as so often, is on the drab side! The call is either a chinking sound or is shrill while its song has been variously described as irritating and dreary.

When you reach a huge expanse of boulders in the Swale's channel, look up to the north to a farm set against a small wood. This is Park Hall. The predecessor to the present hall was the seat of Lord Wharton in his manor of Healaugh. The house bears a datestone "Lord TW 1700". This Thomas was 5th Baron Wharton, 1st Earl (from 1706) and 1st Marquess (from 1715). In the fields below the hall you will note a few parallel banks. Historic definitely, ancient . . . who knows?

In no time at all the riverside path negotiates a step-over stile for the final few metres back to the starting point.

Place-name meanings

Blades	–	from the surname Blades
Feetham	OE/ON	the homestead by the meadow
Gale Lane	OWSc	the lane by the steep ravine
Gallows Top	–	probably as it sounds
Harkerside	ON	the open field or acre field
Haverdale	ON	the valley where oats were grown
Healaugh	OE	the high forest clearing
How Hill	OE/ON	hill
Scabba Wath	OE	? ford
Smarber	ON	the hill where butter was made
Swale	OE	the swift or turbulent river
Thiernswood	OE/ON	the wood with thorn bushes

Discovery Walk 12

A Final Fling in the Dales: a Walk in Arkengarthdale

Start and Finish: on the Reeth to Langthwaite road, 3 kilometres from Reeth (Grid Reference NZ 018 013).

Parking: there is room to park on the roadside at the junction with the access road to West Raw Croft Farm.

Public Transport: no public transport services operate up Arkengarthdale. The nearest is Reeth on the Richmond-Keld route (United 01325 468771).

Facilities en Route: none on the route itself. Reeth has a full range of services as well as a good museum and a National Park Information Point. A Park Information Centre was due to open during 1996. Langthwaite offers meals at the Red Lion Inn, a shop, telephone box, and toilets on the top road near the Wesleyan chapel.

Outline of the Walk: road – Calver Hill – Black Hill – Castle – Heggs – Storthwaite – Raw Croft – road.

Length: 10.8km (6.7 miles) for the long route or 7km (4.3 miles) for the shorter version.

Ordnance Survey Maps: 1:25,000 Outdoor Leisure 30 1:50,000 Landranger 92 and 98.

Introduction

We have met Alan of Brittany on an earlier walk (see *Discovery Walk 8*). In gratitude for commanding the Breton contingent at the Battle of Hastings, he was created Earl and granted the expansive Honour of Richmond which stretched up Swaledale and Arkengarthdale. How noble of the Conqueror to give away what was not his to dispose of! When Alan's daughter Matilda married Walter de Gaunt he gave her much of the area as a dowry. "Here you are, dear. Have a dale or two." The rest – much of Arkengarthdale – became Alan's private hunting ground, called New Forest, apart from pockets which he granted to Jervaulx Abbey to salve his soul.

And so the dale remained right through the medieval centuries. It changed little until the blossoming of lead mining in the early modern period. Mind you, mining here can be traced back to Alan's days. He had lead mines in production, not mines with deep shafts and a network of levels but more likely coffin workings (see *The Southern Dales*) or maybe very shallow shafts. There are also reports of lead being despatched in the late thirteenth century to Windsor Castle and Waltham Abbey. For its era, lead mining was clearly well developed. It was about that time, too, when we see the beginnings of organised coal mining high up the dale. Some was destined for Richmond castle, some for lead smelting.

Arkengarthdale is dominated by Reeth which guards the entrance to the dale as well as controlling traffic up Swaledale. Reeth boomed partly because of lead but also owing to the turnpiking of the Arkengarthdale road in 1770. More lead and coal could be exported on the improved road, so the village collected its dues and prospered. The height and grandeur of the buildings facing the green speak loudly of Reeth's erstwhile importance.

From Elizabethan times to the nineteenth century Reeth also acted as a major centre for the knitting industry in both dales. This was no rural idyll: Reeth was an industrial settlement, no more and no less. Alas, all good things seem to come to an end. One by one the industries collapsed or moved away where conditions were more suitable. The later nineteenth century saw profound economic and social change, with mass unemployment and a rapid slither into destitution and paupery for many, or emigration for the fortunate. In just one year, 1882, the school roll in Reeth halved.

This final walk largely steers clear of the mining areas and sticks to the tranquil part of the dale. The route provides you with a variety of landscapes. There is open heather moorland up on the lower flanks of Calver Hill, with the chance to see red grouse at close quarters. Elsewhere there are delightful wooded reaches close by Arkle Beck. For almost the entire walk the backdrop is provided by the towering height of Fremington Edge, only 400 or so metres high yet dwarfing everything below.

The walk is arranged in a circular way but, as usual, flexibility is there. The first half of the route, taking in Calver, could make a walk in itself, if you were to return to the start by road. For this ignore the first section, "The Short Route: Rawcroft", but follow the rest of the narrative up to and including "Heather Moorland".

Alternatively, you could miss out Calver by staying within the dale itself. If this be the case, read the next section but then jump to "Fremington Edge", and follow the narrative to the end.

The Short Route: Rawcroft

The first part of the short route is easy enough to navigate: **leave the road and walk down the access track to West Raw Croft Farm. A path branches to the right just before the farm buildings, passes through a bridle gate and heads upslope to a squeeze stile above the line of trees.** Whoever planted them either had an eye for variety of form and colour, or else could not make

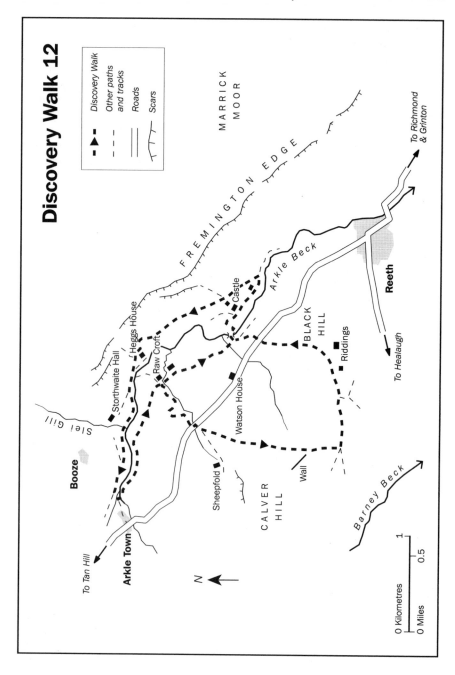

Discovery Walk 12

Discovery Walk
Other paths
and tracks
Roads
Scars

MARRICK MOOR

FREMINGTON EDGE

Arkle Beck

To Richmond & Grinton

Castle

Heggs House

Storthwaite Hall

Raw Croft

BLACK HILL

Riddings

Reeth

To Healaugh

Slei Gill

Booze

Watson House

Sheepfold

CALVER HILL

Wall

Barney Beck

To Tan Hill

Arkle Town

N

Kilometres   0   0.5   1
Miles   0

a firm decision, as almost every tree is of a different species: alder, Scots pine, ash, sycamore and sessile oak.

As you follow the path from here and look up and down the valley, you soon realise how well-wooded lower Arkengarthdale is compared to most of the other dales. **The path, not clear on the ground, runs through a series of fields, more or less at the same level, to join another access track down from the valley road opposite Thorn Dale.**

– At this point you rejoin the full route of today's walk. Pick up the narrative later in the section "Fremington Edge" –

Calver: The Full Route Begins

You could be forgiven for wondering why Calver sits amidst what is known as Reeth *Low* Moor when it is anything but low. A perusal of the Ordnance Survey map tells all. Away to the west of this enormous pasture Reeth High Moor rises a good 80 metres higher.

Calver is one of those hills that does not seem to attract the hordes as yet another summit or trig. point to tick off. I have walked around its edges on numerous occasions but I have only been to the top once. There is something both mysterious and mystical about Calver. When I come near it I feel both drawn to it, compelled to scale its screes and yet, at the same time, I also feel repelled by something I cannot begin to explain. Even when I did go to the top, I did not hang about and was glad to be down again.

I do not wish to sound trite but could it have something to do with the amount of Bronze Age remains around the hill? Or could it be the lingering aura of centuries of mining up there? I shall explore both of these in due course – in facts, not in feelings.

The Ordnance Survey map shows a path passing to the east of Calver from the starting point (018 011) but the map is deceptive, I regret to say. For the first section there is no sign of anything on the ground, and even the fingerpost is pointing in a different direction. By all means try and follow it through the heather, or take the easy way out.

A traceable path does leave the road at our starting point heading south-west towards the quarried butt end of Calver. This path leads to a sheepfold at the foot of the hill, at the end of an old cart track (at 014 009).

Turn left at the sheepfold on the track (which frustratingly fizzles out almost immediately) **and then contour along the east side of Calver on a faint path. Once you reach the quarry workings by the fenced in water out-take, the path improves and is easier to follow.**

Grouse Shooting

This is grouse country again. The line of grouse butts and the patchwork quilt of heather at various stages of growth illustrate the importance of shooting here. You will doubtless see grouse, and more than likely will flush them out of the heather by the path. Why do they always wait till the very last minute before noisily flapping and flying off, giving one palpitations?

I have seldom met any country person (dweller or lover) who maintains a neutral stance on grouse shooting. People either seem to be for it or against it. It is not for me to encourage you one way or the other. For the moment I shall sit on the fence though you may well say I am leaning heavily to one side. First, though, let me sketch in a few facts.

Grouse shooting began to figure largely as a country pursuit in the 1850s. Better road access, the spread of the railway system, and the introduction of safer guns (safer for the shooter, that is) contributed to its popularity, and estate owners quickly seized the opportunity to widen their economic base and consolidate or improve their social standing in the ranks of the gentry or lesser aristocracy.

Management of the moors, husbanding of heather and a kind of breeding of grouse entered the rural scene. Birds of prey and mammal predators were seen as a threat and curbs were widely introduced.

Lines of grouse butts were built across the moors and shooting cabins, with their two "upstairs-downstairs" rooms, appeared in the remotest places. The "Glorious Twelfth" entered the social calendars of shooters, beaters and hangers-on. Social traditions rapidly developed and grouse shooting was soon to be equated with other aspects of our supposed national heritage.

There are now many moors long since abandoned with derelict heather, neglected butts, and ruinous cabins. The First World War sounded the death knell of many shooting estates. The loss of so many "sons" in the war and the social revolution that came afterwards made the shooting party an element of a past to be nostalgically remembered – or forgotten.

In other areas, however, grouse moors are still managed and grouse are still shot, not necessarily just by the high-born, but by those with the money. It is not a cheap sport. Many decry the whole business and will object to my use of the word "sport" in this context. Fair enough, but there are benefits. Carefully managed heather moors ensure healthy growth and regeneration. Think of the abandoned moors with sparse, woody heather. Which is the most attractive? The patchwork quilt left by burning or swathing may offend the eye but this ten to twelve year rotation does maintain the heather.

And not only does this benefit the grouse and us, shooters or not. On one walk across this particular moor my bird count reached nineteen, and I was not particularly making an effort. I have seen six species of raptor on grouse moors around here. Then there are all the insect species that proliferate in a heather habitat, and the mammals that the careful observer may spot. Again, I have seen on Swaledale moors fox, rabbit, hare, voles, weasels, and badger setts. I shall consider moorland ecology a little later on.

Follow the path southwards, using Calver's forbidding slopes as a loose handrail, to the lower end of a stretch of ruinous wall that begins where it ends . . . nowhere.

A Poetic Interlude

Running alongside the wall is a path up to the old mines on the summit plateau. There are many isolated mines in the Dales, but this must have been one of the most gruelling and windswept work places of all.

Bale hills (early primitive smelting hearths) have been located on Calver and dated to the late sixteenth century. Peat was immediately at hand as fuel, and chopwood was brought up from coppiced woods on the valley slopes below. Altogether 30 bale hill sites have been identified by archaeological field surveys between Kisdon and Calver.

Wordsworth provides an insight into the miner's lot in his work *The Excursion*, published in 1814. In Book Sixth, "The Churchyard among the Mountains", his central character The Wanderer happens upon the remote dwelling of a miner. Let me quote a few lines from this poetic masterpiece.

> "High in these mountains, that allured a band
> Of keen adventurers to unite their pains
> In search of precious ore: they tried, were foiled –
> And all desisted, all, save him alone . . .
>
> And trusting only to his own weak hands,
> Urged unremittingly the stubborn work,
> Unseconded, uncountenanced; then, as time
> Passed on, while still his lonely efforts found
> No recompense, derided; and at length,
> By many pitied, as insane of mind . . .
>
> Hope after hope, encouraged and destroyed."

And further on . . .

> "He vanished; but conspicuous to this day
> The path remains that linked his cottage-door
> To the mine's mouth; a long and slanting track,
> Upon the rugged mountain's stony side,
> Worn by his daily visits to and from
> The darksome centre of a constant hope . . .
>
> And it is named, in memory of the event,
> The PATH OF PERSEVERANCE."

This could almost have been Calver.

On a recent walk around Kisdon a friend remarked that we cossetted folk have no idea what life was like, even a hundred years ago. How true that is.

Before you move on you may wish to spend a moment or two pondering the prodigious efforts that went into surveying and erecting the stone walls that carve up the northern slopes of Swaledale above Low Row as well as the subsidiary dale of Summer Lodge, across to the south-west. Due south is an extensive tract of heather moor, forming the watershed between Swaledale and Wensleydale: High Harker Hill, Gibbon Hill, High Carl may seem barren from this vantage point but they, too, are peppered with lead mines and grouse butts.

A Bronze Age Landscape

Once you turn your back on the old wall and the miners' track and head downhill you enter an area rich in surface remains of the Bronze Age. **So, lead on due south from the wall end on the grassed path through the heather.** Do not be drawn by the sight of the gate down below. Head to the right of that. **The path joins a stony track at the level of the walls you see down there. Turn left here.**

Have you seen any signs of the Bronze Age yet? Almost certainly you are shaking your head. They are there but, like so many archaeological remains, you only see them when someone has pointed them out. There is an extensive field system stretching all round the southern flanks of Calver and across Black Hill, as well as above Fremington Edge.

As you walked downhill you crossed low stone bankings running diagonally across the contours, aligned roughly north-east to south-west. These were field boundaries, called *reaves* by archaeologists, and the system in Swaledale is (as far as I know) the best preserved outside Dartmoor where an incredible reave system has been mapped. Dotted around are small enclosures, possibly stock pens.

I have discussed life in various stages of our past (Iron Age, Romano-British, Norse, Medieval) in *The Southern Dales*. The field systems here are much older. The first real impact on the natural landscape was the woodland clearance and agriculture of the Neolithic period (say 4000 to 5000 years

Looking up Swaledale from Calver

ago). As this culture progressed into the Bronze Age, clearance was intensified and it has been estimated locally that the tree cover had been reduced to less than one fifth of its original area.

Stock were reared: pigs, domesticated from wild boar; cattle, from aurochs; and sheep. They cultivated a range of legumes and cereals such as einkorn, emmer and barley. They supplemented their diet with the fruits and nuts of the forest and by hunting with dogs.

During the later Bronze Age the climate took a turn for the worse and many of the higher settlements and field systems had to be abandoned. Increased rainfall and reduced temperatures led to acidification of the soil, peat began to form, and heather began to colonise the former cultivated areas. By 3000 years ago, the late Bronze Age, the landscape on Calver looked much as it does today. It is hard to imagine crops ever having grown up here. It was also around this time, incidentally, that the cursed and invasive bracken began to gain what seems like an irreversible hold on upland slopes.

Our present knowledge of the past has been enhanced by a very intensive archaeological survey involving the National Park, English Heritage and the Royal Commission on Ancient Monuments. The Dales Project operated from 1989 to 1993 and aimed to identify, record, schedule and interpret as much as possible, using existing source material and new aerial photography. Thousands of new sites have been added to the Park record, bringing the total to around 25,000. Of these, maybe 120 are actually scheduled as ancient monuments. The task of interpretation will go on for many years, such is the quantity of material.

Black Hill

When you stand at the junction of the path off Calver and the stony track, you are at the limit of the most recent attempts to win farmland from the moors. To left and right, and down below, are dozens of small, walled fields. Their lack of regularity indicates enclosure before the main Enclosure Movement (see *Discovery Walk 11*). These fields have been hacked out piecemeal, some of them by squatters. Look at the Ordnance Survey map. There are several areas just west of here where walled fields stand surrounded by moor. These can only have been the creation of families who needed to find land. Presumably population pressure drove them out of the valley, or maybe they were made by miners wanting to minimise their daily journey to work.

Straight ahead downhill is the village of Healaugh (see *Discovery Walk 11*). The woods to your right run along Barney Beck. **Head off now from the path junction at 016 996 eastwards along the track above the intake fields.** When you come to the first break in the walls you can see down to the Swale below, to the suspension bridge and to the expanse of rocks and gravel where the river meanders sharply across the plain. From this height it is easy to appreciate that much of the dale was a lake at one time.

Ice Again

As the glaciers were melting water was dammed up behind a terminal moraine, a mass of rock and clay banked up across the valley. Sediments from the surrounding fells and valleys built up in the lake to produce the present flat floor. Eventually the force of water broke through the moraine draining the lake. The remnants of this glacial dam can still be seen at Ewelop Hill and across the river at Grinton where our predecessors constructed a set of defensive earthworks.

Early Farming

South of the river you can also make out the banks of an early field system sloping down to the edge of the floodplain. It is thought that the walled fields between you and Harkerside date from as early as the sixteenth century, and the banked fields obviously pre-date them. We have come across medieval field systems on many of these Discovery Walks.

One of the methods of agriculture in use then was *swidden*. Fields were initially cleared or burned, then ploughed and cropped for between one and three years, to be left fallow for a few seasons to allow the soil's fertility to be restored. Given the marginal quality of soils in the Dales I can well imagine swidden being an integral component of land management.

To ensure parity among the villagers of any given township, all were granted equal grazing rights on the areas left fallow, in addition to rights of pasturage on meadows or common rough pastures.

Individual medieval cultivation strips were always long and narrow, whether parallel or at right angles to the slope, for good reason. The ploughs were pulled by oxen, cumbersome beasts that took quite some turning round at the end of a furrow line. The longer the field, the better from the ploughman's point of view. On the other hand the width of the individual strip was controlled by how many furrows the beasts could manage in a day. Plough teams were normally owned on a communal basis, to spread the costs, and ploughing slots were worked out on a rota basis.

Some land in Reeth parish was still being cropped well into the nineteenth century. The Tithe Map for 1840, for example, shows nearly fifty arable fields in the vicinity, including one or two directly below you. There are none now.

Stay above the wall until the end of the second break just north-west of Riddings. At this point the grouse beaters' track heads east along the wall, but your path swings north-east along the foot of the heather, past old mine pits. Contour round Black Hill on the same level, through a shallow valley, and then due north across the moor. There is no actual path on the ground so use the two houses across Arkengarthdale – Castle – as a target point. Head slightly to the left of Castle. Have you picked out any Bronze Age reaves yet? I can assure you they are there.

Heather Moorland

I cannot possibly write a book about the Dales without mentioning heather moorland in some detail. Climb out of the valleys and more often than not you are among the heather, unless a particular fell has been over-grazed. This is a serious problem in the Pennines generally and, as a result, since 1963 there has been a 50 per cent decrease in heather cover.

Moorland is often cited as one of our remaining wilderness areas, a natural habitat largely left alone by mankind. As we have seen earlier, if you go back to the early Bronze Age there was no heather moorland. Agricultural practices, linked with climatic deterioration and soil degradation, changed the whole picture.

Moorland soils are highly acidic with a pH often below 5.0, leached of nutrients, podsolised and often waterlogged. Not very encouraging for plant growth, you might think. Far from it, I am glad to say. Plant diversity does not begin to approach the richness of limestone grasslands but is there nonetheless. Mosses and lichens abound, particularly in the boggier parts; there is a range of grasses, sedges and rushes; and ground-hugging berries like crowberry and bilberry. Then there are specialised bog communities that include cotton-grass *(Eriophorum angustifolium)*, bog asphodel *(Narthecium ossifragum)* and sundew *(Drosera rotundifolia)*. Let us not forget the three varieties of heather: ling *(Calluna vulgaris)* growing most widely, bell heather *(Erica cinerea)* colonising drier islands, and cross-leaved heath *(Erica tetralix)* preferring damper patches.

Bird populations are healthy as, unfortunately, are a number of species of bothersome insects: clegs, house flies, midges and ticks to mention the most insufferable of all.

Heather moorland is a fragile and precious habitat under threat, one that is recognised as having international importance. A new conservation scheme was introduced by the government in 1995, open to farmers outside the Pennine Dales ESA. The Moorland Scheme expects participating farmers to reduce their stocking rates on the moors. For every ewe taken off the fells, compensatory payments are made annually. A moorland management plan has to be drawn up to preserve the integrity of the habitat. In short a holistic approach is adopted . . . and for those who grouse about shooting parties, management of heather moorland is synonymous with management of grouse. You cannot have one without the other, and red grouse occur only in northern Britain – nowhere else.

The "path" drops down to the road and hopefully you will hit it at the right place, at a fingerpost two fields down from the barn near Watson House. If you have strayed north, make your way to the gate at the fingerpost. Go through the gate (or stile) and head down the track towards the wooded valley bottom,

– unless you intend to return by road to your car –

Fremington Edge

– As you enter the wood the short route rejoins the full route –

Cross Arkle Beck, go through the two gates and walk up the access track, turning right at the junction towards Castle Farm House. The right of way traverses the croft in front of the house and exits through the bridle gate at the barn. At this point a walled lane bears uphill to the right of Castle Farm: this is not a right of way, so no short cuts please!

Carry straight ahead through the "stile", more a chaos of stones, and through a series of small fields and dead walls at the foot of the slope, to an abandoned farmstead. Whoever first chose this spot did so with foresight. Regrettably it could not survive changing farming and domestic needs.

This is just one of many lost homes in the Dales. In a way it is surprising there are not far more. Many have been saved from dereliction to become holiday homes and weekend retreats, very often for town and city dwellers. In my humble opinion, though, I would much rather see them preserved and restored for whatever use than watch them slowly crumble away.

The population of Swaledale and its tributary valleys boomed in the heyday of the mining industry in the nineteenth century. It reached its peak around Reeth in the 1831 census, having grown by a third since the start of that century. Numbers remained fairly constant for thirty years after which the population total plunged, bottoming out in the 1901 census. In 1891 it was calculated that no less than 38 per cent of the houses in the area stood empty . . . and how long could Reeth's 15 public houses survive such a loss of clientele? Imagine the social upheavals of the late nineteenth century. Perhaps it puts our current economic situation in perspective.

The path enters a wood and, just before a redundant wall and gateway, you should double back uphill below old quarry workings, below a wood almost as dead as the wall and the farm.

Chert Quarrying

Fremington Edge was long important for stone extraction. Some of the sandstone layers were extensively quarried for building stone while the cherts that form the topmost strata were mined till the Second World War. Despite this late date, the methods of extraction were, let's say, traditional and had changed little in decades

Chemically chert is an impure oxide of silica (SiO_2), just like flint in chalk. Both are forms of chalcedony (as are jasper and agate). Chert is either dull grey or black in colour and its properties – hardness and ease of splitting – made it a prime choice for fashioning prehistoric stone implements. If flint was unavailable, chert was favoured. No one is totally sure how chert (or flint) formed. One theory is that silica was deposited locally on the sea floor as the limestone deposits were being laid down. This seems plausible.

More modern uses of chert vary from road construction to aggregate for concrete manufacture. Chert is also used for *burhstones* used for grinding and for whetstones.

Dry Stone Walls

The bridleway climbs uphill by the wall that bounds a relict ash and hawthorn wood, and then flattens out as it follows the headwall of the lower fields. **You pass above Castle Farm,** restored but no longer a working farm.

A path branches off at the top of the lane at Castle Farm, to climb steeply up and over Fremington Edge to the huge mining area around Hurst.

Your path continues to contour along, entering the very large field called Heggs Pasture just before another old and decaying wood with a lot of coppiced hazel, formerly managed to supply the mines.

All the land between the rim of Fremington Edge and the old intake below you was enclosed by Act of Parliament in 1777. I have discussed the Enclosure Movement in Discovery Walk 11, and have mentioned walls on a number of occasions but have kept discussion of the process until now because, in my opinion, the walls that march up to the Edge Top are the apotheosis of the whole movement.

Ruler-straight walls like these paid no heed to details of slope or land surface. If the commissioner said build a wall just there, the wall was dutifully built. To us the walls are an essential and integral part of the landscape. Swaledale *is* stone walls and barns. They have not always been viewed kindly however. Writing as the walls and fences were going up all over the country, the leading Romantic poet, John Clare, penned many verses decrying the whole Enclosure process. His own father was a landless agricultural labourer so I suppose he had a vested interest. He referred to the "vile enclosure" in one of his poems and in another, *Remembrances,* he wrote

> Inclosure like a Buonoparte let not a thing remain
> It levelled every bush and tree levelled every hill.

Comparing the rural scene before and after Enclosure in his poem *The Mores* he was equally graphic with his use of language, perhaps over the top in his use of metaphors, when he said

> Unbounded freedom ruled the wandering scene
> Nor fence of ownership crept in between
> To hide the prospect of the following eye
> Its only bondage was the circling sky

when referring to the time before, whereas afterwards he scathingly wrote

> Inclosure came and trampled on the grave
> Of labours rights and left the poor a slave . . .

> Fence now meets fence in owners little bounds
> Of field and meadow large as garden grounds
> In little parcels little minds to please
> With men and flocks imprisoned ill at ease

He was none too keen on punctuation!

It has been estimated that about 320,000 kilometres of wall were built in England and Wales during the Enclosure Movement as a whole. That is sufficient to stretch eight times round the equator. A recent estimate has put the figure still existing at less than half that.

The sad fact nowadays is that many of the walls are crumbling. Just look at the Edge. There is not one single wall still intact. Most are ruined beyond repair. The latest survey, carried out by ADAS (the agricultural advisory service) classified walls into five categories:

A	excellent condition	4 per cent
B	minor defects	9
C	deteriorating markedly	38
D	no longer stockproof	20
E	derelict	12
F	merely remnants	17

The figures refer to length as a percentage of the total in the UK. ADAS's estimate, in 1995, for restoring Category C walls alone was £1 billion. Meanwhile the Ministry (MAFF) has reduced walling grants from 50 to 30 per cent of the total cost per job.

Within the National Park in excess of £100,000 is spent under the excellent Barns and Walls Conservation Scheme for walling repairs. When you consider this is enough to put right less than one per cent of the problem, you will realise the magnitude of the problem. The cash available has been diminishing annually: £155,000 in 1995-96 but only £120,000 for 1996-97. The fault is central government's, not the Park's. A welcome boost of £66,000 was allocated from Northern Uplands Objective 5(b) funds for 1996-97. The maximum grant is 80 per cent of the total cost of a particular job. By early 1996 12 kilometres of wall had been repaired in Swaledale and Arkengarth-dale, and 26 per cent of the 750 barns needing attention had been put right. It is a significant start, and the scheme will continue.

The dilemma is that time is money for farmers and they have neither time, labour nor money to take on such a gargantuan task. It is easier and cheaper to erect a wire mesh fence. And the problem is not new. I remember seeing a photograph taken in 1870 showing an Enclosure wall riddled with gaps. Water gets inside, in winter it freezes and expands. Eventually the wall "bellies" and collapses. Sheep then use it to gain access to where they should not be and, before you know it, a small gap has grown wider. Some farmers just throw the stones back as a "temporary" measure as a "singled up" gap, or place an old gate against it. And that's that.

Walls do not just control stock. They also provide shelter from wind and rain. I am sure you have seen sheep lined up along the lee side of a wall to escape the elements. This can, of course, lead to problems in blizzards. The Big Snow in February 1996 caused problems throughout the Dales as sheep were buried in deep drifts of wind-blown snow. The sheep will not think to escape – maybe the insulating cover of snow gives them no reason to flee. A farmer with sheep on the fells will be out with his best dog and a long pole to locate and extricate the victims before it is too late. Inevitably some are lost. With that morbid thought, let us move on.

Heggs Pasture

As you walk through Heggs Pasture the detail of Fremington Edge is etched clearly before you. Most of the rocks in Swaledale and Arkengarthdale, as we have seen, belong to the Wensleydale Group. Between Arkle Beck and the rim of the Edge there are four main limestone bands. The most prominent scars up there are part of the Main and the Underset Limestones. Above the rim, forming the plateau of Marrick Moor, Millstone Grit overlies the Wensleydale Group.

To the fastidious Fremington Edge and Heggs Pasture probably look a mess, with tumbled walls, mine spoil and bracken encroachment. Maybe it is but it is a recognised habitat in its own right as scrubby slopes. Bracken undoubtedly is a growing problem as it is virtually impossible to get rid of because it expands vegetatively as clones. In the good old days bracken was harvested for stock bedding and this practice helped to keep it in check, but abandoned pastures and degraded heather moorland are now prime targets for bracken infestation.

Habitats like this are good for birdlife. If you are prepared to sit for a while you should catch sight of meadow pipit and skylark anywhere on Heggs. In late spring you could well hear a cuckoo calling from the lower slopes, and in summer wheatears hopping from boulder to boulder. Birds of prey are often spotted high up with little owls amongst the rocky parts.

At the end of Heggs Pasture pass through the bridle gate, ignoring the miners' path up to the right, **and zig zag down to Heggs House. The path goes through the gate, behind the house, and out along its access track.**

– If time is pressing you could foreshorten the walk at this point –

You will see Raw Croft across the valley, and the walled lane that connects it with Heggs. Do not risk the ford but walk a few metres upstream to the footbridge, then double back to the lane. Otherwise you should continue on the path upstream.

The Final Lap

Straight ahead, dominating the view, is the gorge of Slei Gill, a valley deepened and shattered by a combination of glacial meltwater, frost and mining operations. The gill contains an abundance of mining remains and a path that for centuries was a very important and busy packhorse road bringing salt from the Durham coast to the heart of the northern Dales. Clinging to the hillside is the former mining village of Booze. The whole scene is one of utter devastation: some would argue desecration; others would disagree. Whatever one's viewpoint, the scene has many a long story to tell.

Stay close to the riverbank, following the line of mature alders. A disease new to Britain, and of unknown origin, began to hit alders in 1993. The disease affects the root system and kills off the tree. There is no cure at present. At the time of writing the disease had spread as far north as South Yorkshire so I presume it is just a matter of time before it reaches the Dales. Alders are such attractive habitat for birds, bankside mammals and aquatic life: we simply cannot afford to lose them.

Cross the footbridge at Slei Gill, past yet more mine remains and so straight ahead on the path. The remains here are part of the Fell End lead mine. There was a level near Storthwaite Hall and another here in Booze Wood driven in 1870. There are remnants of the ore dressing floor and wheelpit, and the bed of a tramway leading out from the mine, hence the tunnel.

The path joins the road from Storthwaite in ornamental Booze Wood. Follow it to the footbridge across Arkle Beck.

– If you wish to avail yourself of the facilities in Langthwaite, stay on the road, returning here later –

It is around one kilometre there and back.

Cross the bridge and turn left immediately. If you turn right you will end up in Arkle Town, once larger than Langthwaite. **Follow the path along the**

Storthwaite and Fremington Edge

riverside and later slightly higher up in a series of fields. You will have observed the contrast between the floor of Arkengarthdale and that in Swaledale. There was no lake just here. The floor of this dale is too hummocky to have been under water. Here you see the result of deposition by ice, under the glacier. It is all till, or boulder clay, an unsorted mix of rocks, stones and clay.

From this vantage point you see Fremington Edge from a different quarter, and can pick out the extensive areas where landslips occurred in the immediate post-glacial period. Also proclaiming itself to the world is the expanse of scree, rock shattered by frost action in those frigid millennia after the glaciers had melted.

Lichen

The way later descends again towards the wood to follow a high and sturdily built sandstone wall. Note the quantity of green coloured lichen on its stones, *Rhizocarpon geographicum*. Lichens are amazing life forms and repay closer inspection under a hand lens. They come in so many shapes and shades. They are exceptionally slow growing and, exceptionally, can take up to 60 years to spread across one square centimetre of surface.

Lichen comes in two parts, algae and fungi. The fungus part of the duo produces and exudes acids which dissolve chemicals within the rock, thus sustaining the other half of the team. The algae capture the sun's energy and use water and carbon dioxide from the atmosphere to make sugar for both parts of the duo. Peaceful, mutual and sustainable co-existence – perhaps mankind can learn a thing or two from them! The loser, of course, is the rock which is ever so slowly eaten away.

Follow the wall to West Raw Croft Farm, then head up the access track back to the tarred road . . . and farewell.

Place-name meanings

Arkengarthdale	ON	the valley with Arkil's (pers. name) enclosure
Arkle Beck	ON	from Arkil
Booze	OE	house on a curve (in the hill)
Calver	OE	(possibly) the clearing for calves
Fremington	OE	Frema's (pers. name) farmstead
Langthwaite	ON	the long clearing
Marrick	ON	the ridge with horses
Raw Croft	OE	the rough pasture
Reeth	OE	(at) the stream
Riddings Rigg	OE/ON	the ridge with a clearing
Storthwaite	ME	the bull field or clearing

Common or Black Alder
Alnus glutinosa

Status: native to all parts of Britain, favouring riversides and damp ground.

Height: rarely exceeds 20 metres.

Trunk: often divides into two boles low down; ascending branches.

Bark: purple brown in young trees, turning grey with age; becoming highly fissured and split into small plates.

Crown: conical with an open canopy.

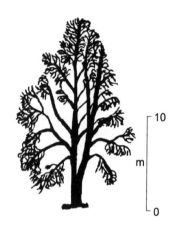

Fruit: small and ovoid and in clusters; distinctly purple in autumn, becoming woody in texture and black in colour, looking like tiny cones; often staying on the tree throughout winter each fruit hangs on a stalk 1cm long male flowers are dangling catkins 2 to 8cm long.

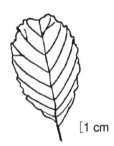

[1 cm

Leaves: broad and cuneate (wedge shaped at the base); flat or slightly indented at the tip, but not always; very dark green and quite shiny with 7 pairs of white veins; up to 10cm long.

Uses: formerly used for making clogs, for wooden sluice gates or for any use requiring immersion in water for long periods; extensively coppiced in the past; nowadays it has few timber uses though it is valuable as a planting to provide a binding for loose soil and for river banks.

Glossary of terms used in the text

Geological terms discussed in *The Southern Dales* are omitted here.

Accommodation Road   see Occupation Road

agger   the raised foundations forming the central part of a Roman road.

allotment   an area of fell or moorland (in the Pennines) parcelled up into individual fields during the Enclosure Movement (q.v.).

bail hill   a simple smelting hearth in the form of a bowl-shaped depression, lined with puddled clay, with a collecting dish for smelted lead metal. The hearth was surrounded by a low stone wall.

banjo   a truck turning area within a forest plantation.

barmkin   a courtyard either walled or surrounded by buildings, attached to a pele tower (q.v.).

Barns and Walls Conservation Scheme   a National Park scheme eligible to landowners and farmers in Swaledale, Arkengarthdale and Littondale, for restoring traditional field barns and dry stone walls.

bield   a dry-stone wall feature, of any shape, built as shelter for sheep.

bingsteads   see bouse teams

block gliding   the process whereby a section of solid rock slips or slides, through lubrication, over less solid layers, eg. clay or shale.

boskins   stone or timber panels separating individual stalls within a cowshed or barn.

bouse teams   the ore (called bouse) was piled in stone hoppers (the team) awaiting processing.

burhstones   a type of grinding stone for sharpening tools.

carding   the process of combing wool with a card to straighten and separate the fibres.

chantry   a chapel within a church for the chanting of masses for the soul of its endower.

chase   a hunting forest owned by a lord rather than by a king.

chopwood   green branches, up to 8cm or so thick, dried in a simple hearth for use in smelters.

collegiate church   an Anglican church with a chapter (or college) run by a dean with a number of canons.

common land   an area of open land, owned by no individual but available for use by all inhabitants of a parish or township.

conversi   lay brothers, part of a monastic community who wore habits, took part in prayer, carried out manual labour, but whose precise role is not known.

coppice   a wood within which small timber is harvested on a rotation basis with trees being cut close to the ground, to allow regrowth of new shoots.

corpse road   a road or path along which the deceased were carried for burial at the nearest parish church.

Countryside Stewardship	a scheme set up by the Countryside Commission in 1991 to reward farmers outside ESAs (q.v.) for farming with conservation interests in mind.
crenellate	to add defensive embattlements to a building.
crinoids	fossils in the form of sea-lilies, with arms at the end of a long stem.
curtilage	the land attached and belonging to a house.
Dales Project	a major documentary and aerial survey of the archaeological remains of the National Park from 1989 to 1993.
dame-school	a small school, often in a private house, for young children and run by a woman.
debris fan	a fan-shaped mass of rock deposited at the mouth of a tributary valley.
dressing floor	the area where ore was crushed, sieved and sorted prior to the smelting process.
drift tail	large concentrations of glacially deposited material in the lee of a hill, running away from the hill, tapering to the bottom.
drove road	a road developed for driving cattle long distances to market.
elling hearth	a simple kiln used for drying out chopwood (q.v.).
Enclosure Movement	the period, mainly from 1770 to 1820, when tracts of open land were enclosed and divided up by Act of Parliament.
Environmentally Sensitive Area (ESA)	an area whose environment is special enough to warrant extra protection, and in which farmers can claim grants to manage the land in sympathy with nature. Introduced in 1987.
furlong	a group of cultivation strips (or lands q.v.).
gait (sheep)	the right to graze one sheep on the common fell pastures.
grange	a farm acting as a monastic outpost, a centre for farming operations.
hearth tax	a tax imposed on domestic property according to the number of fireplaces, in force from 1662 to 1689.
holloway	a track, now sunken, worn by the passage of countless feet and by rain water.
horse litter	a type of roofed and curtained stretcher slung between two horses used as a conveyance for high-born women.
hotching tub	an 18th century wooden sieve. Crushed ore was added to water in the tub which was riddled to separate heavier ore from lighter waste. The tub was hand-operated.
hushing	the process of damming gullies and then releasing the water to scour the surface rock and expose the ore vein.
in-bye	enclosed land around a farmstead.
jagger	a packhorse man or an itinerant pedlar.
keep	the innermost and strongest building within a castle.
kneeler	decorative feature, like a step, at the lower end of coping stones on a roof.
land	a single, medieval cultivation strip.
leat	an artificial watercourse leading to a water wheel or dam.

mail-coach	stage-coaches primarily used for carrying mail on fixed routes, with passengers.
manor	the land and villages belonging to the local lord over which his authority held sway.
metallophyte	a plant that either requires or tolerates pollution from metals.
Moorland Scheme	a government scheme to compensate farmers who agree to manage moorland in sympathy with landscape conservation.
motte and bailey	an early Norman castle comprising a raised mound (the motte) and an outer, defensive courtyard (the bailey).
mullions	vertical stone divides in windows, typical of the late 17th century.
Natura 2000	a Brussels-inspired conservation umbrella including Special Protection Areas (q.v.) and Special Areas of Conservation (q.v.).
nunatak	an Inuit (Eskimo) word describing a mountain totally surrounded by an ice sheet or by glaciers (plural nunatakkr).
Objective 5(b)	a European Union scheme to fund projects in deprived or marginal areas of member states.
Occupation Road	a walled lane built through the in-bye (q.v.) to open or higher pasture.
outrake	a road whose primary function was for bringing sheep from fell to farmstead.
packhorse road	a routeway along which goods were transported using ponies carrying goods slung across or from their backs.
pele tower	a fortified tower house found in the Border regions, dating from the late medieval period.
pinfold	a walled enclosure used for impounding stray stock until claimed by the owner.
podsolisation	the natural process by which iron and aluminium oxides are leached down to the lower soil levels.
pollard	a tree repeatedly harvested (above head height) for young timber.
post-road	a route with regular post-stations (usually inns) where horses were exchanged. Used for carrying mail.
reaves	low stone and earth banks forming divisions in early field systems.
reiver	a cattle or horse thief given to hit and run plundering raids.
river capture	interceptions and diversion of the headwaters of one river by a more forceful river.
salterway	a packhorse route along which salt was a major commodity.
serf	a villager who was virtually a slave to the lord of the manor, and was landless. In the Norman period serfs made up 10 per cent of the rural population.
soke (soc) mill	a corn mill owned by the lord of the manor who had the juridical right to take a portion of each tenant's corn.
solar	a hall either part of or attached to a castle or fortified tower-house.
Special Areas of Conservation (SAC)	a European Union designation under the Habitats and Species Directive to grant protection to areas of outstanding floral importance.

Special Protection Area (SPA)	a European Union designation under the Birds Directive to grant protection to areas of outstanding importance for birdlife.
SSSI	Site of Special Scientific Interest: a small or large area worthy of protection because of its flora, fauna or geology.
stackgarth	a yard or hard-standing on which hay was stacked.
stage-coach	coaches designed for carrying passengers and parcels on fixed routes.
stage-waggon	waggons that carried goods, and some passengers, on fixed and timetabled routes.
standard	a tree left to grow to maturity in a coppiced wood.
statesman	a small landholder owning his own land (or estate).
statute labour	enforced, unpaid service on road maintenance required of villagers.
stinting	the process of assigning right of pasturage to a tenant within pre-determined stocking limits.
stoop/stoup	a stone post used for waymarking or as a gate post.
street-green village	a village built in a linear fashion along a green with the green acting as the route through the village.
swidden (swithen)	farm land originally cleared by burning.
turnpike road	a maintained road with toll gates at intervals.
vaccary	an enclosure within a hunting forest set aside for farming purposes.
villein	a villager bound by service to the lord of the manor in return for the right to farm land. They were of higher status than serfs. In the Norman period they formed 41 per cent of the rural population and held 45 per cent of the land. (The balance was made up of cottagers – 32 per cent of the total on 5 per cent of the land – and freemen – 14 per cent of the total on 20 per cent of the land – and serfs (q.v.).
wallet	a cloth bag used by miners (and others) as a kind of travel bag.
waywarden	an unpaid parish official first appointed to oversee local road maintenance in the late sixteenth century.
wood pasture	woodlands open to stock grazing by farmers with common rights in the parish.
worsted	cloth made from finely woven wool.
yeoman	a freeholder farmer, of lesser status than a gentleman.